FISHING MEASURES

FISHING MEASURES

A critique of desk-bound reason

DANIEL BANOUB

Library and Archives Canada Cataloguing in Publication

Title: Fishing measures : a critique of desk-bound reason / Daniel Banoub.
Names: Banoub, Daniel, author.
Series: Social and economic studies (St. John's, N.L.) ; no. 89.
Description: Series statement: Social and economic studies ; no. 89 | Includes bibliographical references and index.
Identifiers: Canadiana (print) 20210360216 | Canadiana (ebook) 20210360410 | ISBN 9781894725972 (softcover) | ISBN 9781894725989 (PDF) | ISBN 9781894725996 (EPUB)
Subjects: LCSH: Cod fisheries—Newfoundland and Labrador—History—19th century. | LCSH: Cod fisheries—Newfoundland and Labrador—History—20th century. | LCSH: Science and state—Newfoundland and Labrador—History—19th century. | LCSH: Science and state—Newfoundland and Labrador—History—20th century.
Classification: LCC SH351.C5 B36 2021 | DDC 333.95/663309718—dc23

Cover images: istock.com
Cover design: Alison Carr
Copy editing: Richard Tallman
Page design and typesetting: Julianna Smith

Published by Memorial University Press
Memorial University of Newfoundland
PO Box 4200
St. John's, NL A1C 5S7
www.memorialuniversitypress.ca

Printed in Canada
27 26 25 24 23 22 21 1 2 3 4 5 6 7 8

Funded by the Government of Canada

"How many barrels will thy vengeance yield thee even if thou gettest it, Captain Ahab? It will not fetch thee much in our Nantucket market."

"Nantucket market! Hoot! . . . If money's to be the measurer, man, and the accountants have computed their great counting-house the globe, by girdling it with guineas, one to every three parts of an inch; then, let me tell thee, that my vengeance will fetch a great premium here!"

"He smites his chest," whispered Stubb, "what's that for? Methinks it rings most vast, but hollow."

— HERMAN MELVILLE, *Moby Dick* (1851)

CONTENTS

This book is dedicated to my Nan and Pop, and all those summers spent down Champney's, going 30-for-60 on the kitty.

ACKNOWLEDGEMENTS

This book has deep roots. It was first drafted as a dissertation in the Department of Geography at the University of Manchester. It was completed as a postdoctoral fellow at Memorial in Geography (SSHRC, OFI) and History (ISER). The Department of Geography at the University of Manchester provided a very welcoming and inspiring environment to complete my dissertation. Umberto Eco wrote that it is in bad taste to thank one's supervisors, for if they helped you, they were only doing their job. This greatly underestimates the work Noel Castree and Erik Swyngedouw put in to shepherding me through the writing of the thesis. I should also thank Gavin Bridge, who supervised me for my first eight months before moving to Durham. Despite our brief time spent working together, his thinking was an intellectual lodestar for this book. My cohort provided an amazing level of support and friendship, over lunches and pints, throughout my time at Manchester. I'd like to thank Martín Arboleda, Creighton Connolly, Melissa Garcia Lamarca, Julie-Ann de los Reyes, and their partners, for making the potentially lonely time in Manchester so enjoyable.

As a postdoctoral fellow at Memorial, I can confirm that this book would not have been completed without the support, encouragement, and guidance of Dean Bavington, Kurt Korneski, Charles Mather, Christine Knott, and Sarah Martin. They helped me navigate an otherwise quite challenging period of uncertainty and ennui. The staff at The Rooms and the Centre for Newfoundland Studies made the research process easier. A late-night conversation with archivist Allan Byrne at a Tibb's Eve party in St. John's was particularly important in my decision to pursue archival research. A particularly lively group of students in History 4215 and Geography 4600 really taught me how to communicate an idea clearly. If this book succeeds at all, it is through their teaching.

I would like to formally declare my fealty to the Rothermere Foundation, the Social Sciences and Humanities Research Council of Canada, Memorial's Institute of Social and Economic Research, and the Ocean Frontier Institute for funding this research and writing process. I hope that this book goes a small way in repaying my debt to society for allowing me to complete this work while paying my bills. My editor, Fiona Polack, at Memorial University Press has improved this book immeasurably, and has been a sage guide and support throughout this process. I would compare her to Virgil in Dante's *Divina Commedia*, but it wasn't *quite* a journey through the nine rings of Hell. Richard Tallman and Alison Carr were indispensable in guiding this manuscript from my desk to yours.

Writing a book — especially one based on an extended period of archival research — can be a lonely endeavour. Without a supportive group of friends and family, one can easily slip into Jack-Torrance-from-*The-Shining*-style working habits. I really leaned on Caley Venn, Dave Bridger, and Andrew Schuldt and my immediate family — Judith, Joe, David, Mel, and Kathryn — to get me through the publication process.

It is a fiction of Western imagination that knowledge progresses through the successive contributions of "great thinkers." Knowledge production is a collective, collaborative process. This book, and any contribution it might make, is indebted to the people mentioned above, and to so many others. I *can* take credit, however, for any omissions, oversights, inconsistencies, infelicities, errors, boners, spoonerisms, *lapsus plumæ*, malapropisms, misattributions, and downright stupid ideas.

Finally, to you, dear reader, I quote Marx's preface to the first edition of *Capital*: "I welcome every opinion based on scientific criticism. As to the prejudices of so-called public opinion, to which I have never made concessions, now, as ever, my maxim is that of the great Florentine: '*Segui il tuo croso, e lascia dir le genti.*'" The Florentine is Dante, and the quote is roughly translated as "Go on your way, and let the people talk."

PART I ∽ MAKING FISH

Come all you good people, I'll sing you a song,
About the poor people, how they get along;
They fish in the spring, finish up in the fall,
And when it's all over they have nothin' at all.

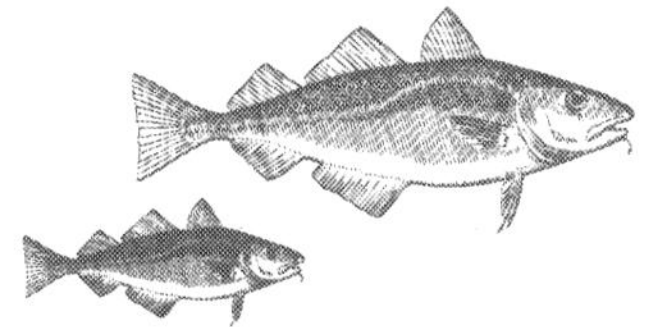

1

THE LOCAL FETISH

One evening in early March 1936 a very frustrated Sir John Hope Simpson sat down at his writing desk in the little office next to his bedroom in the Newfoundland Hotel and wrote a letter to his son, Ian. In it, he vented about his job as Commissioner of Natural Resources in the recently organized Commission of Government. Sworn in on 16 February 1934, it was comprised of six British-appointed Commissioners — three from the United Kingdom, and three from Newfoundland — with the Governor acting as chairman. The Commission of Government aimed to resolve Newfoundland's immediate fiscal crisis and to bring the economy out of the Great Depression, following the relinquishment of self-rule in 1933. As Commissioner of Natural Resources, Hope Simpson — a seasoned British administrator, with over 20 years' experience in the Indian Civil Service — was charged with governing and modernizing Newfoundland's key resource industries: fishing, pulp and paper production, and mining. This was a daunting task that demanded a gruelling work schedule, a real intellectual and physical challenge, especially for someone on the verge of retirement. "I am tired frequently," he wrote to his youngest daughter Betty on 16 June 1935, ". . . I almost said 'generally,' and that would be true at the end of the day."[1]

In his letter to Ian, Hope Simpson complained that Newfoundlanders refused to acknowledge that living conditions in Newfoundland would continue to be deplorable until circumstances improved in the country's primary industry: the export of salted and dried cod to Southern Europe and Latin America.[2] For most of the nineteenth century and early twentieth century, the country's saltfish trade was organized around the credit system.[3] Under this mode of production, fishing families spent their spring and summer catching *and* curing cod, with the necessities of fishing and living supplied by merchants on credit. Known locally as "making fish," the labour process entailed removing *fish from water*, by hook, line, or trap, and removing *water from fish*, by sun, salt, wind, and weight. In the fall, merchants would "break the price," determining the price for both supplies and saltfish, and settling their accounts with fishers. In a good year, fishers would repay the supplies in full, or even in excess, with the products of the season's labour. In bad years, fishers would accrue debts, to be repaid, one hoped, by the next season. It is in this context that one ubiquitous outport saying takes on a profound resonance, resigned, but cautiously optimistic: "We must live in hopes, supposing we dies in despair."[4]

Hope Simpson viewed this mode of organizing the economy as inefficient and demoralizing for fishers and merchants alike. In his letter, he argued that the credit system was an inherent barrier to modern industrial progress for two reasons. First, it encouraged the "extreme individualism" of the merchant-exporter, which limited the government's ability to regulate production and marketing for the common good. "The St. John's merchants are a reactionary crowd," he noted in a different letter. "They see no further than the ends of their noses, and have no interest outside their own profits."[5] The second reason was that it encouraged too many people to remain engaged in the fishery. He proved his assertion by a "simple arithmetical exercise." Dividing a generous estimate of the profit received by producers from the annual export of saltfish (£240,000) by the number of people engaged in the fishery (34,000) yielded an annual profit of £7.10 per producer.[6] Although this "impossible figure" was bolstered by the sale of other products and extra-economic subsistence practices, "the standard of the average fisherman's life is deplorable."

For Hope Simpson, raising the industry's productivity — by reducing the number of fishers and increasing the amount of fish produced — was vital for overcoming poverty in the outports. Yet, he felt, it was consistently stifled by the conservatism of both the mercantile-cum-political elite and the toiling masses. "When I argue along these lines," he groused, "people think I am mad." Despite this local entrepreneurial inertia, Hope Simpson and the Commission of Government wanted to place the industry on a modern and scientific basis by bringing an entirely new mode of production into existence through legislation, one based on cash transactions, a division of labour between fishing and processing, standardized output, government inspection, and co-operative marketing. They were engaged in an effort to reorganize entirely the production and marketing of saltfish in Newfoundland.

But in his letter to Ian, Hope Simpson identified a curious solution to this problem of industrial organization: ". . . what is required is not *knowledge of fishing*, but *knowledge of arithmetic* and the application of a little common sense" (emphasis added). The industry had been "so pampered and so spoon-fed" over the past two decades that they could not recognize the absurdity in the present order of production and marketing. "Fishing," he wrote, "is the local fetish." The methods had been sanctioned by centuries of practice, "and so have proved that they are inevitable and right." Hope Simpson, in contrast, argued that rational production and industrial efficiency required the abstract calculation of modern science, not the practical, embodied knowledges of fishing peoples. But when championing this line of thinking, he noted sardonically, "I am regarded as still less sane."

Concealed by his administrative mindset as simply "a little common sense," Hope Simpson's private letter articulated two opposed forms of knowledge and expertise — "knowledge of fishing" and "knowledge of arithmetic" — engaged in a conflict over the future of the saltfishery. The former was qualitative, embodied and "sanctioned by 300 years of use." It emerged through the sensuous, practical activities of fishing people and was passed down generationally. Located in the dory and on the stage head, the knowledge of fishing was attuned to dynamic uncertainty of fish, weather, and sea. The latter was quantitative, abstract, and quintessentially modern. It emerged in the laboratory, classroom, and government office, and was located behind a desk. It was replicated through the practices of institutional authority and expertise, and it sought to domesticate so-called nature through the model, map, and mathematical equation.

As a veteran British civil servant, Hope Simpson erred on the side of arithmetic.

I.

As jarring and novel as Hope Simpson thought his division between fishing and arithmetic was in Commission-era Newfoundland, it had far deeper historical-geographical roots than he acknowledged or recognized. The quantitative perspective on fishing encapsulated in Hope Simpson's pithy opposition had been fomenting in Western networks of science, industry, and government since at least the mid-nineteenth century. Despite nineteenth-century English biologist Thomas Huxley's famous 1883 assertion that fish stocks "in relation to our present modes of fishing . . . are inexhaustible," they were increasingly being recognized as quite the opposite, and for a very simple reason: *they were being exhausted.*[7] The technical intensification and spatial extensification of fishing effort in Western large-scale fisheries had led to palpable marine fisheries crises in Great Britain, Norway, Canada, and the United States.[8] These crises inspired new levels of state intervention into fishing, and galvanized a new scientific interest in understanding, predicting, and controlling the dynamics of fish populations and ocean processes through the collection of fishery statistics.[9] When British fishery researcher John Cleghorn coined the term *overfishing* in 1854, a new knot was tied between fish populations and human activity, to be unravelled by emergent practices of quantitative science.[10]

Read any history of fisheries science and you will notice a steady proliferation of increasingly complicated mathematical formulae. The incessant "mathematization" of fisheries science may in part reflect a deeper and more granular understanding of the ocean and fish life, but it definitively exposes the ever-more deeply rooted conception of *nature* as mechanical and predictable and *knowledge* as quantitative and scientific.[11] In this context, Hope Simpson's opposition between practical and arithmetical knowledge takes on a new relevance. The very framework of his argument highlights a foundational shift in capitalist world history. It articulates an epochal transformation in the historical-geographical relationship among knowledge production, the environment, and capitalism in the global fishing industry.

Fishing Measures is the story of the troubled and messy emergence of arithmetical expertise in Newfoundland's saltfish economy between the late 1880s and the late 1930s. The title plays on the double etymological roots of *measure*, as both the process of ascertaining the size or amount of something *and* as a plan or course of government action. This book documents a variety of innovations, schemes, and failed proposals that aimed to reform and modernize the country's saltfish industry in fundamentally novel fashion: through the application of quantified forms of scientific measurement. From artificial propagation, to scientific analyses of ocean currents and fish migrations, to improved methods of fish and by-products processing, these scientific, technological, and organizational innovations were framed as a panacea to the troubles in the country's saltfish trade.

Students of Newfoundland history will know that most of these schemes — perhaps more accurately described as half measures — did not result in placing the country's saltfishery on a sound economic footing. But, as we will see, the politicians, merchants, scientists, reporters, and fishers advocating for and against them *did* succeed in an important and under-acknowledged way. They succeeded in introducing and legitimizing a new form and location of fisheries expertise and authority: from the knowledge of fishing to the knowledge of arithmetic, from the dory to the desk. This was an early and underappreciated moment in the development of modern fisheries management. *Fishing Measures* tells the story of that shift, and in doing so points to how that very opposition might be overcome.

But first we must set the theoretical grounds for the critique by delving into a subterranean strand of Marxist political economy. It begins, like Marx, with the commodity.

II.

Of all Marx's contributions, and there are many, perhaps the most radical and profound concept is that of *commodity fetishism*. Introduced at the end of the long first chapter on the commodity in Volume 1 of *Capital*, Marx makes the stunning insight that, under capitalism, humans experience the world as comprised of disconnected *things*, as commodities, as objects. But this "thing-ness" masks the *social relations* behind their production and reproduction. Commodities are the products of the "expenditure of human brain, nerves, muscles, and sense organs" on the material environment, but they *appear* as "autonomous figures endowed with a life of their own, which enter into relations both with each other and with the human race."[12] The commodity-form is thus fetishistic — mysterious, fantastical, ghostly — and this is an *inherent* feature of capitalism, "which attaches itself to the products of labour as soon as they are produced as commodities, and is therefore inseparable from the production of commodities."[13]

A subterranean strand of Marxist political economy, known as "form analysis," has built upon Marx's reflections on commodity fetishism to develop a nuanced, subtle reading of the historical-geographical dynamics of capitalism. This school is rooted in Marx's more open and exploratory analysis in the *Grundrisse*, his notebooks from the winter of 1857–58. Intended as his preparatory studies for *Capital*, the *Grundrisse der Kritik der politischen Öekonmie* (Outlines of the Critique of Political Economy) differs from *Capital* in key ways: it is more deductive and abstract; it uses less illustrative material; and it features numerous digressions that were excised from the final product.[14] Roman Rosdolsky (1898–1967), a Ukrainian Marxist scholar and revolutionary, described the *Grundrisse*'s German publication in 1939 as a "veritable revelation," which "admitted us, so to speak, into Marx's economic laboratory, revealing all the ingenuities, all the winding paths of his methodology."[15]

Form analysis builds on Marx's thinking in the *Grundrisse* on fetishization, reification, and alienation as rooted in the commodity-*form*. Situated in the traditions of Critical Theory, Open Marxism, and *Neue Marx-Lektüre*, form analysis has flowered in Latin America with the work of Enrique Dussel and scholars working in the Centro para la Investigación como Crítica Práctica in Buenos Aires, under the directorship of Juan Iñigo Carrera.[16] Martín Arboleda offers a master class in *Planetary Mine*, his study of the novel politics and territorialities of global resource extraction.[17] For these thinkers, the fetishistic commodity structure is not simply a problem for economic theory; rather, it is "the central, structural problem of capitalist society in all its aspects."[18] Like the chapter on Being, Non-Being, and Becoming in *Science of Logic* for Hegel, Marx's section on commodity fetishism in *Capital*, "contains within itself the whole of historical materialism."[19] It is, as Isaak Rubin argues, the "basis of Marx's entire economic system."[20] This perspective is unconventional, even strange, but it has profound implications for thinking about Hope Simpson's opposition between the knowledge of fishing and arithmetic.[21]

For Marx, commodity fetishism is grounded in the contradictory unity between use-value and value at the core of the commodity. The commodity, at first blush, *appears* as "an extremely obvious, trivial thing."[22] It is an object, produced by human labour, that satisfies a human want, need, or desire. It has a *use-value*. Humans, through practical, sensuous activity, transform the raw materials they find in their environment through social knowledge into use-values. But, under capitalism, the commodity turns out to be a "very strange thing, abounding in metaphysical subtleties and theological niceties."[23] As an object produced for exchange, not use, it requires an equivalence that is detached from its material use-values. Commodity exchange on the market requires an *exchange-value*, some kind of socially acceptable quantity that can be compared between commodities and "that transcends sensuousness." The common element cannot be a "geometrical, physical, chemical or other natural property."[24] Exchangeability itself, therefore, implies a more abstract concept: value. If one disregards all physical, sensuous properties of commodities, then one remains: "they are merely congealed quantities of homogeneous human labour."[25]

The commodity, for Marx, embodies a *contradictory unity* between use-value and value. It is a material, concrete expression of the law of value. Marx explains this through the example of a table (or, for that matter, we can add, a desk). The form of wood, he argues, is obviously transformed when a table is made out of it, but it remains wood, an ordinary, sensuous thing. But as a concrete embodiment of value, as a commodity, it sheds its material form. "It not only stands with its feet on the ground," Marx writes, "but, in relation to all other commodities, it stands on its head, and evolves out of its wooden brain grotesque ideas far more wonderful than if it were to begin dancing of its own free will."[26]

In the section on fetishism, Marx grounds the contradictory unity of use-value and value embodied in the commodity in practical, sensuous human activity: in labour. But commodity-producing labour under capitalism is peculiar. It, too, is contradictory and double-sided. Marx distinguishes between *concrete labour*, which produces use-values, and *abstract labour*, which produces value. These are not two different activities or sorts of labour, but two aspects of the same labour performed in commodity-determined capitalist society. Commodities as use-values are material, and the labour that produces them is sensuous and physiological. It is *concrete*. However, as values, commodities are produced by *abstract labour*. They are purely social: immaterial, but historically determinate and real. "Not an atom of matter enters into the object-ness of commodities as values," he writes. "In this it is the direct opposite of the coarsely sensuous object-ness of commodities as physical objects."[27]

For Marx, the commodity is not a transhistorical object, but a historically specific objective *form*: "a structuring and structured form of social practice that constitutes a radically new form of social interdependence."[28] People relate to one another through commodities. They subsist on commodities, and their own labour-power is itself a commodity they sell for wages. But it is a fetishized or reified form. The social relations behind its production are masked; they "acquire a 'phantom objectivity,' an autonomy that seems so strictly rational and all-embracing as to conceal every trace of its fundamental nature: the relation between people."[29]

Marx's idiosyncratic, dialectical method is the fulcrum upon which form analysis turns, revealed in his notebooks and fulsomely, systematically expounded in *Capital*.[30] Reminiscing on his life's work in old age, in his *Marginal Notes on Adolph Wagner* (1880), Marx reflected on his method of critiquing of political economy:

> In the first place, I do not start out from concepts, hence I do not start from the "concept of value," and do not have "to divide" these in any way. What I start out from is the simplest social form in which the labour-product is presented in contemporary society, and this is "the commodity." I analyse this, and indeed, first in the form in which it appears.[31]

The commodity-form, in this framework, is the simplest determination of value-form, the structured and structuring "core" of capitalist social relations. From this simple determination, Marx unfolds his analysis of the structuring forms of capitalist social relations: value, labour, money, capital, class, etc. The unfolding of these increasingly complex determinations strives towards the "reproduction of the concrete by way of thought," or the meaningful theoretical reconstruction of capitalism as a way of organizing social relations.

Marx described his method as "rising from the abstract to the concrete." His critique of political economy begins with the commodity, "the simplest social form of the product of labour in present day society" or the concrete embodiment of the abstract value-relation. The law of value is the "essence" behind the "appearance" of wealth as an immense accumulation of commodities under capitalist social relations. But Marx goes deeper, to explain the appearances themselves, to examine the "intermediate links, or mediations, which enable essence and appearance to be reintegrated in a unity once again."[32] Marx did not ontologically presuppose the essence behind the appearance, nor did he confer upon essence the determining role in human history.[33] He merely grasped the bifurcated nature of social reality under capitalism, as an effect of the unfolding of the law of value in historically determinate forms or modes of existence. The very division of essence/appearance is *itself* an outcome of commodity fetishism. His dialectical method grasped the progression from the abstract to the concrete as "a movement from the parts to the whole and from the whole to the parts, from the appearance to the essence and from the essence to the appearance, from the totality to the contradiction and from the contradiction to the totality, from the object to the subject and from the subject to the object."[34]

Form analysis, like Marx's later works, begins from a specific starting point: the commodity. Marx struggled to figure it out. He begins his August 1857 draft of *Capital* in the *Grundrisse* from a very different starting point: "The object before us, to begin with, *material production*. Individuals producing in society — hence socially determined individual production — is, of course, the point of departure."[35] Through the drafting process, he decided on a different point of departure. By 1859, when he published *A Contribution to the Critique of Political Economy*, which presaged *Capital* in key ways, he started with the commodity. His famous first line of *Capital* — "The wealth of societies in which the capitalist mode of production prevails appears as an 'immense collection of commodities'; the individual commodity appears as its elementary form"[36] — was hard fought. This starting point was not arbitrary, and it was not chosen *a priori*, before the analysis. It is not logico-deductive — that is, it does not begin with first principles from which his analysis is derived — but is curiously reflexive and immanent. The point of departure is validated *retroactively* by the argument as it unfolds. Form analysis centres the contradictory form of the commodity as the structuring core of capitalist social relations, a determinate mode of existence of capital that structures the higher-order concepts of Marx's analysis. As historian Moishe Postone contends, "What appears as an '*a priori* construction' is a mode of argument intended to be adequate to its own historical specificity."[37]

Marx recognized the potential misreadings and misrepresentations that this method might allow: "If this is done successfully, if the life of the subject matter is now reflected in the ideas, then it may appear as if we have before us an *a priori* construction."[38] This is central to Marx's idiosyncratic method and mode of argumentation, and has been fundamentally misunderstood and lost over time, which helps explain the rigid, stultified, deterministic readings of Marx that have so muddied his legacy. Without an eye to his dialectical method and writing style, his open thinking can be coagulated, reduced to the strict teleologies of base-superstructure. As Marx famously said to his son-in-law Paul Lafargue, whose newly formed Parti Ouvrier left the Old Moor unimpressed: "*Ce qu'il y a de certain c'est que moi, je ne suis pas marxiste.*"[39]

The section on commodity fetishism encapsulates Marx's idiosyncratic, dialectical method and his overarching analysis of capitalism. But Marx recognized the challenge in adopting it. "If I state," he argues,

> that coats or boots stand in a relation to linen because the latter is the universal incarnation of human labour, the absurdity of the statement is self-evident. Nevertheless, when the producers of coats and boots bring these commodities into a relation with linen, or with gold or silver (and this makes no difference here), as the universal equivalent, the relation between their own private labour and the collective labour of society appears to them in exactly this absurd [fetishized] form.[40]

Without reckoning with commodity fetishism, the world appears as disconnected and fragmented. Reality is thus comprised only of immediate experience; commodities exist as things. The table or the desk appears as objective form ("standing on its feet"), but this veils their reality as concrete modes of existence or reified forms of contradictory social relations under capitalism ("standing on its head"). As Czech philosopher Karel Kosik notes, fetishism allows people to "use money and carry out the most complicated transactions with it without ever knowing, or having to know, what money is."[41]

Marx's method begins by showing that those things we encounter in our everyday lives are actually reified products of social relations, concrete forms of the contradictory core of the commodity. This is often derided as *economic determinism*, as a process of abstraction that views the "superstructure" as determined by the "base." But this critique, argues Hungarian Marxist György Lukács, is "itself the product of the habits of thought and feeling of mere immediacy where the immediately given form of the objects, the fact of their existing here and now and in this particular way appears to be primary, real and objective, whereas their 'relations' seem to be secondary and subjective."[42] Marx's method starts with the assumption that social relations are real and objective, historically determinate (not simply determining), and the product of the contradiction inherent in practical, sensuous activity under capitalism. It's systemic, structured, totalizing qualities are not presupposed ontologically, but a product of the determinate forms of social practice. They are historically specific. They are an outcome of the contradiction between use-value and value.

Marxist form analysis entails abandoning the view that objects are simply things, rigidly opposed to one another. "It is necessary," writes Lukács, "to elevate their interrelatedness and the interaction between these 'relations' and the 'objects' to the same plane of reality."[43] This framework has risks. Perhaps it bends the stick back too far, but, as Neil Smith reminds us, "without bending the stick, it is impossible to tell whether it is bent back too far."[44]

III.

In his letter to Ian, Hope Simpson was venting his frustrations at the organization of Newfoundland's saltfish industry. Governed by the centuries-old knowledge of fishing, it was in a state of constant crisis. His solution was simple, just a little common sense: the application of the knowledge of arithmetic. It is safe to say he didn't realize it, but he articulated one of the clearest, most succinct expressions of what Lukács calls the "antinomies of bourgeois thought."[45] Rooted in the commodity form as a contradictory unity, capitalism is riven by antimonies, by oppositions between concrete/abstract, subject/object, thing/relation, essence/appearance, form/content, quality/quantity, mind/body, mental/manual, thinking/doing — and, we can add, fishing/arithmetic and dory/desk. Form analysis grounds these oppositions in lived, material conditions. They are the fetishistic outcome of practical, human activity, of paid and unpaid labour. "According to Marx's analysis of capitalism," writes Moishe Postone, "the dual character of commodity-determined labour constitutes a social universe characterized by concrete and abstract dimensions."[46]

This bifurcation is readily apparent in the world of commodities. The table or desk is wood, a material object standing on its feet, but it also is abstract, standing on its head and evolving "out of its wooden brain grotesque ideas," in Marx's evocative image. But the fetishistic division between abstract and concrete even has implications for *the perception of reality itself.* Immediately given reality — the world of material, sensuous *things* that confront our perception — is understood as concrete. But behind this world of things, another dimension appears as abstract and homogeneous. The concrete world is the world of appearances, controlled by the fundamental essences of abstract laws. For many, this is the basic understanding of nature and reality as conceptualized by Enlightenment science and rationality. An apple falling from a tree is concrete, and might leave a bruise, but to a perceptive observer it also reveals the abstract laws of gravity. To the "enlightened" mind, the abstract laws that govern reality can be discovered, understood, and controlled objectively through quantification and the scientific method. For Hope Simpson, and the elite mindset he personifies, this was simply a "little common sense."

But as banal and self-evident abstract forms of quantitative measurement may appear to the late capitalist Western mind, it is important to remember that the expansion of scientific consciousness did not emerge in a historical vacuum, nor indeed an "air-pump."[47] Despite scientific claims to neutrality, objectivity, and rationality, it was far from apolitical. The proliferation of quantitative measurement was imbued with social values.[48]

For Marx, the very division between concrete/abstract and essence/appearance was not immediately given. It was a historically specific outcome of the contradiction at the core of the commodity, grounded in practical human activity, in human labour. Hope Simpson's quantitative common sense, framed around the knowledge of arithmetic, was deeply historical and profoundly political.

For millennia prior to these diffuse scientific-cum-metrical revolutions, measurement was embodied, qualitative, contingent, and highly contentious. Polish historian Witold Kula, in his study of measurement in Europe, gives many charismatic examples. In Christian lore, it was sinful to count and to measure. It was the devil himself that gave King David the idea to count the people of Israel.[49] Towards the end of the eighteenth century, Czech peasants believed that children under the age of six would stop growing — and become stunted "measurelings" — if cloth intended for their clothes was measured.[50] A 1699 mural in a Polish village church depicts the devil seizing a female innkeeper, with the inscription, "She never poured full measure."[51] Kula pleads that we do not laugh at the peasants' anger towards the innkeeper, but recognize the central role innkeeping and vodka played in the organization of peasant society. "Those drops our lady innkeeper held back," he reminds us, "contained the very calories the peasants failed to get in other ways."[52]

Prior to the scientific revolution, time, space, and nature in Europe were considered organic, not mechanical.[53] Work was task-oriented, "in which the day's tasks . . . seem to disclose themselves, by the logic of need," not ruled by the "measured clank of the clock."[54] Physical quantities were measured by what Kula calls "a system of anthropometric metrology," using human limbs as the primary unit of measurement: the foot, the finger, or the ell (elbow).[55] Larger distances that exceeded human dimensions were measured by other embodied units, such as the bowshot, the carrying distance of a human voice, the amount of human labour required for plowing, or the amount of seed required to sow the field.[56] In Newfoundland, for example, a nineteenth-century missionary noted that fishers measured distance in terms of spells: "'two shoulder spells' is the distance a man would ordinarily carry a burden on his shoulders, resting once in the midst."[57] Following a sudden drop, the temperature would be described as a "jacket colder" than before.[58]

The shift from qualitative to quantitative measurement is the result of century-spanning scientific, religious, artistic, commercial, military, and administrative processes and technologies. Innovations as diverse as the mechanical clock, new cartographic techniques, advances in mathematical symbology, perspectival painting, notation and polyphony in music, and double-entry bookkeeping all contributed to the emergence of the modern "character of calculability" in Western Europe.[59] The quantification and standardization of measurement aided both the emerging commercial elite and expanding state administrations. Factory labour required greater synchronization and time-exactitude in labour processes, and both large-scale trading networks and central state bureaucracies required commensurable and uniform measures to facilitate trade and accounting.[60] Quantification, lastly, was not extended unopposed. It often required the backing of state power. "The metric system," as historian of science Philip Mirowski points out, "tended to follow the barrel of a gun."[61]

But how to account for these changes? Under what social conditions did they emerge? This shift in perception is most often explained as a co-product of the emergence of scientific rationality and the development of new technologies. In his comprehensive history of technology, for example, urbanist and historian Lewis Mumford concludes, "The clock, not the steam engine is the key machine of the modern industrial age."[62] He described the mechanical clock, somewhat counterintuitively, as a piece of "power-machinery" that *produced* seconds and minutes. It "dissociated time" from human events and "helped create the belief in an independent world of mathematically measurable sequences: the special world of science."[63] It materialized, or made concrete, Isaac Newton's conception of "absolute, true, and mathematical time [that] flows emphatically and equably without relation to anything external."[64] It inspired further technical developments, and emerged as the symbol of the mechanical age: "it marks a perfection toward which other machines aspire."[65] Perfected and diffused between the fourteenth and seventeenth centuries in Western Europe, the mechanical clock, and its division of time into commensurable, exchangeable units, marked a fundamental shift in human perception.

Moishe Postone, in contrast, argues that the roots of this shift cannot be reduced to technology. Abstract time was not simply a *product* of a piece of power-machine. Rather, the appearance of the mechanical clock itself, and the parallel materialization of Newtonian time, "must be understood with reference to a sociocultural process that it, in turn, strongly reinforced."[66] For example, various forms of water clocks in Hellenistic and Roman society used a uniform process, the flow of water, to represent variable hours. Complicated technical mechanisms were developed to translate a continuous, regular flow of water into a variable, seasonal understanding of time. For Postone, this was not technologically determined: temporal variability was, in fact, more technically challenging to accomplish. The reasons were social and cultural: "variable hours apparently were significant, whereas equal hours were not."[67]

"The mechanical clock," Postone concludes, "does not, in and of itself, necessarily give rise to abstract time."[68] The rise of abstract time must be understood *socially*, not simply as an *effect* of technology alone. Postone argues that the dual emergence of mechanical clocks and abstract time must be grounded in the circumstances under which Newtonian time became meaningful for the organization of social life. He situates it historically in the generalization of the commodity-form as the structuring core of social relations under capitalism, and its subsequent bifurcation of reality into concrete and abstract dimensions.

Alfred Sohn-Rethel, in his landmark book *Intellectual and Manual Labour*, goes the furthest in analyzing how the process of abstraction and quantification is rooted in the commodity-form. Sohn-Rethel argues that abstraction, the mental process underlying science, is not transhistorical; it is not a fundamental aspect of human consciousness. It is time-bound. Sohn-Rethel demonstrates this by extending Marx's critique of political economy to the critique of bourgeois epistemology. He seeks to apply Marx's critique of Ricardo and Smith to the thinking of Kant, Galileo, and Newton. Building on Marx, he argues that forms of thought arise from practical activity. "It is not the consciousness of men [*sic*]," writes Marx, "that determine their being, but, on the contrary, their social being that determines their consciousness."[69] Forms of cognition — thinking itself — are one of the reified expressions of the contradiction at the core of the commodity.

Sohn-Rethel argues that abstraction is a practical outcome of the process of commodity exchange. Sohn-Rethel proves his assertion both historically and logically. In terms of history, he notes, commodity relations coincide quite neatly with the Western philosophical tradition, pointing out the historical coincidence between classical Greek philosophy and the development of coinage (*c.* 670 BCE), and between Smith's *The Wealth of Nations* and Kant's *Critique of Pure Reason* (1776 and 1781, respectively). Logically, he argues, this is rooted in the commodity as a social form. Commodities as use-values are sensuous, material, qualitative. They are a product of the brains and muscles of the producer. However, the process of exchange involves abstraction: different commodities must be compared and equated in terms of value. Their use remains important, but it is purely a mental projection, an imaginative use. As commodity exchange is generalized, thought is increasingly separated from activity, individualized and privatized. The conceptual mode of thinking, and the separation of head and hand that it entails, is peculiar to the societies based on capitalist commodity production.

In non-capitalist societies, human consciousness and knowledge emerge organically from practical activity. "Conceiving, thinking, the mental intercourse of men [*sic*]," Marx wrote in *The German Ideology*, "appear at this stage as the direct efflux of their material behavior."[70] The relationship with and knowledge of nature is organized around producing and consuming use-values. The historical trend towards production for exchange — with the accumulation of value as the primary driver of human activity — introduces a distinction between manual and mental labour. Knowledge of nature is abstracted from practical activity and limited to certain classes. "Just as the process of exchange abstracts in practice from the use-value of the commodities being exchanged," Neil Smith concludes, "so the human consciousness can abstract itself from the immediate material conditions of existence."[71] The growing dominance of exchange-value on the world scale under capitalist social relations entrenches and intensifies the division between mental and manual labour. Capital requires constant technical innovation to maintain profits, made possible by the constant development of scientific knowledge.[72] Simultaneously, the work process is increasingly divided and regulated, and workers are alienated from their traditional knowledge, increasingly functioning as appendages to the productive machinery of capital.[73] "It is no exaggeration to say," concludes Sohn-Rethel, "that one can measure the extent of division of head and hand by the inroad of mathematics in any particular task."[74]

This is a radical assessment of bourgeois thought, one that connects the seemingly independent fields of political economy and classical philosophy. Both, he argues, strive towards the same goal: "to prove the perfect normalcy of bourgeois society."[75] He frames the emergence of science and Enlightenment rationality as historically specific, shaped by a particularly androcentric, Eurocentric, and capital-centric standpoint.

The value of this perspective is demonstrated through a comparison with different cosmologies.[76] For example, Glen Coulthard and Leanne Simpson demonstrate that the very conceptual divisions of mind/body, thought/feeling, human/nature that structure European bourgeois thought are anathema to the ways of being that characterize Dene and Anishnaabeg societies.[77] Those philosophies are forms of "grounded normativity." Intelligence in Dene and Anishnaabeg societies is developed and nurtured in, on, and through the land.[78] "Knowledge" is not created by an abstract thinker — a brain in a vat — calculating and measuring abstract space and time. Intelligence is a relational, reciprocal process of land relations guided by knowledge, emotion, spirituality, and experience. Bourgeois thought, in contrast, is a form of particularly *un*grounded normativity. As Marx points out, "For the landowner ground and earth mean nothing but ground-rent; he lets his land to tenants and receives the rent; a quality which the ground can lose without losing any of its inherent qualities such as fertility."[79] By projecting the division between head and hand as timeless, "the bourgeois order must run according to its self-appointed norms until the end of time,"[80] regardless of the socio-ecological destruction at its very core.

The coterminous development of Enlightenment science and capitalist development, then, and the forms of cognition that undergird them, can be grounded in the double character of labour in capitalist society, arising from the dualistic form of the commodity. Bourgeois thought, as embodied in classical political economy and critical philosophy and articulated succinctly by Hope Simpson, reached its apotheosis in pure mathematics, logic, and geometry. But as we have seen, its development is not an apolitical process of human progress towards truth. The division between manual and mental labour — between the knowledge of fishing and arithmetic — is not natural, ahistorical, or apolitical. It is socially determined and historically determinate. It "springs from the reified [fetishized] structure of consciousness."[81]

~ ~ ~

The word "fetish," defined as a material object regarded with awe as having mysterious powers, is derived from the Portuguese *fetiço*, meaning "charm, sorcery, allurement." Etymologically, the word has coalesced an interesting set of denotations, from the Latin *facticius* (artificial) and *facere* (to make, to produce) to the Middle English *fetis* and *fetice* (a cleverly made thing, or an attractive person) to the Middle Age Romanic derivatives of *feitixeria* (sorcery, witchcraft) and *feiticeiro* (sorcerer, wizard). First documented in 1610, it was brought to English by Portuguese sailors and traders — perhaps via the Newfoundland fishery? — who used the word to describe the talismans, amulets, and witchcraft of the people of Africa's Guinea coast, the location of Europe's earliest colonial atrocities. It was popularized in anthropological writing by Charles de Brosses's *De culte des dieux fétiches* (1760). It did not take on psychosexual connotations until (surprise, surprise) the late Victorian period.

If fishing was the local fetish, as Hope Simpson argued, then the knowledge of arithmetic can be thought of as the elite, bourgeois fetish. Both fetishes, and the very distinction between the two, I argue, are a dialectical expression of the commodity fetishism at the core of capitalism. *"When I argue along these lines, people think I am mad."* The mode of thinking that Hope Simpson articulates so succinctly can thus be understood as a fetishized expression of the underlying contradiction between use-value and value in the commodity-form. *"And when I point [this] out . . . I am regarded as still less sane."* Recognizing this, I will try to show, points us towards a way to overcome the very opposition itself.

IV.

Sitting at his little writing desk in the small office next to his bedroom at the Newfoundland Hotel, or at his loftier desk in the aptly named Colonial Building — or "ploughing along through the slush"[82] on Military Road between the two — Hope Simpson had an interesting vantage point from which to observe the political-economic organization of Newfoundland's saltfishery. The situation, in his assessment, was appalling. Inefficient production methods, declining quality, lost markets, vicious local competition, and a morally degraded and racially degenerated population had wasted the island's resource bounty.[83] "The people have become demoralized, and many of them lazy," Hope Simpson lamented in a different letter, "and they seem to prefer to sit down and eat flour and drink tea, rather than attempt to get their living for themselves."[84]

This situation demanded novel solutions. He proposed the development and institutionalization of the knowledge of arithmetic. As we will see, this was intended to reform the problems of an industry guided by the knowledge of fishing. It was meant to make the saltfishery modern, calculable, and predictable. The knowledge of fishing was developed over centuries through the sensuous, practical engagement between European settlers and the North Atlantic environment. The knowledge of arithmetic was meant to grasp the world — conceptually, abstractly, *numerically* — and to thereby give humans control over the frustratingly uncooperative characteristics of cod and a vast ocean. This was framed as a question of science. However, as I have argued in this chapter, despite the rhetoric of the scientist as "an Olympian standing high above all the 'earthly' technical and economic interests of his time, and soaring only in the empyrean of abstract thought,"[85] *scientists*, like any other humans, and *science*, like any other human activity, must be located within specific material, historical conditions.

With these stakes in mind, *Fishing Measures* is divided into three parts, followed by a short conclusion. The rest of Part I introduces readers to the knowledge of fishing. It examines how merchant credit overcame the inherent problem of fluctuation in fishing to ensure a steady stream of saltfish commodities, and why this system was breaking down by the 1880s. Although left unacknowledged in Hope Simpson's letter, it was this period that witnessed the first attempt at institutionalizing fisheries science and management in Newfoundland.

The subsequent two parts are dedicated to an empirically rich examination of the uneven development and trajectory of arithmetical institutions and innovations between the last two decades of the nineteenth century and the first three decades of the twentieth. Part II documents attempts to exert control over the *quantity* of fish extracted. It examines early attempts to regulate fish reproduction and predation (Chapter 3, "Controlling Quantity"), and early efforts to render cod and ocean-space legible and predictable through fisheries science (Chapter 4, "Predicting Quantity"). Part III shifts focus to attempts to control the *quality* of saltfish exported. It examines scientific reform and improvement of processing and marketing techniques for both saltfish (Chapter 5, "Improving Quality") and its key by-product, cod liver oil (Chapter 6, "Discovering Quality"). The conclusion (Chapter 7, "From Dory to Desk") reflects on the bifurcation of the knowledge of fishing *and* arithmetic, and points towards its possible overcoming in the form of a liberated, socially grounded, egalitarian, and sensuous science.

We are about to embark on a journey through 50 years of schemes, hopes, and desires aimed at modernizing and improving Newfoundland's saltfishery, its fishing families, and its society. Before leaving port, however, we need a crash course on saltfish production as organized by the credit system, and how it confronted what I call the problem of fluctuation.

"To understand the market," writes environmental historian William Cronon, "open the boxes; see the objects inside, then ask where they came from, who brought them there, who will buy them, and where they will go next."[86] Cronon follows this advice with a simple instruction, almost an incantation, for tracing the elaborate choreography of saltfish, supplies, labour, credit, and debt: "Follow the seller, follow the buyer."[87] The next chapter adopts Cronon's method by opening the boxes, or really, by opening the stage-door and peeking at the piles of saltfish produced through the strenuous labour of fishing families. It begins by examining a particular shipment of saltfish that landed in Valencia, Spain, on 13 December 1924, one that "set loose a chain of endless troubles."[88]

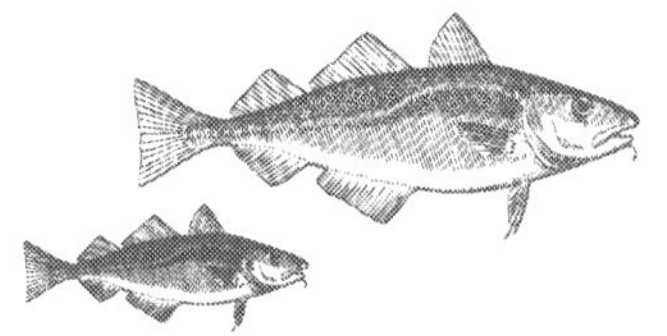

2

A CHAIN OF ENDLESS TROUBLES

One Saturday afternoon in mid-December 1924, Spanish fish merchants Mr. Francisco Romeu and Mr. Rafael Gavara were waiting at the port of Valencia for their latest shipment of Newfoundland saltfish, sent by the St. John's firm Colonial Products Ltd. and arriving on the S.S. *Paliki.* The Spanish merchants were expecting to receive 300 casks of large, prime-quality shorefish, 250 for Romeu and 50 for Gavara. As the ship was being unloaded, Romeu and Gavara took the opportunity to see what they were receiving, as some of the casks were open, "probably due to rough handling."[1] The Spanish fish merchants were shocked. Despite the certificate of inspection provided by the Newfoundland Board of Trade, guaranteeing a shipment of large, prime quality:

> the Shorefish in question (safe an insignificant portion) was exceedingly thin, without colour characteristic of Shorefish, but instead entirely white, burned or say overcured, defects, which all of them come from the place of origin and which could not have been caused while in transit.[2]

The "shorefish sent," they concluded, "in our humble capacity, . . . is absolutely inadmissible."[3]

Romeu and Gavara, furious, wanted to refuse the shipment, claiming deliberate fraud on the part of the Colonial Products Ltd. and the Newfoundland Board of Trade. For them, the shipment was useless. "Even offering the fish to the public at a ridiculous low figure," they argued, "no better result is obtained than to lose your customers, and a bad reputation in the bargain."[4] They were convinced to accept it by Hugh Haneberg, director of the Valencia Overseas Trade Company. Haneberg had negotiated the shipment between St. John's and Valencia, and he believed that it was in the interest of all involved to work towards a "square deal."[5] The fish business, he reminded the managers of the Colonial Products Ltd., was based on respect and reputation. Merchants in St. John's and Europe negotiated and traded through documents, promises, and trust. Fraudulent, dishonest, or simply negligent shipments threatened this mode of distribution. As Haneberg wrote to Aaron Stone, the managing director of Colonial Products Ltd., "If you have had the intention to kill further business, we must admit, that you couldn't have employed a more effective method to reach that end."[6]

Despite the threat of criminal proceedings against both the firm and the Board of Trade, the outcome of this conflict has slipped from the archival record. But the contours of the grievance lay bare the fundamental genius and flaws of Newfoundland's credit system. The conflict over the S.S. *Paliki* shipment highlights the uncertainties involved in the production, transportation, and consumption of saltfish. Actors involved in the trade had to negotiate the materiality of cod, the organization of labour, flows of financial capital, cultural norms regarding consumption, and far-flung networks of trust and respect. Getting saltfish to the consuming markets, in sum, confronted what I call *the problem of fluctuation.* This was rooted in the materiality of cod and ocean-space, in their specific characteristics and capabilities under certain technologies and social conditions. Fishers and merchants, bankers and brokers, bureaucrats and politicians all had to respond to this complex layering of environment, markets, culture, knowledges, and technology. Collectively, they developed geographically uneven and historically specific ways of accommodating and overcoming this problem.

This chapter covers a lot of ground. It delves deeper into how the problem of fluctuation shaped the credit system and the knowledge of fishing, and why this mode of production was reaching a crisis point in the late nineteenth century. Both questions, I argue, are grounded in the whirling, swirling materiality of ocean-space, rooted in geophysical processes that stretch back deep into planetary time. Let us dive in.

I.

The ocean, despite its appearance as a singular mass of water, is a highly complex, patterned system of differentiated moving water masses, each with distinct properties and boundaries.[7] Ocean water masses vary in terms of temperature, salinity, and nutrients. These variations cause differentiation in terms of water density, which drives ocean circulation, because denser (cold, salty) water sinks. Ocean currents, driven by density differences, orbital forces, and wind, distribute these variegated water masses across the ocean's volumetric space. Ocean currents, alongside light and depth, help determine the biological productivity of ocean ecosystems, fostering or inhibiting the production of plankton and fish life.

Off the coast of Newfoundland, on the part of the North American continental shelf known as the "Grand Banks," the icy, southerly flowing Labrador Current meets the northeasterly flowing Gulf Stream.[8] The differentiated water masses cause constant churning, as the warmer water is pushed upwards, bringing the nutrient-rich warm water closer to the surface. Here, in the "euphotic zone," microscopic organisms known as phytoplankton feed on the nutrients brought to the surface, while remaining close enough to the surface to successfully transform sunlight into chemical energy via photosynthesis. Phytoplankton form the basis of the aquatic food chain, feeding increasingly larger species, from zooplankton to crustaceans to fish to marine mammals to, let's not forget, humans. These millennia-spanning biogeophysical processes produced the conditions of possibility for the spectacular abundance of maritime life in the eastern North Atlantic. In Newfoundland, it turns out that one historically abundant form of life was particularly important for European civilization:

Gadus morhua, or Atlantic cod — so abundant, and so important, that it was commonly referred to by a more general name: simply "fish."[9]

Atlantic cod have two biophysical characteristics that make them particularly valuable to humans, especially urbanizing and colonizing medieval European humans. The first characteristic is that they are wonderfully, staggeringly fecund. Early tales of Atlantic cod's abundance off the coast of Newfoundland and Labrador, while perhaps apocryphal, speak to the species' fecundity. John Cabot, who "discovered" the island in 1497, reported cod so plentiful off the Grand Banks that they slowed the passage of his ship and could be scooped from the sea in buckets.[10] "These descriptions," writes historian Jeffrey Bolster, "which have sometimes been dismissed as extravagant propaganda, are numerous, and they corroborate one another, though written by different authors, in different languages, with different agendas, over more than a century." Regardless of their literal accuracy, they communicate something of the fecundity of that marine space.[11] A single large female may hold five to ten million eggs. Fishery scientist George Rose notes, "At its peak, the large northern cod stock included 300 million adult females that released about 500 trillion eggs each year."[12] Yet, in favourable environmental conditions, an adult cod is literally one in a million, due to very low survival rates. Unsuccessful eggs, regardless, are still huge infusions into the metabolic processes of ocean life, being recycled as food for zooplankton, pelagic and bottom invertebrates, and even cod larvae.

But cod exhibits a second characteristic that makes it valuable to human civilization: the specific biochemical composition of its flesh makes it particularly amenable to preservation after it is caught and killed. Fish decompose rapidly when killed. This occurs through three primary mechanisms: lipid oxidation, enzymatic autolysis, and microbial growth.[13] Lipid oxidation and enzymatic autolysis are *internal* biochemical changes, which involve the breakdown of the complex chemical substances of the tissues that leads to spoilage.[14] Microbial growth, in contrast, is the result of *external* contamination of the flesh. In order to extend the geography of consumption beyond the immediate locality, fish-based economies must exert some form of control over these processes of decomposition. This can be accomplished in two ways: first, by lowering the temperature, altering the acidity, or reducing water content of fish tissue to prevent microbial and enzymatic action; or second, by destroying the microbes and enzymes through heat and/or smoke.[15]

Simply put, different fish are more or less amenable to different forms of preservation. Cod flesh, on average, contains around 81 per cent water, 18 per cent protein and 0.1 per cent fat.[16] Unlike fish species with higher fat contents, such as herring, mackerel, and salmon, decomposition via lipid oxidation in cod is not a serious threat.[17] As the Department of Marine and Fisheries noted in 1905, "Different from oily fishes . . . its [cod's] flesh is rich and gelatinous, without being fatty, and readily lends itself to a simple and efficient cure by salting and being dried in the sun."[18] The most common way of limiting the processes of enzymatic autolysis and microbial growth in cod was by the removal of water. Dehydrating cod has the added benefit of concentrating the protein content of cod flesh, rising to almost 80 per cent protein by weight, and radically expanding the geographical distribution of marine protein across the globe.[19]

Saltfish was perfectly suited to the demands of the expansionary dynamics of capitalism: abundant, protein-rich, transportable over long distances, and cheap in relation to other sources of protein — not to mention, *delicious*, "the piscatory equivalent of salt-cured hams."[20] It literally fed the proletarianization and urbanization of the Southern European peasantry and the processes of colonization and enslavement in the plantation economy. "The discovery of gold and silver in America, the extirpation, enslavement and entombment in mines of the aboriginal population, the beginning of the conquest and looting of the East Indies, the turning of Africa into a warren for the commercial hunting of black-skins," Marx wrote, "signaled the rosy dawn of the era of capitalist production."[21] To this list of "idyllic proceedings," we should add the integration of the Grand Banks as a source of protein and profit in the metabolism of European capitalist production.

Despite their useful qualities as fecund and preservable, however, cod also exhibit characteristics that pose *obstacles* to the efficient production of fish commodities and the accumulation of capital. Cod fisheries are plagued by *the problem of fluctuation*.[22] This problem has two dimensions. First, cod fluctuate in terms of *quantity*. "From the earliest times," begins Johan Hjort's foundational text in fisheries biology, "a characteristic feature in all branches of the fishing industry has been fluctuations in the respective yields from year to year."[23] The ocean is profoundly, staggeringly, almost sublimely dynamic. Fish populations, accordingly, surge and decline over different time scales and in different areas.[24] They have highly variable diets, stitched together in complex food webs. As they grow and age, the predator–prey relationships shift, adding further complexities. For example, adult salmon prey on herring, but herring also prey on young salmon. This is unparalleled on land. As zoologist Peter Larkin points out, "Lions eat zebras, but zebras do not eat lion cubs."[25] Removing fish from water by hook, line, or trap was rife with uncertainty, due to the inherent fluctuations in annual yields. This had deep implications for the livelihoods of fishers and merchants, not to mention the urban poor in the consuming markets.

When cod leave the water, however, they enter a socio-economic system equally characterized by flux. This is the second dimension of the problem of fluctuation. Saltfish production had to confront and overcome *qualitative* fluctuations after extraction, in the processing, distribution, sale, and consumption of saltfish. The quality of saltfish varied due to weather and production methods, the price of fish varied due to conditions in world markets, and the consumption of fish varied due to season, religion, and local preferences. Saltfish had to arrive at the foreign markets in a palatable and culturally appropriate form. Like extraction, this was a difficult and risky process, shaped and constrained by the processes of decomposition and the dynamics of the global saltfish market. The quality, economic value, and cultural preferences for saltfish were dynamic and unpredictable, with equally profound implications for the economic geography of the saltfish industry as fluctuating yields.

In order to enjoy cod's use-value and profit off its exchange-value, European capitalists and settlers had to develop systems to overcome the inherent uncertainty of fishing arising from the quantitative and qualitative problem of fluctuation. Sheer biophysical abundance, in other words, was necessary, but not sufficient for economic development in Newfoundland after colonization. As David Harvey pointed out 40 years ago, "It is often erroneously accepted that scarcity is something inherent in nature, when its definition is inextricably social and cultural in origin."[26] Resources are only scarce (or abundant) in relation to historically and geographically specific social needs and ends. There are many abundant forms of life, both now and historically, in Newfoundland's waters, only some of which are socially/commercially "valuable." For example, geomicrobiologists have recently uncovered a vast microbial ecosystem under the surface of the ocean's floor. They note that "subseafloor basaltic crust," in fact, represents the "largest habitable zone by volume on Earth."[27] These stunning new discoveries should help problematize the relation between sheer abundance and social abundance.

Atlantic cod's abundance does not necessarily make it socially useful. Rather, its usefulness makes its abundance legible. In Newfoundland, merchants and financiers used the system of production known as the "credit system" to harness the problem of fluctuation, rooted in the material properties of fish and ocean-space, seeking to profit off this abundance. But as the Romeu and Gavara shipment demonstrates, this system was fraught with pitfalls. For most of the nineteenth century, however, the credit system *did succeed* at moving fish from the Grand Banks to the bellies of the urbanizing, global working class, proletarian and enslaved, in Southern Europe, Brazil, and the Caribbean. The material properties of cod provided both opportunities and obstacles for the transatlantic accumulation of capital in the saltfish industry, shaped by cod's seasonal patterns of abundance and its rapid decomposition after death.

Emerging over the course of the nineteenth century, as the saltfish industry shifted from a migratory to a resident, family-based mode of production, the credit system negotiated the obstacles and opportunities afforded by the "nature" of fishing to ensure a steady stream of saltfish commodities to the importers and traders of the consuming markets in Southern Europe and Latin America. This mode of production proved remarkably persistent, still dominating saltfish production when Hope Simpson arrived in the 1930s. Let us now turn to charting the contours of this way of organizing the fishing industry as it operated in *fin-de-siècle* Newfoundland.

II.

The word "fishing" evokes a wide array of referents. It might induce the romantic vision of the "hardy fisherman" rowing his wooden dory a few miles offshore to hand-line fish, straining to pull the fish aboard. Or, one might conjure up the image of a massive steel trawler, many days away from land, manned by alienated industrial labourers, mechanically hauling in thousands of pounds of fish with massive nets.[28] It could also bring to mind someone wading hip-deep into a river, casting off and hoping to reel in a large salmon or rainbow trout. These different images have one thing in common: they focus on the extractive moment. Fishing remains the act (or art) of "catching" fish, the process of extracting fish species from their aquatic environment. As Alicja Muszynski notes in her superb and underappreciated book on salmon canning in British Columbia, fishing is often romanticized in literature and popular culture as a masculine, adventurous pursuit.[29] Melville's *Moby Dick* and Hemingway's *The Old Man and the Sea*, she notes, are typical examples of the Western construction of fishing as manly and heroic.

Once fish are caught and landed, however, this sense of romanticism quickly evaporates. The activities associated with preparing fish for consumption, commonly the purview of women's labour, are not celebrated in literature.[30] "Cleaning and processing fish," she writes, "is not a heroic activity."[31] Studies of fishing, like literature and popular culture, often focus on the moment of extraction. Removing fish from water, by hook, hand, or net, remains the most charismatic moment in "fishing." Accordingly, fishing appears most powerfully shaped by two biophysical factors:

the maritime environment and the life histories of fish. But as we have seen, the problem of fluctuation is not resolved when cod are removed from the water and turned into saltfish. Saltfish, once cured, enters a socio-economic system equally uncertain and capricious: the quality of saltfish varies due to weather and production methods; the price of fish varies due to conditions in world markets; and the consumption of fish varies due to season, religion, and the local preferences of foreign markets. Fish are highly perishable, and this fact shapes the geography of production as much as their biophysical abundance or scarcity. The credit system had to confront and overcome both dimensions of the problem of fluctuation.

"Fishing" began long before fishers woke up and rowed towards their fishing grounds. Fishers required both the social knowledge of production and the fixed capital necessary for extraction and curing, namely: a boat (equipped with a gasoline engine by the early twentieth century), fishing gear (bultows, cod traps, handlines, etc.), and the land-based processing facility (the stage). This *fixed* capital was accumulated very slowly, often intergenerationally, and required constant maintenance.[32] Fishers also required annual inputs of what Marx calls *circulating* capital, which, as Gerald Sider points out, were "basic" in a dual sense of being both plain and essential: "salt, twine, nails, boots, jackets, flour, salt meat, tea and lard."[33] The Kent Commission report, an important Commission-era investigation into the saltfishery, adds a few others — hard bread, sugar, molasses, peas, beans, and tobacco — as well as items that grew in importance in the twentieth century, such as batteries, lubricating oil, and gasoline.[34]

This basic circulating capital, however, only covered the *counted* costs of the reproduction of labour-power, only those marked in the merchant's ledger. They were subsidized by a variety of unpaid, subsistence practices that made life reproducible with just those basic inputs, not to mention the gendered division of unpaid housework and emotional labour that make *all* economies possible.[35] Commissioner Hope Simpson learned this first-hand from a group of prominent merchants and politicians, as they sat chatting after dinner. He wrote to his daughter that when he brought up the precarious conditions in the outports, the "merchants at once piped up: 'They are used to nothing else. They are perfectly happy. They have blueberries and pay nothing for their firewood. In winter, they can snare rabbits.'"[36] Fishers would bring the fixed and constant capital together, through their labour-power, to produce saltfish and, more importantly for global finance, to produce value. Fish merchants advanced these costs on credit against the summer's catch, and in the process struggled with fishers over the distribution of value. Both groups extracted a livelihood from the ocean through cod, but some were more concerned with profiting than living, or really, living through profiting.

Newfoundland's late nineteenth-century saltfishery was not only divided socially. It was also divided in terms of geography, processing methods, and output. Three geographical regions of extraction emerged over centuries of settlement: the shore fishery, the Labrador fishery, and the Bank fishery. The *shore fishery* was the oldest and largest sector, employing about three-quarters of Newfoundland's fishers, spread across the island's 6,000-mile coastline. This fishery was prosecuted on the inshore grounds between June and October, in small boats with crews of two to five men, mainly using baited handlines or cod traps.[37] The *Labrador fishery*, which emerged in the early 1800s, was initially conducted on the southern coast of Labrador but extended northward over time. Residents or fishers travelling from their homes on the island, on schooners of 50–70 tons, prosecuted this fishery between July and October. It was divided into two types: the "stationers," who mimicked the techniques of the shore fishery, and the "floaters," who lived aboard their larger boats, fishing from smaller dories, and splitting and salting the fish on board before returning home for final processing.[38] The *Bank fishery* was operated on the Grand Banks, 50–300 miles southeast of the island from March until October, on large schooners of up to 150 tons, with crews of 20–24 men and 10–12 dories.[39] Fishers would fish from the dories around the "mother ship" with baited longlines of up to one thousand hooks, and the fish would be gutted, washed, split on the vessel, and placed in *salt bulk* to be processed later, or exported *green*.[40]

Although all three sectors produced "saltfish," they did not produce the same commodity. There were a number of different *styles* of saltfish, varying primarily by the amount of salt used and the intensity of drying. "In the beginning," writes biochemist N.L. Macpherson, "local conditions of the locality of fishing dictated different procedures in the methods."[41] In other words, the method of catching and local weather conditions determined the curing method. The shore fishery produced *shore fish*: a light-salted, hard-dried product, "unique to the weather conditions and curing skills of the island."[42] Inshore fishers fished close to their homes and processed their fish daily, which limited the amount of salt required to halt decomposition. Moreover, Newfoundland's weather conditions were uniquely suited to producing shore fish: it required warm and windy conditions, but was damaged by *too* much sun or heat. Labrador and Bank fish, in contrast, produced *heavy-salted fish*. For the Bank fishery and the Labrador floaters, their extended geographies of extraction required split fish to remain in salt for a much longer time before drying. Labrador stationers and residents required larger salt inputs than the shore fishery, due to the region's shorter summers and more northern climate.[43]

We have, then, three different extractive methods, producing two different styles of fish. The production of saltfish commodities entailed an almost dizzying level of differentiation and heterogeneity. Shipments of saltfish to the foreign markets were made up from fish from "a hundred of different hands,"[44] representing, "in reality, nearly as many different cures and qualities, on account of the fish from two fishermen being seldom found alike, and puzzling often the best culler to cull properly."[45] Yet, as British administrator Thomas Lodge points out, these heterogeneous labour processes reduce themselves to the "essentially simple process" of extracting and preserving codfish, known in Newfoundland as *making fish*.[46] It entailed both removing *fish from water*, by hook, line, or trap, and removing *water from fish*, by sun, salt, wind, and weight.

Once caught and returned to shore, fish were landed onto the *stage head* where they were cleaned and split.[47] Work was centred on the splitting table, divided between three essential tasks. First, the *cutter* or *cut-throat(er)* would cut the throat from gill to gill, and then cut down along the belly from nape to vent. The fish would then be passed to the *header* who gutted and headed the fish. The header would first remove the liver, and place it in a bucket for rendering into cod oil. The rest of the internal organs were then removed and would be discarded through a hole in the floor. The header would then place the fish's head over the edge of the table, and using the table as a cutting edge, would rip the head off with a "violent jerk" and pass the fish to the *splitter*.[48] Splitting required the most skill and dexterity, and had the greatest effect on the final quality and thus price fetched.[49]

Before salting, the fish was often washed and scrubbed to remove any blood, guts, or *slub* (slime), which were all sources of accelerated decomposition.[50] Fish were salted in two ways. First, by placing alternating and slightly slanted layers of the fish and salt in *pounds*, to drain off the excess pickle by pressing, known as the *kench cure*.[51] Second, by alternating layers of salt and fish in casks or puncheons to cure in brine, known as the *pickle cure*.[52] Salting was an extremely complex task, which required years of experience to successfully account for the different variables that affected the process: the size and thickness of the fish, weather conditions, such as temperature and humidity, the characteristics of the salt, and the different styles of cure. Too much salt could cause *saltburn*; too little would not sufficiently halt the processes of bacterial and autolytic decomposition.[53] These complexities were compounded by the wide variations in the types of salt used. Fishers used both mineral and solar salts, which varied in terms of grain size and potency.[54] "It is a skilled art, judging the salt," concluded one local biochemist.[55]

After the appropriate amount of time left under salt — three to five days for light-salted pickle cure, five or six days for light-salted kench cure, and up to 20 days for heavy-salted kench cure — the fish was taken out of its pickle or pile and washed for the final time, removing any blood, slime, and excess salt.[56] The washed fish was then piled and re-piled, in a stack known as a *water-horse*, often with a weight on top, to help press out moisture and prepare the fish for drying.[57] Fish would be left in the *water-horse* for a few hours, most often overnight, but could be stored for up to three or four days if the weather was too damp for drying.[58]

The drying process entailed the alternating spreading and piling of the fish to remove the water content by air circulation and by pressing.[59] Fish were spread on *flakes*.[60] At first, the fish was very delicate, requiring gentle handling, but as it dried and hardened, it became more resilient. Fish were spread out for the day, piled into *faggots*, and covered with a bough each night or if the weather became too wet. These piles increased in size as the fish was cured. After a week or so of good drying, the fish were piled into very large *faggots* known as *round piles* to *work* (to press out moisture) for approximately a week. The fish were then re-spread and re-piled, until the desired level of dryness was achieved, and then stored for shipment.

Like any product dependent on the vagaries of the ocean and weather, saltfish commodities also varied greatly in terms of quality. The quality of saltfish was "a function of the size of the fish, the amount of salt in which it has been cured, the cleanliness which has attended its preparation, and the weather."[61] For consumers, the quality of saltfish ultimately depended on three factors: durability, appearance, and reversibility.[62] Saltfish had to survive shipment from the outports to the consuming markets in Southern Europe and the Caribbean, overcoming both the biophysical processes of bacterial and autolytic decomposition in storage and shipment, and the rough handling of culling, packing, and unloading. To further complicate matters, quality and durability in saltfish were somewhat at odds: the most attractive and reversible product, light-salted shore fish, was also the most delicate and perishable.[63] Fish makers had to balance a complex set of risks and rewards when curing saltfish.

These decisions were complicated, and often frustrated, by the reliance on a key input into the drying process beyond human control: the weather. Drying was done outside, and its success relied on local temperature, humidity, and precipitation conditions. Newfoundland is well known for its highly unpredictable and variable weather. This was often blamed for the inferior cure of Newfoundland fish. As research scientist N.L.

Macpherson argued in a 1932 analysis of the industry, "By far the greater part of the difficulties in obtaining a product of high quality lies in the unfavourable drying conditions prevailing."[64] But fluctuating weather was also *essential* to the process because curing fish entailed the alternating drying *and piling* of fish. Fish makers removed moisture from cod by air drying and *by pressing*.[65] Piling was an essential part of the drying process, as it pressed inner moisture to the surface, which was evaporated when spread out and gave the fish a smooth, even surface.[66] Newfoundland journalist, politician, and eventual Governor of the Bahamas Sir Ambrose Shea summed up the issue concisely: "Unbroken sunshine is not desirable, while a long continuation of wet produces deterioration of quality; the best cure is effected when the weather is variable."[67] Newfoundland's geography was ideally suited to this process, but as the Spanish fish merchants Romeu and Gavara were frustratingly aware, a lot could go wrong in this process. The smooth conversion of saltfish into money and commodities and profit was constantly under threat.

Spread over thousands of miles of coast in hundreds of small communities, the labour process of making fish was largely unsupervised, but it was not disorganized. Often derided as governed by "rule of thumb" methods, it nevertheless required a refined, embodied knowledge of the techniques, inputs, and weather, knowing how much salt to use or when to move to the next step by look and feel, intuition, and experience. As the complaint that opened this chapter demonstrates, this process was susceptible to a number of threats that could lower the quality of the final product, "defects, which . . . come from the place of origin."[68] If the weather was too wet, the fish could not dry; too fine, and the fish would be *sunburnt*. In the summer, flies could lay eggs on the fish and turn the fish *maggoty*. Moreover, as only a *semi*-perishable food commodity, decomposition was an ever-present menace, which could turn the fish "slimy" or "sour." While in storage, fungal infections such as *dun*, characterized by black or brown spots on the fish, and bacterial infections such as *pink* or *red*, characterized by the fish turning a pinkish hue, similarly plagued the industry.

Making fish, in sum, was inherently uncertain and incessantly unpredictable. That Romeu and Gavara received anything even remotely edible — even if it was "exceedingly thin, without colour characteristic of Shore-fish, but instead entirely white, burned or say overcured"[69] — was a remarkable social and technical achievement. The uncertainties that plagued the labour process, however, were not resolved when the commodities were laid out in round piles, awaiting shipment, or stacked in bulk in the holds of transatlantic sailing vessels. As we will see in the following section, they were multiplied.

III.

As we know from the conflict that opened this chapter, we have a sense that the saltfish went *somewhere*, namely the markets of Southern Europe, Brazil, and the Caribbean. But an important question remains: how *did* saltfish get from the *stage head* in Newfoundland to the bellies of the urban poor in Valencia, not to mention Oporto, Patras, Maceió, or Bridgetown? As Marx points out in Volume II of *Capital*, the circulation of commodities, "their actual course in space," is a product of the transport industry, an independent branch of production.[70] On the other hand, transportation "is distinguished by its appearance as the continuation of a production process *within* the circulation process and *for* the circulation process."[71] The production of saltfish, then, extends beyond the local labour process of making fish to incorporate the circulation of saltfish through space-time via circuits of financial capital in the form of merchant credit. Somewhat counterintuitively, therefore, a plantation worker in Jamaica, eating a plate of ackee and saltfish, was as central to the production of Newfoundland saltfish as an English or Irish settler facing the North Atlantic gale.

Saltfish, in order to be consumed in Spain or Barbados, had to be exported: collected, culled, stored, transported, and sold. Moreover, to be produced, saltfish required supplies and equipment to be imported and distributed to fishing peoples. In Newfoundland, fish merchants conducted both activities, acting as both exporter and supplier. There was a pronounced seasonal disjuncture between these two activities: supplies were required in the spring, fish was made over the summer, it was exported and sold in the autumn, and fishing families had to survive the winter to start the cycle anew. Credit, thus, emerged as a central, enabling feature of Newfoundland's economy by overcoming the seasonal disjuncture between production and realization.

With the season's catch cured, the saltfish would pass from the fisher to the merchant. This could happen in a variety of ways: saltfish could be delivered by the fisher to the merchant/exporter in the fisher's immediate vicinity, a nearby settlement, or an exporting centre; saltfish could be transported to an exporting centre with means of transport provided by the merchant; or a merchant could travel to the fishing settlement on a schooner to trade goods for fish, on full-time freighters or on ships previously engaged in fishing.[72] Generally, fishers sold their fish to their supplying merchant. Except in the case of insolvency, this was not a *legal* obligation, but it was considered a *moral* obligation.[73] For fishers, this was also a *practical* decision. Knowing that they would need supplies on credit in the future and that credit was advanced more liberally to "honest" fishers, they balanced these moral demands with attempts to circumvent their current supplier to receive better prices by selling to peripatetic "traders."[74]

To determine the amount paid to fishers and to settle credit accounts, the saltfish would be culled: sorted into grades by style, size, and quality. Culling was a key moment in the process of making fish that determined the prices paid for the season and the standard of living for the following winter. Cullers, employed by the merchant, evaluated the quality of saltfish produced by fishers, and sorted it into different market categories. Cullers examined the look, feel, and thickness of each fish and measured the length of the fish on a culling board. They were sorted by grade and then weighed, with the final amounts of each grade placed on the credit side of the fisher's account. Saltfish was divided into a range of grades (merchantable, Madeira, thirds, West India, cullage, and damp), and subdivided within grades on the basis of size (large, medium, small) and between No. 1 and No. 2.

The grading of saltfish had a huge influence on the prices received and profitability of a season, for both fishers and merchants. Often paid by per quintal culled, and trying to evaluate a staggering amount of diverse saltfish, the culler worked quickly, often handling the fish quite roughly.[75] With the culler in the merchant's employ, the cull was thus highly politicized, viewed less as an accurate assessment of quality than "an expression of opinion on the part of the purchaser as to what he chose to regard as value for the various grades."[76] To further complicate matters, culling standards varied depending on market conditions. "If the market goes down after the buyer has bought he is going to examine the fish carefully and you will not get off with any defects in the fish. . . . Minor defects, if the market has gone up, will be overlooked."[77]

After the cull, saltfish would be stored on the merchant's premises in buildings of various quality and cleanliness, awaiting resale or export. Before export, the product would be re-culled, which often differed from the first cull between fishers and merchants. Differences in first and second culls were occasionally the result of overt deception, on the part of either fisher or merchant, but, structurally, they resulted from deterioration within the merchant premises.[78] The concentration of saltfish from many different places into premises of varying quality and cleanliness tended to spread and intensify halophilic organisms, such as the bacterial infections known as "pink" or "red," and the mould known locally as "dun." Stocks of saltfish could be stored on a premise for 10 to 12 months, competing with the following year's "new" fish, but this risked deterioration and depreciation.[79]

From the merchants' stores, saltfish was shipped to the consuming markets. The traditional method of shipping fish was in bulk by locally owned or English sailing vessels. Saltfish was exported in small cargoes of 100–150 tonnes, arriving in a staggered fashion over the season.[80] Transportation in bulk was often detrimental to the overall quality of the fish shipped: "The fish is shipped in apparently good condition, but in transit deterioration of quality takes place."[81] Handling, packing, and unpacking the cargo, often multiple times due to its transshipment through New York or Liverpool, and careless storage led to damaged fish.[82] Storage in piles in the ship's holds — reminiscent of the *water-horse* phase meant to drain salt and water off saltfish in production — led to loss in weight and shrinkage of the cargo. Finally, the journey from Newfoundland's milder summer to the much hotter climates of the Southern Europe, Brazil, and the Caribbean often accelerated the processes of decomposition in saltfish.[83] All told, saltfish often arrived in the foreign markets a different quality than it was shipped.

The uncertainties of shipping were a constant source of tension between the Newfoundland shippers and foreign buyers. Sales were either made through direct contact with buyers, or through brokers in Newfoundland, London, New York, or other commercial centres.[84] Shipments would then be weighed and inspected to account for shrinkage and deterioration and to finalize the sale terms — another obvious source of contestation between buyer and seller, this time between Newfoundland and foreign merchants.[85] Methods of payment varied as well, but the usual method was "to draw a Bill of Exchange upon the buyer, with the shipping documents attached, payable at sight, or so many days or months after sight, in Newfoundland currency or in sterling."[86] Generally, however, payment was on the basis of 90 days' sight, meaning that it took a long time for merchants to receive payment on their shipments. One merchant complained that because "it took 40 days for the voyage, 10 days to discharge, 20 days for the drafts to reach London, and 90 days before maturity of the draft, shippers would be nearly 6 months getting their money."[87] As merchant H.R. Brookes pointed out, large shippers often had multiple cargoes overlapping, further tying up capital.[88] The extended terms of payment, moreover, left merchants vulnerable to fluctuating currency exchange rates.[89]

Once the sale was completed between the Newfoundland merchants and the foreign merchants and retailers, saltfish entered the biological and social realm of consumption. For Marx, this final step is not the *opposite* of production, but *an important part of it*. "Only by decomposing the product does consumption give the product the finishing touch."[90] Saltfish was a very popular food in Southern Europe and South America: "partly on account of the facility of salted cod being resistant to hot climates, and partly due to most of the people being of Catholic religion."[91] Saltfish consumption had distinct seasonal patterns, related to both the biological reproduction of cod and the religious calendar.[92] Saltfish, moreover, was primarily consumed by the urban poor, which, as David Alexander points out, imposed a strict *ceiling* on prices, but not much of a *floor*.[93] It was in direct competition with other sources of food, being favoured more for its low price than its culinary qualities.[94] However, when the price for saltfish approached the price for meat, it was often the second choice.[95] "When fish becomes dearer than beef or pork or mutton in the Latin countries," noted one observer in 1930, "consumption soon falls off; when cheaper than national foods, the consumption grows rapidly."[96]

In the early days of Newfoundland's saltfish trade, fisheries "did not have an order for fish of a certain type from certain places."[97] Rather, various types of products of various grades were offered in different markets, until demand began to differentiate. Eventually, a stable hierarchy of styles, grades, sizes, and markets had emerged for shore and Labrador fish.[98] For example, Spain, Italy, and Portugal preferred the highest-quality "merchantable prime" and "merchantable No. 2," Brazil preferred the medium-quality "Madeira," and the lowest-quality "West India" was sent to the Caribbean.[99] The wetter, heavy-salted Labrador cure was sent in two qualities, No. 1 and No. 2, to Spain, northern Italy, and Greece.[100] Market preferences varied internationally, but also intra-nationally, with different ports having different requirements.[101] For example, in contrast to the preference for thick fish in most Spanish ports, Barcelona preferred thin and very salty fish. Seventeenth-century colonial bureaucrat Sir Joseph Williamson sums it up perfectly: "Some sorts of fish are for some places and go off better, others at other."[102]

The process of making fish, at first glance, appears as the transformation of commodities into saltfish into commodities, or C-M-C, in Marx's classic formula.[103] In Newfoundland, saltfish is often referred to as "Newfoundland currency," highlighting its role as a medium of exchange in the economy.[104] Newman, Hunt and Co. of London stated this view explicitly in 1864: "We wish you to understand that our business in Newfoundland is not to buy Fish but to sell goods, and that we only take Fish in payment because the Planters [fishers] have no money to give us."[105] Saltfish occupied the place of money in the circuit of capital. This circuit is most apparent at the scale of the community and to the lived experience of fishing peoples and, subsequently, to social history and ethnography.

But this circuit was nested in a broader one: the transformation of money into commodities into more money, or profit, visualized as M-C-M' by Marx.[106] This is the realm of historical-geographical materialism. It must be remembered that the saltfish commodity chain extended far beyond the shores of Newfoundland and Labrador. The Kent Commission report is one of the few analyses of Newfoundland's saltfish trade to point this out. The report spells out a five-stage "cycle of finance for the fishery":

> First, the fisherman with his boats and gear and knowledge of production; second, the Banking Institutions and large merchants with their cash and stocks; third, the merchants in the outport settlements, who with the help of the larger merchants, supply the outfits; fourth, the fishermen who catch the fish, and sell the results of their labours to the merchants; and fifth, the Banks, who are called into assist in the collection of the value of the catch from the foreign buyers.[107]

Saltfish is most commonly regarded as occupying the role of money — as "Newfoundland currency" — but it should also be understood *as capital*, as value *in motion*.

IV.

We are now in a position to understand how saltfish produced in "isolated outports" made its way to those fish merchants in Valencia, Spain, mediated by a merchant firm in St. John's, a broker in Spain, transportation infrastructures, and international centres of finance. The credit system successfully overcame the inherent obstacles to accumulation emerging from the material characteristics of fish: its seasonal patterns of abundance and its rapid decomposition after death. But these obstacles were also opportunities; those very characteristics made the credit system possible in the first place. As George Henderson demonstrates in an incisive analysis of Californian agriculture, the very disjuncture between production and realization arising from the seasonality of agriculture "opens up temporal and spatial channels for the extraction of surpluses by means of fictitious values and fictitious capitals."[108]

As the conflict that opened this chapter demonstrates, this mode of economic organization was rife with contradictions. A rift in the smooth metabolism of cod protein from the Northwest Atlantic to inshore fishing stages and stores to the stomachs of the urban poor could happen at any point in the circuit of capital. And, indeed, by the late nineteenth century, this was happening more and more often. The credit system's internal contradictions were sharpening, with profound repercussions for the industry and the colony as a political-economic entity.

Despite the inherent uncertainty of an economy based on fishing, for most of the nineteenth century the credit system in Newfoundland succeeded in overcoming the problem of fluctuation and producing a large quantity of highly variegated saltfish commodities. For individual fishers in Newfoundland, catch failures were common, and potentially devastating to their social reproduction. Yet even a cursory examination of the various fishery reports shows that while catch failures occurred almost every year in some areas, they were offset by good or fair catches in other areas or by held-over stocks from the previous year.[109] In other words, despite persistent, even recurrent, local catch failures, *overall* production was very rarely seriously affected. "One can easily get the mistaken idea," states historian Shannon Ryan, "that such failures were widespread and a major threat to the whole economy."[110] But, as he notes, crises were usually limited to specific regions. As Governor MacGregor concluded in a 1906 report, "The most remarkable feature of this Cod fishery is its perennial character."[111]

Nevertheless, by the late nineteenth century Newfoundland's economy was struggling, even in the context of the steadily increasing world demand for saltfish.[112] This proves somewhat counterintuitive: how could Newfoundland struggle when there were ever-more people wanting saltfish? Three intertwined issues fundamentally altered the economic landscape of saltfish production in the late nineteenth and early twentieth centuries: the emergence of new patterns of consumption; increased competition from other saltfish producers; and the introduction of steam into Newfoundland's economy.

By the end of the nineteenth century, there was a revolution in consumer demand. As one fisher explained succinctly in a letter to the Newfoundland Board of Trade: "People is more particular over food nowadays than they were years ago."[113] Rather than basing food purchases solely on price or flavour, new consumer standards emerged. Attractiveness, uniformity, year-round availability, and ease of preparation emerged as key determining factors in fish purchases.[114] Many people noted that Newfoundland shore fish was favoured in the foreign markets for its "fine flavour and good keeping qualities."[115] By the end of the nineteenth century, however, its appearance deterred many consumers, who preferred "a clean white and delicate looking article and a somewhat uniform type of the different kinds."[116] Consumers, noted merchant W.A. Munn, "are dainty and must see a nice appearance or they will not be tempted to purchase."[117]

This shift in consumer demand, however, was made possible by the increasing competition from saltfish producers. In other words, without more attractive saltfish to choose from, consumers would not have been able to cultivate their new demands. Indeed, this point is highlighted by the fact that Newfoundland's Labrador and Bank fisheries were decimated by the new competition, but its shore fish industry remained less affected. This is because Newfoundland's light-salted, hard-dried shore fish was the result of the island's particular climate and processing methods, and was very difficult to reproduce.[118] The wetter, saltier Labrador-style fish faced more intense competition due to the fact that other countries could produce a similar, and superior, product, even retaining the name "Labrador style."[119]

Newfoundland's main competitors in the saltfish industry over the course of the nineteenth century were Norway, Iceland, Scotland, France,

Portugal, Canada, the United States, and the Faroe Islands, with France, Norway, and Iceland as the most important competitors. They significantly eroded Newfoundland's market share by the end of the century. For example, in 1814, Newfoundland exported roughly 400,000 quintals of saltfish to Spain — fully *100 per cent* of Spain's importation — but this was reduced to 80,000 quintals by 1914, only *10 per cent* of Spain's total importation.[120] The French government subsidized their fishery through an extensive system of bounties, as a way to train sailors and to stimulate saltfish exportation, allowing French bounty fish to be sold under production cost.[121] The Norwegian and Icelandic fisheries received significant support from their governments to improve their production methods and marketing arrangements.[122] For Newfoundland's Department of Fisheries, the reasons behind Newfoundland's declining market share were simple. Their competitors were beating them "by their improved methods, better handling, intelligent and intimate business relations with the purchasers, and their anxiety to please the customer in every way."[123]

The case of Iceland is particularly instructive. For most of the nineteenth century, Iceland was not a major producer and exporter of saltfish.[124] However, by the turn of the twentieth century, Iceland had captured a large portion of Norway's and Newfoundland's former markets.[125] For example, Iceland had almost completely replaced Norway as the main source for saltfish in Barcelona, formerly a Norwegian "stronghold."[126] Similarly, Icelandic "Labrador style" saltfish outcompeted "authentic" Labrador saltfish by producing a uniform, attractive commodity "in boxes, nicely packed and finished off with white salt [making] it an attractive article of food to the purchasers."[127] Again, this is despite the supposed superiority of Newfoundland saltfish: ". . . customers to-day buy from the look of the fish, and when they come in to purchase it is no use telling them that Newfoundland fish is of better flavour when it does not look as white and clean as does the Iceland fish."[128]

As one commentator noted, "there is something in the nature of a war between Iceland and Newfoundland, which is being carried on by using fish as the weapon."[129] Iceland was winning for two reasons. First, Icelandic production methods were better suited to making high-quality fish. With catching and curing separated and centralized, merchants could control production more closely and efficiently.[130] Second, the Icelandic government had instituted rigid inspection and established standard grades of quality and size.[131] Icelandic fishery inspectors travelled to foreign markets to gather information on local requirements, improving grading standards.[132] This gave buyers confidence that their contracts would be fulfilled. "They can quote to arrive as required — Extra Large, Large, Medium, and Small — giving the price per kilo, and the number of fish contained in each box for each size."[133] These guarantees encouraged payment against documents, rather than on consignment, speeding up the turnover of capital.[134]

Newfoundland's decline in market share was radically accelerated by the introduction of steam technology in the transportation and distribution sectors during the last quarter of the nineteenth century. Steam power was first introduced in Newfoundland's seal fishery in the 1860s and was introduced to the fish-carrying trade by the 1880s.[135] Prior to this, saltfish was shipped in small-capacity sailing vessels, arriving at the markets in small batches over the course of the season. The introduction of large-capacity steamers, however, upset this system. Saltfish arrived in much larger cargoes, often flooding the market and depressing fish prices.[136] These gluts "induced something akin to panic as sellers anxiously underbid each other, trying to dispose of their fish before the price dropped even further."[137]

On top of the larger shipments, the faster transatlantic journey exacerbated the annual "rush to market." The first shipments to arrive in the fall tended to fetch better prices than subsequent shipments.[138] George Hawes stated that the reason for this is quite simple: "Supply and demand — at the beginning they can buy more than you can supply and they are not fussy about the price."[139] Newfoundland shippers were anxious to capture these extra profits, which led to keen competition between them. "Every shipper," wrote merchant and politician James Murray, "wants to supplant his neighbour — to anticipate, to over-reach him" — or, in his memorable phrase, to "wolf" the competition.[140]

To speed up the process of buying and exporting fish, merchants turned to the practice of *talqual* purchasing, derived from Latin "*talis qualis*" meaning "such as it is."[141] Under this system, rather than strictly culling the fisher's catch, an average price was "fixed for the whole of a fisherman's catch without any exact regard to the varying qualities of the fish comprising the catch."[142] Talqual purchasing was first introduced in the 1850s, and was fairly common in the Labrador fishery by the 1890s.[143] By 1907, it began spreading to the shore fishery, and was regarded as common by the 1910s and "almost universal" by 1915.[144]

This practice had two effects. First, it eliminated the price incentive fishers received for curing high-quality fish, because improperly cured fish often received the same price as properly cured fish.[145] In 1897, a fisher writing to the *Evening Telegram* articulated the fisher perspective regarding talqual: "I have lost my time in handling my fish so often; I have lost on its weight by drying it so much, and now it does not bring me as much money as if I had only half-dried it; I have had my pains for my labor and less money for more trouble."[146] Fishers began selling as much partially or poorly cured fish as possible, realizing that quantity was more profitable than quality. Second, it had a "prejudicial effect" on Newfoundland saltfish in the foreign markets.[147] Importers no longer felt secure buying fish outright and began purchasing fish on consignment; that is, they waited for the fish to arrive and be inspected before processing payment.[148] This shifted bargaining power to the importers, leaving the Newfoundland shippers open to the risk of gluts, price drops, deterioration, and claims against quality. Talqual buying was regularly criticized as "the result of mistrust, avariciousness, and inexcusable folly" that demoralized fishers and discouraged efficiency, yet it remained stubbornly prevalent.[149]

This context helps explain why Newfoundland's saltfish economy was struggling in the context of growing world demand. Consumers were demanding new facets of quality — attractiveness, uniformity, ease of preparation — and saltfish producers from other nations were able to respond to these demands. Newfoundland, in contrast, was swimming against the current: the quality of Newfoundland's saltfish was in steady decline. For many commentators, the poor cure was blamed on the use of family labour in Newfoundland. Rather than blaming women and children, however, we can see that this issue was deeply rooted in the organization of production. Shipments of saltfish to the foreign markets, as we have seen, consisted of fish from many independent fishers that varied greatly in quality and cures. Once a strength of the system, by ensuring the differentiated qualities required by different markets, this was now framed as a problem with consumers demanding uniformity.

V.

The 1924 shipment on the S.S. *Paliki* to Romeu and Gavara in Valencia was thus deeply symptomatic of contradictions embedded in the organization of production that had plagued the industry for decades. Organized around credit, saltfish production in late nineteenth-century Newfoundland overcame the problem of fluctuation in fishing by ensuring that a large aggregate amount of highly differentiated saltfish was exported each season. Fishers and merchants, buyers and sellers, producers and consumers all had to confront and overcome the problem of fluctuation in saltfish production, in terms of both quantity and quality. They had to overcome quantitative fluctuations prior to extraction, shaped by the materiality of fish and ocean-space, and qualitative fluctuations post-extraction, shaped by the material properties of biochemical decomposition and socio-biological consumption. Fishers made saltfish, but more importantly they produced value. Merchants controlled the distribution of this value across the circuit of capital through the price-fixing mechanism of supplying fishers and exporting saltfish. Fishers, too, struggled to appropriate more value by selling their fish to peripatetic traders, or by deceiving the merchants or cullers. The credit system was a chain of endless troubles, but this chain was also the source of all profit.

How, then, can we describe and characterize the knowledge of fishing? If, as early German sociologist Georg Simmel argues, the metropolis, as the seat of the money economy, inculcates a calculative mindset, then what sort of mindset was inculcated in St. John's and the outports by the *credit* economy? How did fishers and merchants understand and confront the problem of fluctuation?

Newfoundland's *fin-de-siècle* credit system was characterized by a persistent lack of *precise* information. It was governed, primarily, by the embodied "knowledge of fishing" in Hope Simpson's terms, knowledge gathered over hundreds of years through practical labour: the accumulated knowledge of past and living experience. Fishers used experiential knowledge to determine when and where to fish, to intuit weather patterns, and to "read" ocean dynamics. For example, Commissioner of Natural Resources Hope Simpson encountered this on his journey to Newfoundland: "A Newfoundland skipper, Capt. Whiteley, who is on board, told me yesterday morning that he 'smelt' ice. The captain had not told him anything, so I suppose there must be something in it."[150] This knowledge was often devalued and derided as hearsay, anecdotal, or simply absurd. Take Fisheries Superintendent Adolph Nielsen's assessment of the "lower class" people in Newfoundland: "They are terribly ignorant and probably no more than 10% of them can read or write. To read the many theories that are set about the fishery here in the local papers are ridiculous."[151]

This form of accumulated knowledge extended beyond the extractive process. Processing methods in Newfoundland, like extraction, were governed by the accumulated knowledge of fishers: "curing by rule of thumb and every one a law unto himself."[152] *Making fish* was a complex procedure that required a granular knowledge of the process and the conditions of production. The way the fish was gutted and headed, the amount, type, and quality of salt used, the time left in pile, *water-horse*, or on the *flake*: all profoundly affected the finished product's quality and price, and the fishers' and merchant's profits. In biochemist Norman Macpherson's estimation, this knowledge was "rather vague."[153] For example, regarding the optimal amount of salt to use, he stated that the fisher knew "the old 'rule of thumb' methods, but he has never studied the thing from the point of view of a science."[154] The fishers did not know the specific properties of the different salts used, and thus could not calculate the optimal amount to use for each type of salt. Consequently, fishers had "to salt by guess."[155]

Like catching and curing, the marketing and distribution of saltfish were characterized by a profound absence of information. Merchant W.G. Gosling, in a letter recommending the formation of a Board of Trade in Newfoundland, wrote that the lack of information regarding Newfoundland's competitors and customers was "a very serious drawback to us in the proper management of the business."[156] He continued:

> We go on shipping there [Southern Europe] in an absolutely blind way, very few ever knowing what vessels are loading for market at one time. Every now and then it is suddenly discovered that there is an excessive quantity of fish on the way to that market. . . . A little consultation and forethought would have avoided such an unhappy condition of things.[157]

Merchants shipped fish without knowing the conditions of the market. In response, they turned to hyper-competitive practices, trying to undersell and outsmart their competitors, or to "wolf" them.[158] They were so competitive that they often actively impeded the collection of information and statistics. As the Assistant Collector for Customs noted, both exporters and fishers were reluctant to report their catches and sales, "and unless there is compulsory legislation they will not do so."[159] In the hyper-competitive context of the Newfoundland credit system, science and statistics threatened the ability to "wolf" the competition.

The credit system also functioned without a detailed or precise knowledge of its internal economy. Merchants supplied fishers without determining the price of goods advanced. Rather, each transaction would be logged in an account book, with a price to be settled later in the season: "No money passes between them; but the account of every article that is supplied to the fishermen is entered in the books of their masters."[160] Merchants met in August to "break the price," to collectively settle the price of fish and oil.[161] Fishers laboured without knowing the prices they were charged on goods and the prices they would receive for the fish.[162] This left most fishers "somewhat indifferent about the prices they are charged," concerned more with securing supplies than questioning prices.[163] The price of goods and saltfish, rather than representing an abstract calculation of absolute value, was relational and variable under the credit system. Prices could vary significantly between two fishers supplied by the same merchant, between different merchants in the same locality, and between merchants in different settlements.[164] Despite the use of double-entry bookkeeping — an important early quantitative technology[165] – accounting was primarily negotiable and contingent, not abstract and accurate.

In an analysis of a major financial crisis in Newfoundland in 1894, known as "Black Monday," merchant, politician, and social critic James Murray reminded fishers that they were "an average member of a System that dealt in averages."[166] Individual efficiency was less important than aggregate output. A large quantity of saltfish of varying quality was more profitable than a small quantity of No.1 fish: "When rule of thumb methods prevailed in the past and hurry was the motto, the big idea was to kill a voyage. The making of it was of secondary importance."[167] The hope was that the profits from a large quantity of saltfish would "average" out: good fishers would cover the debts of bad fishers and high-quality fish would cover the cost of shipping low-quality fish. These tendencies were exacerbated by the gradual spread of talqual buying, whereby cargoes of saltfish were purchased at an average fixed valuation, "without any exact regard to the varying qualities of the fish comprising the catch."[168] Often framed as evidence of merchant greed or fisher apathy, perhaps talqual and the imprecision of the credit system are evidence, as French Consul C.R. des Isles suggests, of a more "general tendency" in Newfoundland: the "neglect of details."[169]

The political-economic organization of saltfish production thus created a fundamentally different metrical mindset than the metropolitan money economy described by Simmel. This system — through its imprecise, averaging tendencies — succeeded in producing large quantities of varying quality saltfish. By the late nineteenth century, as we have seen, this system could no longer offset the declining profitability of the saltfish trade. Increased foreign competition and the higher-quality standards of consumers, alongside social and technological innovations that led to declining quality of Newfoundland saltfish, led to a systemic crisis in accumulation. It was at precisely this moment that politicians, scientists, merchants, and fishers turned to novel *fishing measures* — or what Hope Simpson dubbed the knowledge of arithmetic — to reform and improve the industry. They wanted to replace the "rule of thumb" with the "rule of plumb and level," from embodied, qualitative measurements to abstract, quantitative measure. In what remains of this book, I examine a variety of strategies aimed at doing just that.

PART II ∽ FISH OUT OF WATER

Go out in the morning, and the wind it will sing,
And it's over the side you will hear the line ring
Out flows the jigger, freeze with the cold,
And as for the startings, all gone in the hole.

Poor fisherman he's been out all of the day,
Come in in the evening, boats sail off the bay;
Find Kate in the corner with a wink and a nod,
Saying, "Jimmy or John, have you got any cod?"

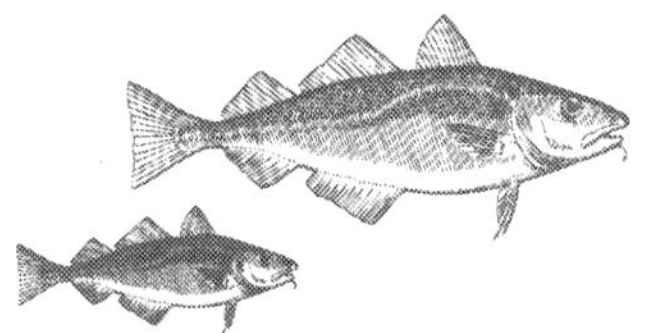

3

CONTROLLING QUANTITY

"There are no people on the face of the earth," claimed D. James Davies, a Welsh chemist working for the Newfoundland government, in a public lecture in March 1919, "who know the meaning of lean years and fat years so well as the fishermen."[1] Farmers, he noted, suffered crop failures and gluts, but these variations tended not to be as extreme as fish fluctuations because farmers had "a certain amount of control over their crops." Fishers, on the other hand, were not so lucky. They had little control over the extreme fluctuations in yield between seasons, and little understanding of the causes behind this variability. "Good and bad seasons might come and go," wrote Irish-born priest, journalist, and naturalist Moses Harvey, in an 1894 guidebook promoting Newfoundland tourism, "but these were believed to be purely providential, and quite beyond human control."[2]

Like all ocean-faring populations, Newfoundland fishers were "only too accustomed" to the precarious nature of fishing due to fluctuating fish yields: "There is nothing unusual or alarming in a failure of the fisheries."[3] Yet, by the mid-1880s, repeated failures of the inshore stocks in Trinity, Conception, and Placentia bays began pointing to a more intractable problem. Rather than being purely providential, declining fish stocks appeared to be the result of human action, flying in the face of English biologist Thomas Huxley's infamous claim that fish stocks were inexhaustible.[4] On top of the sharpening contradictions in Newfoundland's credit system, manifested in declining profitability and productivity of the cod fishery discussed in the previous chapter, the "steady decline, for years, of our shore cod-fishery" in many of the island's principal bays had "latterly become alarming."[5]

Two factors led to the new worries of overfishing in Newfoundland. First, Newfoundland's population had trebled between 1825 and 1885, placing *extensive* pressure on the inshore stocks.[6] Second, a number of new fishing technologies, such as the cod trap, bultow, and jigger, were introduced that greatly increased fishers' ability to harvest fish, placing *intensive* pressure on the stocks.[7] One Trinity Bay fisher, with 20 years of experience fishing the area, explained the decline by noting, "every destructive mode of catch has been tried without interference."[8] In Newfoundland, like most other Western fishing nations, the perceived fisheries decline in the late nineteenth century encouraged new levels of state intervention in the fishing industry. But, in Newfoundland, fisheries crises were especially acute, because the country was so utterly dependent on fishing as a source of employment and national income. The 1884 census, for example, showed that 82 per cent of employed persons were engaged in fishing-related work, and that fishery products comprised 79 per cent of realized national income.[9]

As Harvey argued in his tourist guidebook, the fishery decline in Newfoundland, like that in other fishing nations, "began to impress the minds of thoughtful men, and to suggest the necessity of taking prompt and energetic measures to meet the evil and to protect and restore the fisheries."[10] This chapter examines two such measures: the artificial propagation of cod and the reorganization of the bait supply. These projects emerged out of the newly formed Fisheries Commission and targeted two distinct biophysical processes shaping fish life: reproduction and predation. As we will see, these novel fishing measures, both scientific and governmental, sought to exert "a certain amount of control" over a heretofore providential process — fluctuating fish yields — with the aim of finally overcoming the uncertainties of lean and fat years for fishing people.

I.

On 18 April 1887, English-born merchant Ellis Watson, the representative for Trinity Bay, stood up and took the floor in the House of Assembly to propose a revolutionary resolution in the history of the country's fishing industry. The decline in the quantity and quality of Newfoundland's saltfish output, he argued, "teaches us that the fisheries of this country require more attention, encouragement and scientific care and supervision."[11] He proposed the formation of a commission to investigate the workings of fishery departments in other countries in order to establish a similar department in Newfoundland. This resolution was passed on 26 April 1887, marking the beginning of scientific state intervention in Newfoundland's fisheries.[12] There had been some previous attempts at introducing scientific state intervention in fisheries. For example, in 1876, the government budgeted $2,000 for Professor H.Y. Hind to survey and chart the Labrador fishing grounds.[13] Nevertheless, the establishment of the Fisheries Commission marks a shift in the role of science in Newfoundland's saltfishery. It was a milestone in the institutionalization of quantitative, arithmetical knowledge as the basis of fisheries management.

The Fisheries Commission, with merchant and politician A.W. Harvey as chair and naturalist and booster Moses Harvey as corresponding secretary, sent out circulars to the United Kingdom, United States, Canada, and Norway, requesting information regarding their various fishery departments and seeking recommendations for a suitable superintendent of fisheries.[14] From the responses and reports received, two broad aims for the nascent Department of Fisheries emerged. The United Kingdom recommended placing restrictions on fishing to allow the natural regeneration of fish stocks. Canada, Norway, and the US, in contrast, recommended a second solution: the artificial propagation of cod. When no suitable recommendations for superintendent were offered — one who was "sufficiently scientific while thoroughly practical"[15] — Moses Harvey suggested offering the position to Adolph Nielsen, a Norwegian fishery inspector who had recently visited Newfoundland as part of a research trip in 1887.[16]

Armed with information from the leading nations regarding the workings of their fishery departments, and with a superintendent chosen, the Fisheries Commission recommended establishing a permanent commission. Secretary Moses Harvey argued that science had two options that went "hand in hand" to overcome "the destroying hand of man": first, "immensely increase the number of young fish in the waters by artificial propagation, and thus restore the lost abundance," and second, " to teach us how to protect our fisheries when recuperated."[17] Due to the acute nature of the crisis, Harvey, Nielsen, and the Fisheries Commission emphasized the more proactive remedy, artificial propagation, as "a means of assisting nature against the destructive power ever at work, and in keeping up and improving that natural wealth derived from the sea."[18] Fishing restrictions, they argued, were important, but could be left until a later date, after the exhausted bays had been restocked.

The Commission therefore set two primary goals: first, to start an artificial propagation program and, second, to regulate Newfoundland's fisheries. Members of the Commission were particularly excited by the possibilities of artificial propagation. "If science could now restore that abundance, and restock those exhausted waters," extolled Harvey, "what a boon to our people!"[19] The Commission's faith in artificial propagation reflected a broader Western consensus regarding humanity's ability to control and regulate maritime processes in the late nineteenth century.[20] For these boosters, the science of aquaculture or "pisciculture" promised to rival the importance of agriculture.[21] "Food-factories" would no longer be confined to land, and "coastal waters will become great sea-farms, yielding enormous supplies of food for man."[22] The Fisheries Commission placed its faith in aquaculture to overcome the unpredictable lean years endemic to fishing.

Aquaculture, or fish farming, is an ancient practice. Chinese and Sumerian fish ponds date to *c.* 2000 BCE and *vivaria piscinae* were common in Rome.[23] But aquaculture "in its modern restricted sense" dates to the discovery of the technical means for artificially fertilizing and hatching fish eggs in the mid-seventeenth century and its dissemination in the eighteenth century.[24] This process involved harvesting fish ova (eggs) and milt (spermatozoa) by gently squeezing the bellies of living fish, mixing the materials in a container, and letting the contents fecundate until embryos were hatched. The embryos were protected as they passed from the alevin to juvenile phase, and then were released into maritime environments.[25] First reported in the eighteenth century by German agriculturalist Stephen Ludwig Jacobi, this model quickly spread throughout Europe in the eighteenth century, after it was adopted and encouraged by Louis-Napoleon's Second Empire.[26]

Although most early artificial fecundation projects were focused primarily on freshwater and anadromous species, such as trout, salmon, carp, perch, and bream, an 1864 "discovery" by Norway's first state-employed marine scientist, zoologist Georg Ossian Sars, opened the possibility of control over cod reproduction.[27] Sars conducted a series of studies on the cod fisheries of Lofoten in northern Norway, seeking to understand the causes of wide annual fluctuations in cod landings.[28] During his study, Sars "discovered" that cod eggs floated in the water column, rather than sinking to the ocean floor. Local fishers had told Sars that cod eggs floated, but "as this was in such direct opposition to anything [he] had hitherto known of the spawning of fish," he had assumed they were mistaken.[29] However, after the "microscopic examination" of their development, he "proved" that the floating globules that filled the sea around Lofoten were, in fact, cod eggs.[30] Equipped with this new understanding of the early stages of cod development, Sars believed that the "question might be raised if nature might not be assisted in this respect, so as to prevent the occurrence of unfavourable years" via the artificial hatching and planting of cod ova.[31]

Sars's suggestion was quickly taken up in the United States and Norway. The United States Fish Commission (USFC), under fisheries science pioneer Spencer Baird's directorship, began the large-scale artificial propagation of cod in 1878 at Gloucester, Massachusetts.[32] The USFC later expanded its operations, building cod-hatching apparatus at Woods Hole in 1885 and Ten Pound Island in 1888.[33] In Norway, mariner and aquacultural pioneer Capt. Gunder Mathisen Dannevig established a privately funded cod hatchery at Flødevigen, near Arendal, seeking to repopulate the Skagerrak coast in 1882.[34] Millions of cod yolk-sac larvae were released in the coastal waters surrounding these facilities, a modern techno-scientific panacea to the problems of overfishing. Bolstered by the reported success of American and Norwegian cod-hatching facilities, the members of Newfoundland's Fisheries Commission focused their early efforts on building and developing such a facility.[35] This was recently hired Norwegian fisheries expert Adolph Nielsen's first task upon his arrival in Newfoundland.

Nielsen left Norway in January 1889 to take up his position as Newfoundland's Superintendent of Fisheries, travelling to St. John's via Hamburg and Boston on the Bremen steamer line.[36] While in Boston, Nielsen visited the USFC cod hatcheries at Woods Hole and Ten Pound Island, consulting with Col. Marshall MacDonald, Baird's replacement as head of the USFC, and purchasing the required hatching apparatus.[37] Nielsen arrived in St. John's on 15 February 1887, setting out 12 days later for a tour around Conception, Trinity, and Placentia bays to investigate the most suitable place to erect the hatchery.[38] After measuring water temperatures, densities, and depths at various points around Newfoundland, Nielsen chose Dildo Island, Trinity Bay, as the most suitable place.[39] The land, he determined, was low and convenient to build on, and the water had a "good density" and was fairly deep towards the shore.[40] Construction of the Dildo Island hatchery began on 30 April 1889, with a capacity to hatch and plant 200 million eggs per season — purported to be twice the size of the American and Norwegian hatcheries.[41] Despite some "vexatious delays," construction was completed on 18 July 1889, but it took Nielsen two seasons to get it fully operational.[42]

Nielsen's chief obstacle to ensuring a successful hatching season was to secure an adequate supply of spawning cod. In 1889, he immediately set about trying to collect spawners, but was unsuccessful, despite the assurances of local fishers and a number of unfounded reports of abundant spawners. Recognizing that he would have to wait until the following year to begin the cod-hatching program, Nielsen began hatching lobsters at Dildo Island, releasing 4,039,000 lobster fry that year.[43] The following spring, unseasonably cold temperatures kept the cod in deep water outside Trinity Bay. Spawners were not available until late June and could only be extracted by hook-and-line, the most injurious method.[44]

At the end of the 1890 season, Nielsen developed a new plan to overcome the spawner issue. He decided to keep 260 "fine codfish" in pounds attached to the hatchery's wharf to make an early start next spring. But this experiment was foiled when a large tidal wave, "such as had not been witnessed by any of the present generation," destroyed the wharf and pounds, freeing the overwintering cod.[45] Cod hatching was again delayed the following spring, due to an outbreak of "La Grippe," which caused the complete suspension of fishery operations for three weeks in June, limiting the number of spawners taken.[46]

The end of the 1891 season marked a turning point for Nielsen's cod-hatching program. Two innovations were key to its success. First, at the end of that season, Nielsen had a large saltwater spawning pond constructed to allow cod to spawn in their "natural" manner, following the Norwegian method.[47] Rather than having their ova and milt stripped by hand — a labour-intensive and risky procedure — cod were placed in the pond to spawn naturally, and the materials were conveyed to the hatchery. Nielsen hoped this method, combined with an accurate control of the water conditions, would increase the efficiency of his procedure from around 50 per cent to 70–90 per cent.[48] Second, during a research trip to Newfoundland's west coast, Nielsen noticed that spawners arrived there much earlier than in Trinity.[49] Nielsen believed that this opened the possibility of starting hatching earlier and increasing output by transporting west coast fish to the hatchery on a welled vessel. But Nielsen hypothesized another, more profound and prescient, implication from this discovery. In addition to increasing output, by using the principles of land agricultural stock enhancement, he thought he could improve the size and quality of Trinity Bay fish through cross-breeding with larger regional stocks. "By judicious cross-breeding and the preservation of the best," he argued, "so our sea-stock of food-fishes may in many cases be improved by similar treatment."[50]

The decreased percentage of wasted ova, from 50 per cent to just over 20 per cent, and the improved capture of spawners led to very successful seasons in 1892–94.[51] This was met with increased government support, as demonstrated by the institutional reorganization of the Fisheries Commission into a permanent Department of Fisheries in May 1893.[52] In 1894, Nielsen was awarded use of the steamers *Fiona* and *Lady Glover* to expand the distribution of cod fry, planting 20 million at Bloody Reach, Bonavista Bay, 20 million at Bay Roberts, Conception Bay, and 18 million at Goose Bay, Bonavista Bay.[53] But just as Nielsen's artificial propagation program was hitting its stride, a financial crisis and a period of fiscal retrenchment intervened to kill the government's interest in the program.

On Monday morning, 10 December 1894, the Commercial Bank, one of the country's three main banks, did not open its doors for business.[54] The bank's locked doors were explained by a notice posted outside: "In consequence of the failure of several of our mercantile customers to respond to their liabilities to us, we are obliged to suspend payment for the present."[55] The notice posted on the Commercial Bank's door shocked the citizens of the town, "burst[ing] like a thunder-cloud over the commercial community of St. John's."[56] It shattered confidence, locally and abroad, in Newfoundland's banking institutions, and caused a run on the two private banks. They closed their doors within a few hours.

The closing of the country's financial institutions had an immediate and devastating impact on the country. As contemporary observer P.T. McGrath writes, "The commercial community was stricken almost to death, but the area of the ruin wrought was as wide as the colony itself."[57] Left without a currency, the country's economy ground to a halt: businesses closed, workers were fired, trade was suspended. The crash was augured by a chain of demands for debt repayment, set loose by the death of a commission merchant in London. The crash laid bare the overextension of credit by the Newfoundland banks to merchants, and highlighted the contradictions of allowing merchants to sit on bank boards and approve loans to themselves. Known as "Black Monday, 1894," the financial crisis portended a period of decline for Nielsen's work at the Dildo Island hatchery.

Political opposition to Nielsen's efforts intensified in the wake of the bank crash, with critics repeating that the hatchery was an extravagant waste of money. His work had always faced opposition by the more conservative elements of Newfoundland society. "He [Nielsen] was as much of a party political football," one paper noted, "as he was a piscatorial expert."[58] As he wrote in a letter dated 1 November 1889 to G.M. Dannevig, head of the Flødevigen hatchery, "Politics has a big role to play here and everything that is done has a political aim in mind."[59] Despite attempts to organize the Fisheries Commission on "non-political" lines, the Dildo hatchery, from its inception, was highly politicized, "the central point around which the storm of controversy rages."[60] The conservative political establishment volleyed "rancorous attacks" on Nielsen, seeking to "vilify, abuse and discredit him and his work and to destroy public confidence in the important enterprise."[61]

Nielsen felt these acutely, noting in a letter to Dannevig dated 24 February 1890 that critics "insisted that hatching of fish is the same as throwing money out in the ocean."[62] Opposition to his hatchery, he noted in the same letter, was primarily because "it was the old government that had come up with the idea."[63] In 1914, Prime Minister E.P. Morris, reflecting on Nielsen's work, recalled that the hatchery "became such a standing joke throughout the Colony that eventually the Government of the day . . . dropped it."[64]

The faith in artificial propagation did not survive the financial crisis and subsequent political machinations. With the country in crisis, the hatchery's budget was cut in half, following the "general policy of retrenchment adopted by Government, to the utmost limits that would be consistent with efficiency."[65] In 1896, the hatchery was funded entirely by Nielsen's private funds.[66] At the end of that season, Nielsen returned to Norway to convalesce from a severe asthma attack, marking the end of his tenure as Superintendent of Fisheries.[67] With the election of J.S. Winter's conservative government in 1897, government support for the hatchery was revoked. It was maintained by Fisheries Commission chair A.W. Harvey's personal funds in 1897, focusing on the hatching of lobster, salmon, and trout.[68] By 1903, it was described as being totally unused, and in 1906 it was said to be in "a bad state of disrepair."[69] The equipment and building were finally auctioned off in 1911.[70]

Despite the hope that Nielsen's work would herald a new scientific era in Newfoundland's fisheries, the artificial propagation program did not succeed in restocking the exhausted coves and bays around Newfoundland. Reproduction, however, was not the only biophysical process under scrutiny during this period. Predation, too, occupied the minds of boosters and reformers, offering a different possibility for controlling the recurrence of lean and fat years.

II.

Although cod may be considered the "mainstay" of Newfoundland's fisheries, wrote Senior Naval Officer R.H. Anstruther in a 1906 report on the fishery for the Governor of Newfoundland, "the bait fishes . . . must claim their place as, so to speak, the 'lanyard of the mainstay,' without which it would be of no use."[71] Unlike the cod trap — which worked by guiding cod into a twine box by the use of a *leader* — the extraction of cod by handline and bultow required *bait*, primarily herring, squid, and caplin, although other species were used at times.[72] In both the shore and Bank fisheries, hooks were baited and left in the water to attract and extract the voracious cod. The amount of cod caught, processed, and exported was thus dependent on a steady and abundant supply of caplin, herring, and squid. Bait was considered the "key of the situation for a successful prosecution of all branches of the fishery."[73] Harnessing bait for human purposes was an intervention into the patterns of cod predation. If baitfish were scarce, fish could still eat, but fishers could not fish.

The development and improvement of the cod fishery, thus, required a consistent and abundant supply of bait. Contemporary critics were alarmed at the prevailing "primitive" methods for procuring bait, whereby fishers supplied their own needs.[74] It required "a more rational and certainly a more serviceable method than the present costly, wasteful and haphazard way of procuring bait."[75] A new system was necessary to "bring our most important industry . . . to that degree of efficiency which its supreme position in the business organization of the colony demands."[76] The uncertainties of bait supply limited the quantity of saltfish produced and, therefore, the amount of value extracted by fishers and distributed by merchants each season. Intervening in cod predation was therefore central to saltfish production, and substituting natural food sources for artificially provided bait at the end of a hook offered a possible lever to rationalize the country's fishing industry.

Newfoundland's maritime ecosystem, as discussed in the previous chapter, is highly complex and dynamic. The historical superabundance of cod off Newfoundland was a result of many factors, a confluence of oceanographic features and processes, biological characteristics, and food availability. Like cod, the primary bait species were subject to marked variation over time and distinct spatial discontinuities. Bait could be scarce in some locations at certain times, but plentiful in others, leading to a profound sense of uncertainty.[77] To further complicate matters, groundfish such as cod and the mostly pelagic bait species responded to and were shaped by different, but deeply intertwined, biogeophysical signals. In 1922, Liberal MHA Michael Cashin summed up this problem in the House of Assembly, repeating the ubiquitous complaint: "One year . . . there was no fish and plenty of bait, the next year there was plenty of fish and no bait."[78]

Cod cannot exist without a wild profusion of food. They are opportunistic eaters, devouring almost anything in sight. For example, nineteenth-century US Fisheries Commission scientists G.B. Goode and J.W. Collins stated that cod "are liable to swallow almost anything that comes in its way, so that stories are by no means uncommon of jack-knives lost overboard returning to their owners again when the day's catch of fish was dressed."[79] Fishers, however, were limited in the number of species used as bait for both technical and socio-cultural reasons. "As everyone connected with the fishing industry here knows," stated politician and merchant L.C. Outerbridge in a report on the bait supply, "in the past there has been quite an obsession on the part of all our [fi]shermen [*sic*] that squid is the bait par excellence and that all other kinds of bait fishers are but substitutes."[80] In addition to the *seasonality* and *geography* of bait, fishers were limited by the very *materiality* of bait itself. "The cod regard bait as an article of food," Outerbridge continued, "and it must be preserved as such and not offered to the cod in a stale or putrid condition."[81] Maintaining an adequate and appropriate bait supply was a real challenge, technically and socially.

Fishers and merchants regularly complained that annual yields were negatively affected by the uncertainty and scarcity of bait. "As we all well know," explained merchant W.C. Job, "towards the end of this month every season we hear reports that there is plenty of fish on the ground but no bait."[82] Each year, much fishing time was lost waiting for the bait to strike, which had a "paralyzing effect" on the codfishery.[83] The fishing grounds may have been teeming with cod, but without bait on the hooks they were unattainable for many fishers. "It is annoying," the *Evening Telegram*'s editor noted, "to figure out the wealth we yearly miss through lost time for want of bait, and the too great cost and scarcity of it at all times."[84] A fisher from Old Bonaventure noted that fishers in his area "have often witnessed times of when through the lack of bait have been deprived of a half a year wages."[85] Outport merchant Thomas Fitzpatrick estimated that, over the past 20 years, Newfoundlanders "have lost in cold cash 2½ millions of dollars and the revenue $625,000 dollars for want of bait."[86] The lack of bait had serious pecuniary consequences, and controlling its supply emerged as one of the Fisheries Commission's central preoccupations.

Newfoundland's first organized attempt at revolutionizing the bait supply came in 1890. The recently formed Fisheries Commission, led by Superintendent Nielsen, organized a Bait Intelligence Service with the participation of the international telecommunications firm, the Anglo-American Telegraph Company. The purpose of this service was to collect and distribute "accurate intelligence regarding the movements of the bait fishes . . . to all the principal bait and fishing centres throughout the Island."[87] This system was intended to reduce the time "wasted" looking for bait. "Nothing can be more uncertain and capricious than the movements of these bait-fishes; and only such a system as this, for watching and reporting their movements, could have the desired effect."[88] The following year, intelligence from 56 different telegraph stations was broadcast from the 15 April to 31 October, at about 11:00 a.m. each day.[89] By 1892, however, the Commission reported that the Anglo-American Telegraph Company had discontinued the service, "due to reasons beyond their control."[90] Historian Keith Hewitt notes that this decision was most likely financial, with the service considered too expensive, despite the very minimal operational costs.[91]

The dissemination of accurate information regarding baitfish was considered a boon, but it paled in comparison to the possibilities offered by cold storage, or the preservation of bait by refrigeration. "The importance of cold storage commercially, but more particularly in the preservation of bait fishes, cannot be overestimated, so far as this Colony is concerned."[92] It was so important that "no argument was necessary to prove their utility."[93] Stocking the bait depots when bait was plentiful, it was hoped, would ensure a constant supply throughout the season, finally overcoming the uncertainties of the bait supply.[94] Preservation by ice, it was hoped, would freeze bait in time and space, allowing it to be stored and moved at will.

The Commission proposed the establishment of bait cold storage in 1892.[95] The following year, the first experimental bait freezer was erected at Burin under Nielsen's supervision. He hoped that the successful demonstration of bait storage, and the increased yields resulting from it, would convince fishers of the benefits of cold storage. With early demonstrable success, he argued it "might naturally be expected that private enterprise would speedily erect and keep in operation around our shores, similar bait preserving establishments."[96] That same year, in 1893, a "Mr. P. Sullivan of Presque, Placentia Bay," offered up part of his premises to be used as a bait freezer, operated under his own expense, using the "salt-and-ice" method.[97] In 1894, Nielsen exhibited a new Norwegian technology: the "freezing barrel" for the small-scale preservation of bait, which required only "an ordinary herring or pork barrel, some ice chopped small and coarse salt."[98] Despite some initial successes the following year — 10,000 squid and 40 barrels of caplin were frozen at Burin — a period of abundant fresh bait and a marked indifference from fishers made these ventures ultimately unsuccessful.[99] As E.P. Morris noted years later, reflecting back on his experience promoting cold storage, "In the summer time when there is plenty of fish and no bait, the need for Bait Depots is seen, but when we have plenty of bait we let the question stand aside."[100]

Unlike artificial propagation, cold storage was taken up and encouraged by subsequent governments following the bank crash of 1894. It remained a favoured response to periods of bait scarcity, and by the turn of the century the adoption of cold storage by Newfoundland's competitors contributed to a new sense of urgency. French construction of cold storage facilities at St. Pierre, American usage of frozen squid, and Icelandic use of refrigeration highlighted the importance of cold storage in "modern" fisheries.[101]

In the late 1890s, a renewed period of bait shortages inspired Conservative Prime Minister (and artificial propagation opponent) James S. Winter to once again encourage the establishment of cold storage in Newfoundland. In 1898, his government passed "An Act for the Encouragement of Cold Storage and Other Business," which guaranteed 5 per cent return on investment for at least one, but not more than five years, along with other concessions.[102] This bill, however, enjoyed only limited interest and practical effect.[103] The newly elected government under Liberal Robert Bond — elected in November 1900 as a rejection of Winter's conservative policies — formed a committee to investigate the question of cold storage.[104] The committee recommended the construction of bait depots by entrepreneurs and fisher associations. By 1902, two small bait depots were in operation: Mr. Penny's facility at Ramea and Mr. Clement's facility at Channel. By 1904, six more were constructed at Bay Bulls, Petty Harbour, Port-de-Grave, Fogo, and Channel.[105]

Despite the tentative success of these small-scale initiatives, the Bond government remained focused on the encouragement of large-scale, capital-intensive cold storage projects. Bond sought large-scale foreign investment in Newfoundland, and began courting two Montreal cold storage experts, J.A. Wright and C.W. Vollman. In 1903, future Prime

Minister E.P. Morris, then Minister of Justice under Bond, introduced a bill to encourage the establishment of a colony-wide cold storage system, with very liberal terms, which he justified by arguing that Winter's 1898 Act had been too conservative to attract investors.[106] Although initially rejected by the Legislative Council, a revised version of the bill passed in 1904, but the new agreement began to quickly unravel due to conflicts over the bait purchase provisions.[107] Despite signing the agreement, construction never began. In 1909, E.J. Greenstreet, another cold storage expert, concluded: "nothing practical ever came of it [the 1904 contract], and Wright never accomplished anything beyond signing the agreement."[108]

Between 1906 and 1910, mimicking the mid-1890s, a period of abundant bait obscured the government's failure to secure the establishment of cold storage facilities. In the hotly contested 1908 election, Morris promised the erection of bait depots to supply fishers as part of his campaign for Prime Minister. Morris was an ardent supporter of cold storage, continuing to boost its possibilities well into retirement.[109] After his landslide victory in May 1908, the construction of cold storage facilities became a central preoccupation.[110] Morris communicated extensively with cold storage firms, securing an agreement with the firm Trefethen and Lord in 1910 and tabling a bill in 1911 to encourage the establishment of cold storage depots.[111] The firm agreed to construct five cold storage facilities over five years and to operate a steamer with refrigeration to distribute bait and collect in exchange for very liberal concessions, including large land grants and a guaranteed profit of 5 per cent up to $500,000.[112]

Accused of contravening the Bait Act of 1887 and criticized for the liberal concessions given to entice investment by the company, this contract was mired in controversy.[113] Construction never began, which Morris attributed to happenstance: "Unfortunately one of the principals of the Company went into an insane asylum."[114] Undeterred, Morris travelled to New York and Boston to negotiate with Booth Fisheries Co., hoping the firm would take over the Trefethen and Lord contract.[115] Again, this contract became mired in controversy over whether it contravened the Bait Act.[116] In June 1912, a Booth Fisheries Co. vessel visited Newfoundland to become acquainted with the area and to survey the fishing grounds.[117] Despite these initial satisfactory experiments, however, the project "vanished into thin air."[118]

Over the next 20 years, there were some spasmodic attempts at cold storage by private enterprise, focused primarily on the distribution of fresh frozen fish. Harvey & Co. erected a bait freezer at Rose Blanche in 1914 and one in St. John's in 1915.[119] Between 1915 and 1917, innovative entrepreneur John Clouston operated a large cold storage facility at Bay Bulls.[120] In 1918, one firm, Newfoundland Atlantic Fisheries, built a modern refrigerating plant in St. John's, with eight cold storage rooms and a capacity of 6,000,000 lbs.[121] Job Bros. erected a cold storage plant at their South Side premises in St. John's during the First World War, and bought a cold storage factory ship, the S.S. *Blue Peter*, in 1928.[122] By the late 1920s, four bait freezers — at Ramea, Quirpon, Bonavista, and Bay de Verde — were constructed by local entrepreneurs with small government subsidies.[123]

A renewed period of governmental intervention arrived with the Commission of Government in 1934.[124] With the country unable to pay its debts and threatening default, and with the elite fearing widespread social unrest, the Newfoundland government made progressively more desperate attempts to secure aid from Britain. In 1933, a Royal Commission into Newfoundland's finances recommended suspending parliamentary democracy in favour of a six-person commission until the country was once again financially self-sufficient.[125] Under the Commission of Government, sworn in on 16 February 1934, the Department of Marine and Fisheries was brought under the new Department of Natural Resources (DNR), directed by Sir John Hope Simpson.[126] The DNR greatly expanded the bait service, based primarily on L.C. Outerbridge's 1933 proposals.[127] The government had four additional bait depots constructed at Joe Batt's Arm, St. Mary's, Port-aux-Basques, and Rencontre West.[128] The DNR also converted the steamer *Malakoff* into a floating cold storage unit to collect and distribute the bait around the island.[129] In 1937, it reintroduced the "Bait Intelligence Service," receiving daily reports on the availability of bait that were broadcast via wireless, print, and telegraph.[130] The solutions proposed by Nielsen in 1890 were finally in place, and the question of bait tentatively answered — until, that is, factory trawlers diminished the role of bait in fish extraction.

III.

Artificial propagation and the reorganization of the bait supply were both attempts to extend control over biophysical processes prior to the extractive moment. By extending control over reproduction and predation, reformers sought to resolve the problem of fluctuation in fishing described in the previous chapter. The success of Nielsen's artificial propagation program, like its American and Norwegian counterparts, was, and remains, hard to assess. Artificial propagation sought to control and improve reproduction: "a means of assisting nature against the destructive power ever at work, and in keeping up and improving that natural wealth derived from the sea."[131] Contemporary analyses note that accounts describing the success of hatchery operations rely entirely on the "hearsay evidence" and "unsolicited testimony" of local fishers and citizens.[132] In Newfoundland, there were many reports of immense numbers of small codfish forming a "solid thick mass" in the waters of Trinity Bay, often accompanied by claims that "oldest fishermen declare they never in all their lives saw so much fish in the bay."[133] One newspaper — admittedly edited by fish-hatching proponent Moses Harvey — even claimed that young cod were so numerous that fishers "could catch their fill from the rocks on the shore."[134] By the late 1890s, Nielsen and the Fisheries Commission's eerily prophetic dreams of stocking the bays with judiciously cross-bred and improved cod juveniles were dashed, and these dreams faded into obscurity until the renewed interest in cod aquaculture in the 1980s and 1990s.

The development of the bait intelligence service and bait cold storage was aimed at overcoming the uncertainty of the bait supply. Those projects were, in effect, interventions into the feeding habits of cod. They extended bait in time and space through cold storage, resolving its periodic local scarcity, and rendered it more certain, and thus calculable, by the dissemination of information regarding the presence of abundant deposits.

Improving bait technology was the initial impetus for the development of cold storage; however, a new use for these facilities emerged by the early twentieth century, which eroded the role of bait in fish production: the distribution and consumption of fresh-frozen fish for the North American markets.[135]

Both technologies were "a means of assisting nature against the destructive power ever at work, and in keeping up and improving that natural wealth derived from the sea."[136] Both were aimed to overcome the unpredictable variations between lean and fat years that plagued fishing nations. These innovations were far from perfect and complete. However partial or ineffective, this period witnessed the development of scientific and governmental fishing measures aimed to control the quantity of cod extracted. They were concerted efforts to subsume biophysical processes — reproduction and predation — to the rhythms of capitalist accumulation. They were an attempt to subsume the knowledge of fishing with the knowledge of arithmetic, replacing providence and luck with the certainties of calculation and control.

These attempts at controlling the quantity of cod extracted were tied to a broader shift in the "mental conceptions" organizing production: the development of mathematical fisheries science.[137] Early fisheries scientists aimed to remove the uncertainties regarding cod abundance by allowing humans to accurately predict, and thus more rationally extract, the country's abundant maritime life. "This is no mere flight of fancy," Moses Harvey argued in a speech to the Royal Society of Canada.[138] "Keen-eyed science," he continued, "has taken the matter in hand, and is subjecting to her scrutiny the entire life-history of those finny tribes which can be made subservient to human necessities."[139]

Let us now turn to "keen-eyed science" with the jaundiced eye of historical-geographical political economy.

4

PREDICTING QUANTITY

At around 10:30 p.m. on 19 April 1937, the Bay Bulls Fisheries Research Station's night watchman was making his usual rounds of the premises when he noticed flames spewing from a nearby cod liver oil refinery. The premises, rented from Harvey & Co. by the Commission of Government, housed the recently inaugurated Fisheries Research Commission, a state-financed scientific research institution dedicated to improving and rationalizing Newfoundland's fishing industry. The watchman saw the fire spread to surrounding buildings and alerted the authorities in St. John's. The fire engulfed the Research Station's main premises around midnight, igniting rapidly "when it reached the inflammable chemicals stored there."[1] Around 11:00 p.m., a fire truck was dispatched from St. John's under Fire Superintendent Codner's command, but "owing to the snow and the soft conditions of the road," it became mired in the roadbed about 3.5 miles from the scene.[2] Codner and a few men proceeded to Bay Bulls on foot, reaching the conflagration around 4:00 a.m. By the time they arrived, the Research Station and the adjacent buildings "were all a heap of ruins."[3]

The Bay Bulls fire destroyed a large amount of property — $20,000 worth of saltfish, and the Tors Cove Trading Co.'s cod liver oil refining equipment[4] — but the damage to the Fisheries Research Station was harder to reckon. "As of yet," one paper noted a few days after the fire, "no estimate can be made of the loss sustained."[5] Some scientific equipment was saved — "some cameras, a projector and some microscopes"[6] — but the entirety of the office equipment, the museum's collection of marine specimens, a large collection of raw data, and the library were all destroyed. The destruction of the library was particularly troublesome, as it contained a large collection of textbooks, "which were almost daily in use," and the entirety of the scientific data collected since the Station's inception in 1931.[7] With the destruction of this large collection of fishery data, "much of the work of years has gone up in smoke."[8]

The Bay Bulls fire marked a turning point in the history of fisheries science in Newfoundland, with important implications for the post-World War II flowering of fisheries science and the industrialization of extraction. For the preceding half-century, dating back to Adolph Nielsen's appointment as Superintendent of Fisheries in 1887, the lack of scientific information on Newfoundland's marine environment and the life histories of key species had been persistently identified as a central reason for the industry's — and the country's — backwardness. Modernizing saltfish production required a new framework for understanding fluctuating fish yields. No longer the result of divine providence or luck, fish fluctuations had to be understood as the result of predictable and rational changes in the biology of fish or biogeochemistry of the ocean. Reframing fluctuations in these terms required significant ideological work. This chapter traces the slow, discontinuous emergence of a new understanding of fish and ocean-space, one framed around a quantitative rationality and arithmetical expertise.

I.

"If we want to improve, conserve and regulate our fisheries," Superintendent of Fisheries Adolph Nielsen argued in 1895, "the first step is an accurate knowledge of their present condition, of the causes which are injuriously affecting them, and of the errors in working which lead to their deterioration."[9] Although initially preoccupied with setting up the artificial propagation of cod and lobsters, Nielsen shifted focus in the early 1890s to uncovering the laws regulating fish life and the oceans. For Nielsen and his boosters, the development of fisheries science had an important role to play in Newfoundland's political economy: understanding and predicting fish fluctuations to rationalize saltfish production. Through the development of the scientific knowledge of "fish-life" and the "physics of the sea," Nielsen argued, Newfoundland's fisheries could finally be modernized, and be "placed under an intelligent, scientific supervision."[10]

For Nielsen, the production of "accurate knowledge" required the systematic collection of observations and information "regarding the ichthyological and meteorological conditions of the waters around our shores" by a "careful scientific observer."[11] He organized a number of research surveys to map and measure the biogeophysical conditions of the waters by taking temperature readings at different points and depths, and by examining the biological life at different intervals by using tow-nets and dredges.[12] He circumnavigated Newfoundland, doing just that, between the late fall of 1890 and early summer of 1891.[13] Between 29 August and 29 September 1892 he conducted another field survey, visiting Labrador aboard Wilfred Grenfell's missionary ship, the *Albert*.[14] In 1894, Nielsen hired the banking schooner *Jubilee*, skippered by Capt. John Lewis, to take observations of temperature with the "new and improved Negretti and Zambra's patent standard Deep Sea Thermometers."[15] Capt. Lewis continued these investigations the following year.[16]

Nielsen's surveys both challenged and reinforced the traditional knowledge of the ocean and fish life. By taking temperature readings at a number of different points and depths, Nielsen ascertained that there were distinct "layers" of colder and warmer water. Although he originally attributed this to malfunctioning or inaccurate instruments, Nielsen was eventually convinced by the validity of his findings, correctly raising the question of whether the Gulf Stream, "in opposition to what is generally believed," was powerful enough to affect the coastal waters of Newfoundland and Labrador.[17] Nielsen also began identifying a direct correlation between ocean temperatures and the movements and abundance of fish.[18] Through his experimental work, he determined that cod were most plentiful where the temperature of the bottom water was between 36° and 39°F, with a specific gravity from 1.0260 to 1.0270.[19] Nielsen noted that his scientific observations seemed to help prove "an expression I often have heard among the old fishermen, when the herring are in close to the land, that 'they come in to get the heat of the rocks.'"[20] He continued his analysis of the effects of temperature on cod at the Dildo Island hatchery, noting that cod transferred to colder water became sluggish, and even appeared dead, but resumed normal activity once returned to warmer water.[21]

Regardless of the validity or accuracy of Nielsen's research findings, his research methods were shaped by and helped contribute to a far greater shift in Western perception. No longer a sublime, swirling mass, the ocean was understood as composed of an infinite series of fixed points on a Cartesian grid that extended both horizontally and vertically.[22] There was much work left to do, but the method was established. Measuring temperature, density, and biological life at specific points would unlock the mysteries of fish population and ocean dynamics. For Nielsen, this new knowledge would have profound effects on the country's economy by overcoming the problem of fluctuation through a granular knowledge of ocean temperatures and fish life histories. This knowledge was predicated upon, yet superseded, fishers' knowledge and experience. For example, in his 1892 survey, while Grenfell was treating each harbour's residents, Nielsen hired a boat and men from each settlement, proceeding to the fishing grounds "where the people generally used to fish" to make observations.[23] "I could at last," he stated, "tell the fishermen who took me around on the fishing grounds, where they were likely to get fish and where they would not, by only dropping my instruments down to the bottom and ascertaining the conditions of the waters."[24] Following these experiments, Nielsen concluded that deep-sea thermometers were essential instruments for fishers, claiming that they could remove much of the "guesswork" from fishing.

Despite his early enthusiasm, he did not succeed at fundamentally reorganizing the fishing industry along scientific lines before his resignation in 1896. Subsequent fisheries ministers looked back at his work approvingly, blaming his failure on cynical political opposition. In 1910, Department of Marine and Fisheries Minister A.W. Piccott noted that

Nielsen's investigations would be appreciated in the future, but failed because they were a "Government venture, and thus, became a target for political abuse."[25] Piccott's prediction proved prescient: in 1930, the Department of Marine and Fisheries republished and circulated his still-helpful 1890 report on "The Cure of Codfish and Herring."[26] In 1914, Piccott repeated these claims, noting that, "through some cause unknown to me, the Government of the day did not approve of the methods employed by Mr. Nielsen."[27] Nielsen resigned without modernizing Newfoundland's saltfishery — as we shall see, he would not be the last to fail at that task — but he did much of the spadework.

Interest in scientific research waned in the decade following Nielsen's resignation, a period of modest prosperity in Newfoundland due to large catches, high fish prices, and expanding mining and timber industries.[28] But interest in fisheries science and modernization was regalvanized in the autumn of 1908, when fish prices fell by 50 per cent.[29] The price collapse in 1908 "carried with it an unmistakable scent of depression," and the formation of the Fishermen's Protective Union (FPU) in 1908 and the Newfoundland Board of Trade in 1909 reflected the unease surrounding Newfoundland's saltfish trade.[30] Both the fisher-led FPU and merchant-led Board of Trade formed around similar proposals to resolve Newfoundland's intractable political-economic problems. Both institutions isolated the persistent lack of information regarding Newfoundland's fisheries as the trade's key limiting factor and sought to encourage and systematize the collection of fishing information.[31]

This local interest in accurate quantitative knowledge was encouraged by the country's gradual incorporation into international fisheries research communities. The infusion of foreign expertise further galvanized elite interest in the development of fisheries science. "Sir, as far as I can gather," wrote Harbour Grace factory manager H.H. Archibald in a letter to the *Evening Telegram*, ". . . all are agreed that the guessing process is entirely out of date, and that something better and more reliable must be introduced. That something, sir, is Science."[32] In July 1910, famous Norwegian fisheries scientist Johan Hjort visited Newfoundland as part of the SS *Michael Sars* transatlantic survey, measuring ocean temperatures, salinity, currents, and animal life.[33] In 1911, following a suggestion by W.A. Munn, the government hired M.B. Simonsen, a cod liver oil expert from Lofoden, Norway, to improve production methods in Newfoundland.[34] Simonsen helped modernize cod liver oil production, introduced Norwegian fisheries expertise, and stressed the value of state-funded scientific investigations to the political and mercantile elite.[35]

In 1914, the government hired Walter Duff, "one of the well-known Inspectors of the Fishery Board of Scotland," to visit Newfoundland for a summer cruise and to report on the local fisheries.[36] In a summary lecture at the Grenfell Institute, later published as a pamphlet, Duff recommended the employment of fishery instructors to demonstrate best curing practices, as well as the use of motorboats and the diversification of fish species harvested.[37] In November, Hjort — shortly after publishing his *magnum opus* on the causes of fluctuations in fish stocks[38] — returned to Newfoundland as part of the 1914–15 Canadian Fisheries Expedition, where he and his team conducted fish scale analyses, plankton studies, and hydrography.[39] While in St. John's, he gave a public lecture at the King George IV Institute on the benefits of scientific investigations for Norway's fisheries.[40]

That same year, reflecting the excitement around fisheries science, the newly re-elected government of E.P. Morris decided to act on the problems in the fishery by forming a committee to examine and evaluate the organization of the saltfish trade. The committee submitted its final report on 1 May 1915, roundly critiquing the lack of scientific knowledge concerning Newfoundland's waters and fish life. The committee concluded that "not one-half of the fish producing capacity of the Colony has been reached,"[41] and they recommended hiring a fisheries expert, with both scientific and practical experience, to reorganize the fishery along scientific lines. This call was repeated by the Board of Trade, which sought a "much larger share of the public monies . . . expended in scientific investigation and practical experiment," as well as the creation of fishery schools to introduce a "system to provide a scientific knowledge of the fisheries."[42]

The political will to radically reorganize the country's fishery and institute a system of scientific research, however, evaporated with the onset of World War I. The prosperity brought on by "shortage of supply and interruption of industry arising out of the European war" overwhelmed the desire to combat the structural problems in the fishery.[43] Yet again, a short period of prosperity scuttled attempts at reform. The early extension of scientific knowledge mirrored rising and falling fish prices. Real or perceived crises — in the late 1880s, in 1908 — inspired attempts at understanding the causes of fluctuations through investigations into the life histories of fish and oceanography. Rising fish prices inspired renewed inertia. Despite the momentum in the pre-war period, gathering accurate fishing information was of neither strategic nor economic import during the Great War.

II.

Prosperous wartime conditions, it seemed, had resolved many of Newfoundland's economic problems. Questions of quality and efficiency seemed irrelevant during the war, a period of diminished European supply and high fish prices. Far-sighted observers, however, understood that these conditions would not stand with the cessation of conflict. In an important analysis of the saltfish trade, Governor C.A. Harris predicted that a drop in fish prices and renewed competition following the war was inevitable, and would necessarily cause "serious industrial difficulties."[44] All the pre-war issues would return, but with one important difference: government could now play a more active role in regulating business due to the unprecedented role it played in public life during the war.[45] As a meeting of fishers resolved in 1922, "During the Great War, the authority of Government was exercised with general approval and beneficent results in many matters previously left entirely free from interference," such as the sale of wheat in Canada or the shipping of saltfish in Newfoundland.[46]

The 1919 general election was a turning point. A coalition between lawyer and publisher Richard Squires's Liberal Party and W.F. Coaker's fisher-led Union Party was elected. Unionist, farmer, and telegraph operator Coaker was appointed as Minister of Marine and Fisheries, a concession he negotiated with Squires. He was now in the position to implement the changes he had been arguing for since the formation of the Fishermen's Protective Union (FPU) in 1908. In 1920, the legislature passed three bills — known collectively as the "Coaker Regulations" — intended to reform the marketing of fish in Newfoundland.[47] Alongside new processing regulations, Coaker intended to create a scientific fisheries bureau, financed by an export tax, and to collect fishing statistics.[48] But these regulations did not survive the articulated opposition of certain merchants to any government intervention in business. They were overturned the following year.[49] Respect for the new "authority of Government" did not extend to all sectors of Newfoundland society, and the creation of a robust government-funded scientific research bureau was yet again postponed.

Despite the failure of the Coaker Regulations, the pace of scientific research accelerated in the postwar period through the incorporation of Newfoundland's fishery into international fisheries science organizations and the creation of a number of scientific institutions aimed at fostering quantitative approaches to fish and the ocean. Research was focused on extending methods and theories developed in Europe and Canada to the Newfoundland case. In July 1918, merchant and member of the Legislative Council, John Harvey, who had attended Hjort's lecture in 1914, asked D. James Davies, the Welsh chemist employed by the Newfoundland government that complained of the lean and fat years in fishing, to carry out the "microscopic examination of fish scales with the view of determining age."[50] He provided him with a copy of Hjort's 1914 report, and sent him to the Loggieville Canadian fisheries station, led by A.G. Huntsman, to learn the correct method for fish scale analyses in August 1918.[51] In late July 1922, Michael Graham — who was later instrumental in developing the "maximum sustainable yield" concept in fisheries science[52] — visited Newfoundland, accompanying Dr. S.S. Zilva, who was hired to examine the vitamin content of Newfoundland's cod liver oil.[53] Graham spent one month examining the morphological characteristics of cod landed at four ports — Ferryland, St. John's, Winterton, and Port Union — seeking to understand the basic life history of Newfoundland "shore cod."[54]

The following year, A.G. Huntsman led an expedition to investigate the "ocean around Newfoundland."[55] A joint creation of the Canadian, American, and Newfoundland (and later French) governments, the North American Council on Fishery Investigations (NACFI) was modelled on the European International Council for the Exploration of the Sea (ICES), created in 1902.[56] The Council was intended to co-ordinate the co-operative efforts of the different governments with three main objectives: first, to compile and provide complete fishery statistics for the region; second, to conduct investigations into the key economic species; and third, to accumulate data on the relationship between oceanographic conditions and fish life.[57]

This research continued the work laid out by Nielsen in the 1890s: to correlate the biology of fish with the movement and temperature of the ocean to unlock the mysteries behind fluctuation and to ensure predictable yields. Huntsman's 1923 expedition is instructive. Equipped with two research vessels and several scientific staff, Huntsman wanted to understand the effect of the Labrador Current on the Gulf of St. Lawrence, particularly in relation to movement of the principal economic fish: cod.[58] Huntsman and his crew measured ocean temperatures and animal life at different points and depths and conducted drift-bottle experiments to study the movement of water through the Strait of Belle Isle. This work yielded definitive results: "The water flowed in through the Strait during the flooding tide and out during the ebbing tide, but the inward was stronger than the outward movement on the north side, while the opposite was the case on the south side."[59]

Huntsman then sought to correlate the movement of water with the movement of fish. "Cod, as do men," he wrote, "dislike it to be too warm, or too cold, but prefer it to be 'just right.'"[60] He concluded that the "violent fluctuations" in fish yields in the Strait are the result of highly variable temperature conditions, due to the movement of the cold and warm water he identified. "In the summer," he summed up, "the Strait acts as a machine for producing 'cod water,' i.e. water from 40 to 45°F in temperature. . . . It depends upon the way in which the machine works as to where and in what quantity this 'Cod Water' will be found."[61] For Huntsman, this work established a very simple fix for the problem of fluctuation: fishers simply need a thermometer to predict when the 'cod water machine' was producing the right conditions. "Probably in no other place in the world are the temperature conditions in the water so vitally important for man's livelihood."[62]

The investigations led by Davies, Graham, and Huntsman all pointed to a profound and unacceptable lack of information regarding Newfoundland's fisheries. Each research trip was viewed as provisional and exploratory. As Graham noted in his report, the results "are only given here for what they are worth, namely, as a jumping-off ground for further research."[63] Davies, Huntsman, and British fish merchant J. Allen Taylor, in their public lectures in St. John's, all stressed the need for more scientific research.[64] In 1921, when the Welshman Davies was sent to NACFI's inaugural meeting in Ottawa, Newfoundland's lack of scientific research was glaringly apparent. "It is humiliating," wrote Deputy Minister of Fisheries A.C. Goodridge in the 1921 annual report, "that Mr. Davies representing the oldest fisheries in the New World was not possessed of any information of a scientific or hydrographic nature, which could advance or even assist the deliberations of that Board in any way."[65]

The founding of the colony's first university, Memorial University College (MUC), in September 1925 established a key institutional foundation for the robust local participation in scientific research on fish populations and ocean dynamics. After serving 21 years as Highmaster of Manchester Grammar School, J.L. Paton was hired as the university's first president.[66] An ardent booster of fisheries science and a persistent critic of the conservatism inherent in the Newfoundland fishery, Paton was instrumental in expanding the field of fisheries science in Newfoundland. In an undated letter, Paton summarized his view of the Newfoundland fishery: "No pisciculture — no stations for marine biology. No understanding of life-story of the cod. Troubled with bait — no study of the question. No guidance. All rule of thumb. As it was in the beginning so it is now."[67] Through MUC, Paton hoped to change this situation.

Paton focused his early efforts on establishing a biology department at MUC. He began by contacting fellow Mancunian and professor of botany F.E. Weiss for suggestions on potential candidates.[68] Meanwhile, William Blackall, a member of the MUC Board of Trustees, was in Montreal and heard that George F. Sleggs was looking for an academic position. Affiliated with the Scripps Institute of Oceanography, Sleggs was a doctoral candidate in zoology at the University of California, Berkeley.[69] He had previously worked with the British Ministry of Fisheries on the distribution of plaice and sole in the Irish Sea. In 1926, Paton hired Sleggs, reaching an agreement with the DMF, whereby Sleggs would be seconded to the department to conduct research for the government each summer.[70] Sleggs accepted the position on 10 May 1926.[71]

Sleggs continued the work recommended by previous experts. Following the NACFI meeting in St. John's in July 1926, the Newfoundland government — perhaps sheepishly coaxed to support scientific research after the presence of so many North American fisheries experts[72] — placed a vessel at Sleggs's disposal. He conducted experiments consisting of "the investigation of temperature distribution both at the surface and at sub-surface levels, the putting out of drift bottles, and the taking of plankton samples over a wide area and from accurately known depths."[73] Following his research trip, Sleggs stressed the importance of science to industry in a lecture to the Rotary Club, recommending the scientific study of preservation technologies and the development of new products, as well as research into the life history of fish at sea, with the view to "predict in advance the probable abundance of the fish for a given year or for a given locality."[74] Between 1927 and 1930, Newfoundland-born and MUC-educated George Jeffers of the Biological Board of Canada used similar research methods to examine the relationship between ocean temperatures and catch rates in the Strait of Belle Isle.[75]

Paton continued his efforts to establish a permanent fisheries research bureau in Newfoundland, correctly thinking that the arrangement he negotiated between the DMF and Sleggs was tenuous at best.[76] In a letter to Huntsman, Paton complained that the government's funding was not dependable, and mocked the political response to Sleggs's research, which mimicked the response to Nielsen's work in the 1890s. "Directly 'Brother Ass' gets up in the House of Legislature," wrote Paton, "and asks — 'What's the good of paying a man to be chucking bottles into the sea?'"

Paton viewed the recently formed Imperial Economic Committee (IEC) as a potential source of funding for scientific research in Newfoundland. The IEC was formed in 1925, following recommendations made at the 1923 Imperial Economic Conference, seeking to encourage the consumption of imperial food products in the UK, with a grant of £1,000,000 per annum.[77] In 1926, the British government created the Empire Marketing Board (EMB) as part of the IEC, to advertise products (expanded to include raw materials) in the UK and help finance scientific research into the improvement of products.[78]

The IEC chairman — and the first Reader in Geography at a British university — Sir Halford Mackinder, suggested that Newfoundland should pursue a co-operative research arrangement with the Biological Board of Canada.[79] Paton fully supported this idea, and prepared an application to the EMB to set up a joint Canadian–Newfoundland research laboratory. He proposed renting a research vessel equipped with scientific apparatus each summer, establishing a library with canonical texts in fisheries science, and erecting a fisheries research building at MUC.[80] Nevertheless, nothing concrete materialized from this proposal, as the Newfoundland government was reluctant to commit financially, and the Canadian government was reluctant to devote resources to Newfoundland's research needs.[81] "It is not reasonable to think," lawyer, merchant, and bait enthusiast L.C. Outerbridge stated, "that any Canadian station could or would undertake the pioneer spade work which has to be done here in the almost total absence of data or statistics regarding Newfoundland fishery conditions."[82]

In the decade after the Great War, some strides were taken in rectifying the "humiliating" absence of statistical data and scientific knowledge regarding Newfoundland's fisheries. Despite the conservative backlash against government intervention of the early 1920s, some basic research was accomplished, and certain gaps in knowledge were filled through diverse quantitative technologies, such as deep-sea thermometers, drift bottles, microscopes, and rigorous practices of scientific notation. International and local institutions — NACFI, MUC, the IEC, and the EMB — spread the gospel of fisheries science. This work helped proliferate the abstract, mechanistic understanding of the ocean and fish, articulated so clearly by Huntsman in his description of the Strait of Belle Isle as "a machine for producing 'cod water.'" This was important groundwork, but did not fundamentally alter the organization of production. But calls for rationalizing production received a new impetus in the 1930s, kicked off by the worst economic crisis in living memory. This period would later be described as the "real start" of fisheries science and management in Newfoundland.[83]

III.

The recurrent calls for a robust government-funded scientific fisheries research program in Newfoundland were finally answered in 1929. With Newfoundland reeling from the early effects of the Great Depression, Prime Minister Richard Squires travelled to London to attend the Imperial Conference, where he successfully negotiated a fisheries research scheme with the EMB on behalf of the Newfoundland government, which was "impressed by the urgent need for fishery development on scientific lines."[84] Squires was inspired by the views on the fishery of Dr. J.C. Drummond, professor of physiological chemistry at the University College London. In Newfoundland investigating the vitamin potency of Newfoundland cod liver oil, Drummond made his views on the relationship between science and industry clear in a lecture to the Rotary Club in August 1929, arguing that "the whole fishery will find its salvation in the establishment of a scientific research association."[85] The EMB agreed to provide a capital and annual maintenance fund, to be matched by the Newfoundland government, for an initial period of five years and to split the cost of sending a marine biologist to Newfoundland to conduct an initial survey of the country's fisheries and to prepare a scheme of research and a detailed cost estimate.[86] The agreement also stipulated that the Newfoundland government would set up a "special body" — half nominated by the government, half by the EMB — to supervise the research and administer the funds.[87]

Dr. Harold Thompson was selected to conduct the initial survey.[88] A graduate of the University of Aberdeen, with first-class honours in Zoology and Chemistry, Thompson was employed as a marine biologist with the Fishery Board of Scotland, specializing in the study of North Sea haddock.[89] He conducted his survey between 15 July and 25 October 1930, and submitted his report in December 1930.[90] For a successful research scheme, Thompson stated that the Fisheries Research Commission (FRC) required an adequately staffed and well-equipped laboratory, analyzing information provided by two sources: a scientific research vessel and trained officers on the "wharf-sides."[91] He later summarized this pithily, listing three prerequisites for effective science: "a ship, a laboratory, and a library."[92] Thompson recommended Harvey & Co.'s Bay Bulls plant as the best site for the FRC's laboratory, as it was close to St. John's and had access to abundant seawater. With the addition of scientific apparatus, he felt that the *Cape Agulhas*, the only operating trawler in Newfoundland, would be a suitable research vessel.[93] Finally, to collect information on shore, he recommended the training of four young men at Halifax Research Station.[94] In his final report, submitted to the EMB in December 1930, he repeated these recommendations.[95] The EMB agreed to adopt Thompson's proposal on 18 February 1930, finalizing the terms at a capital grant of £5,000 and an annual maintenance of £5,000 for five years, with Thompson approved as director.[96] The FRC then negotiated the rental of the Bay Bulls premises, the purchase of the *Cape Agulhas*, and the training of four young men — Baxter Blackwood, George Blackmore, Arthur Hearn, and Bertram Mayo — at the Atlantic Fisheries Experimental Station.[97]

With his research laboratory and vessel secured and his staff assembled, comprised of local, British, and American-trained experts, Thompson's salary began on 1 April 1931. The basic requirements for fisheries research were in place, and Thompson expressed satisfaction with the FRC's progress: "As far as things have gone," he wrote Fisheries Minister H.B.C. Lake, "I think we can allow ourselves a preliminary pat on the back."[98]

Under Thompson's direction, the FRC had three main objectives: first, to survey, estimate, and study Newfoundland's fishery resources and to gather statistics of the primary species to establish the "maximum, minimum and normal densities of numbers of the stocks" to predict future catches; second, to examine and improve current fish-processing methods; and third, to find means of utilizing waste by-products.[99] The FRC's research, in other words, spanned both the "biological side" and "processing side" of Newfoundland's fishing industry.[100] With such a broad mandate, the FRC cast its initial field of research very wide, with the hope that the most important subjects would emerge over time.[101] Biological observations focused on the correlation of fish abundance with changing oceanic conditions, with a primary focus on cod and caplin, a key baitfish, as well as investigations into herring, haddock, lobster, salmon, and shrimp, the identification of marine flora and fauna, and the vitamin A content of Newfoundland cod liver oil.[102] Technical investigations focused on the development of artificial dryers to remove the climatic variable from fish processing, the improvement of cod liver oil and canning methods, and research into the production of fishmeal from fish waste.[103] The Commission stressed the need to reach the public through lectures, press articles, fishery inspectors, and technical training.[104] The FRC also strengthened connections with the international fisheries research community, with Harold Thompson attending the NACFI annual meetings between 1930 and 1934.[105]

A 1932 article by George Whiteley Jr. captures the FRC's early research *Zeitgeist*. Raised in a prominent fishing family — his grandfather is credited with the invention of the cod trap in the 1860s — Whiteley spent his childhood summers at his family's fishing premises at Bonne Esperance, Labrador, where he learned the diverse practical skills necessary for fishing. It was as a child visiting Labrador that he first witnessed the effects of the "uncertainty of economic return that continually hovers over primary producers, farmers or fishermen, so dependent on natural forces beyond human control."[106] Trained in biology at MUC, Dalhousie, and the University of Toronto, where he worked under A.G. Huntsman, Whiteley returned to Newfoundland in 1931 as part of the FRC's inaugural research staff.[107] In his 1932 article, Whiteley casts the role of the FRC in explicitly entrepreneurial terms:

> Just as business men, when they reorganize a corporation, first take a complete inventory of stock on hand to find how much of it is valuable and what has to be scrapped, so the fisheries biologists must first possess a complete and intimate knowledge of the life history and habits of each fish before attempting to lead the industry ahead by the scientific application of such knowledge.[108]

Mirroring the separation laid out by Thompson, Whiteley divided the work of fisheries biologists into *technical* problems of cure, processing, and transportation and "life history problems," such as identifying the abundance and location of commercially valuable fish, understanding their reproductive cycles, and developing methods to forecast annual catches over the short term.

Whiteley introduces his readers to the mechanics of routine sea work. In its first survey, the *Cape Agulhas* was 52 days at sea, covered 4,200 miles, and established almost 100 stations, "a fixed position in the ocean of known latitude and longitude where investigations are made."[109] This locational precision allowed future investigations to be repeated and compared, which, if continued over several years, made it possible for the varying conditions at the station to be "accurately pictured."[110] For biological surveys, the crew used a trawl to collect samples, which were hoisted on deck by winch, sorted by species, and examined under Dr. Thompson's direction. Fish were measured, scale samples taken, and stomach contents measured and noted. Elsewhere on the ship, hydrographical workers were taking accurate temperature measurements "at different depths from bottom to surface," pulling up fine cheesecloth and silk nets at specific locations to take "cross-sections of the marine life at that station," and tossing drift bottles to trace currents. "Complete logs and journals are kept," he notes, "so an exact record of everything done is ready for future reference."[111]

Whiteley described the current knowledge of the life history of Newfoundland fish as a blank. "We have no accurate knowledge of a single one of the creatures," he stated, "the barter of which brings to the country ten to fourteen million dollars per year, and whose abundant capture seems so necessary to our very national security."[112] The basic research into the life history of key species — cod, salmon, caplin, squid, lobsters, herring, etc. — by the FRC was geared towards establishing the reliable and accurate capability of predicting future yields. This was made possible by the scientific method, the "essentially rational way of thinking" based on evidence of a particular kind: "objective evidence, evidence outside himself, tested evidence, comparative evidence, experimental evidence[,] ... evidence that can be reduced to measurement — to number."[113]

Despite the FRC's early success — demonstrated by reams of data and new knowledge by the practices described by Whiteley, and popularized by tentative but initially successful public broadcasts of where and when to fish — funding for scientific research was threatened by the continuing economic depression.[114] On 19 September 1931, the FRC received a telegram from the EMB requesting a "substantial reduction" in its research expenditure via "deceleration and economies" in view of the recent financial crisis.[115] The FRC agreed to a 10 per cent reduction in the annual maintenance expenditure, attained through voluntary staff salary cuts.[116] By October 1933, the British government had abolished the EMB, in an effort to reduce the country's financial commitments and following the introduction of actual tariffs that did not rely on consumer preferences to encourage consumption of British goods.[117] Despite the shuttering of the EMB, the Newfoundland government successfully managed to hold Great Britain to its five-year commitment of FRC funding.

Like Great Britain, Newfoundland was also pursuing a policy of retrenchment to help pay down the country's debt, which was reaching staggering proportions. With the governmental restructuring brought on by Newfoundland's debt crisis in the early 1930s, and the subsequent appointment of the Commission of Government, the FRC was abolished, but the research staff, laboratory, and vessel were brought under the direction of the new Department of Natural Resources, under John Hope Simpson. With the initial five-year agreement set to expire on 31 March 1936, the Commission negotiated a one-year renewal on existing terms, barring the cancellation of deep-sea work, which comprised 25 per cent of the laboratory's budget.[118]

Despite the uncertainties of the Great Depression and the country's political machinations, Thompson and his staff continued their work, motivated by the belief that "fishery research is bipartite in nature in that it is concerned equally with a study of the source of supply of raw material and the processing of that material."[119] Consequently, the FRC's work focused on the continuous hydrographical survey of seas and fishing grounds around Newfoundland and biological survey of the country's marine fauna, as well as technical investigations in the production of saltfish, cod liver oil, and canned products.[120] Thompson viewed the short-term extension of the scheme and cessation of the survey work as proof of the government's waning interest in fisheries research.[121]

Disillusioned by his time in Newfoundland, Thompson tendered his resignation as director in September, effective 31 December 1936, after securing employment as founding director of a fisheries research organization in Australia.[122] We can get a sense of his disillusionment from some pointed (and still pertinent) advice he gave aspiring biologist, and his eventual replacement as director, Wilfred Templeman, in the autumn of 1936: "Never take a job with the Newfoundland Government."[123] Dr. W.F. Hampton, educated at MUC, Dalhousie, and McGill, took over as acting director in January 1937.[124] Four months later, the Bay Bulls laboratory burned down, destroying a large collection of data and research material. With much of the investment in fisheries science up in flames and the leading intellectual force departed for Australia, the future of fisheries science in Newfoundland was unclear by early 1937.

Thompson was correct to assume that expiry of the original financing scheme would lead to a re-evaluation of the importance of fisheries research, but he was wrong about the outcome. In 1937, the Kent Commission — constituted by the Commission of Government to investigate conditions in Newfoundland's saltfish industry — concluded that, in a country so dependent on fisheries, scientific fisheries research was "an essential public service."[125] A second committee repeated the call for continued funding of scientific research, and recommended the centralization of government laboratory work in a single building in St. John's, following the Bay Bulls laboratory fire in April 1937.[126] The committee's recommendations were adopted, and the new laboratory was hoped to be in service by July 1938.[127] Until that time, fisheries research was carried out in a small, cramped temporary laboratory at the Court House — where "even routine matters are met with difficulty."[128] After considerable delays, the Newfoundland Government Laboratory, located on Water Street in St. John's with access to the harbour, was opened in 1940, with Hampton as acting director.[129] After a lengthy search for a full-time director, Newfoundland-born Dr. Wilfred Templeman became director of the Fisheries and Analytical Sections of the Government Laboratory in 1944.[130] Following Confederation with Canada in 1949, the laboratory was placed under the Fisheries Research Board of Canada as a permanent biological station.[131]

IV.

By the time of the Bay Bulls fire in April 1937, although a significant portion of the actual research work had gone up in smoke, much of the ideological work of legitimizing science and expert authority had been accomplished. Modernizing the knowledge of ocean-space and the life history of fish, like the attempts at extending control over reproduction and predation described in the previous chapter, emerged as a response to the credit system's sharpening contradictions in the late nineteenth century. These structural shifts highlighted internal problems within the mode of production, which were framed around inefficient and pre-modern "rule of thumb" methods. Boosters of fisheries science derided these embodied forms of practical knowledge as an inherent barrier to rational production. Reforming and reframing the embodied knowledge of fishing around the abstract knowledge of arithmetic was framed as a precondition for rational economic development.

The knowledge of fishing — where, when, and how to extract fish from water — was an essential input to the production process. But the socio-spatial division of labour in saltfish production, outlined in Chapter 2, precluded the top-down, hierarchical reordering of fishing knowledges by experts, as fishing families exercised some direct control over the pace and patterns of work in the saltfishery. For FRC scientist George Whiteley Jr., this was the essential difference between the rapidly developing industrial world and a "peasant community like Newfoundland."[132] The industrial world could place the technical innovations developed by private and public science into immediate effect: "when Ford scrapped his model T and began to manufacture a new car — the product of his scientific laboratories — it would have been useless for the workmen to say 'we don't approve of this new method, we want to continue turning out the old car.'"[133]

Fisheries scientists, from early innovators like Nielsen and Hjort to Huntsman and Sleggs, to the cadre of fisheries scientists under Thompson's direction, applied a range of metrical technologies to fish and the ocean, such as drift bottles, fish scale studies, tagging experiments, temperature readings, and rigorous notation and archiving practices, with a simple objective: "to enable us to predict in advance the probable abundance of the fish for a given year or for a given locality."[134] These investigations produced a new conception of fish and ocean-space. Scientific surveys, for example, proceeded by taking observations at different "stations," or fixed, precisely recorded positions in the ocean. This produced an abstract conception of ocean-space, comprised of infinite series of *fixed* points on a Cartesian grid, and with depth understood as a succession of vertical surfaces.

But Whiteley presents a very different picture of this research trip in his 1982 memoirs, *Northern Sea, Hardy Sailors*. Fog, ice, and rough conditions made it difficult to establish accurate lines of position. "We really did not know where we were with any reasonable degree of accuracy," he conceded. The inshore fishermen aboard the research ship also take a more prominent role in his memoirs. Obscured in his paean to the scientific method, they emerge as friends, offering company and entertainment, and allies, who contributed concretely to the success of the survey through their knowledge, skills, and work ethic. The harrowing stories of survival and loss communicated by experienced fishers highlight the embodied experience of these research trips, which is obscured in Whiteley's more Promethean description of the scientific method. As one fisher on the trawler crew, Levi Parsons, contended, these stories of mysterious happenings and ghostly visitations were proof of the limits of human knowledge of reality. "We people," he stated, "don't know everything . . . now adjust your mind to that."[135]

Fish, too, were transformed. Rather than the lively "swarming fish-life,"[136] they were understood as predictable and manageable, responding mechanically to different environmental signals. Once the variables were decoded, fish abundance and scarcity could be easily predicted. This, it was argued, "would largely remove the element of 'luck'" in fishing.[137] "The knowledge as to the current and the temperature of the waters," stated Drs. A.G. Huntsman and A.C. Gardiner in a 1923 speech to the Board of Trade, "would prove of immense value to the fishermen as it would solve the problem as to where and when the fish could be caught.[138] However insignificant the pre-Confederation (and pre-conflagration) history of fisheries science in Newfoundland may have been in terms of legislative reach and research output, this period witnessed the creation of the institutional, methodological, and, most importantly, *ideological* conditions for the implementation and elaboration of scientific fisheries management and the subsequent proliferation of industrial fishing practices.

~ ~ ~

As I have argued in Part II, extending control over the *quantity* of fish produced annually was a critical preoccupation for reformers — scientists, politicians, merchants, fishers — over the 50 years between the formation of Fisheries Commission and the Bay Bulls fire. Attempts were made to *control* and *predict* the quantity of cod extracted annually, through artificial propagation, control over bait, and the development of fisheries science. But, as we will see in Part III, attempts to introduce novel fishing measures extended beyond simply the *extractive* moment. Getting *fish out of water*, remember, was only part of the problem. Fishers and merchants had to preserve and cure cod by taking *water out of fish* by salt, wind, and weight, in order to distribute and realize the value congealed in the saltfish commodity. Circulation, too, like extraction, emerged as a potential lever of accumulation in the saltfish trade. The *qualities* of saltfish and its key by-product, cod liver oil, not just their quantities, entered the arithmetical gaze of modern science.

Governor David Murray Anderson reading the documents at the inauguration of the Commission of Government, flanked by the six commissioners at the Newfoundland Hotel, 16 February 1934. (TRPAD, A 15-159, Holloway family fonds.)

Stages and fishing boat at Quidi Vidi, St. John's. Extraction in Newfoundland was divided between the inshore and Bank fishing fleets, between dories and schooners, with very different capital outlays and labour requirements. (MUNA, COLL-137, 01 01 003.)

Landing fish from boat onto fish stage. (TRPAD, A 57-82.)

Weighing and piling codfish at Bowring Bros. in St. John's, getting ready for export to the consuming markets in Southern Europe and Latin America. (TRPAD, VA 35-18.4.)

Wilfred Grenfell (third from left) and Norwegian fisheries inspector Adolph Nielsen (fifth from left) at Winsor Harbour Island, Labrador, early 1890s. (TRPAD, Item VA 152-151, Eliot Curwen fonds.)

Fisherman rinsing split cod, Bristol's Hope on the Avalon Peninsula. Curing cod was beset by potential pitfalls: slimy, sour, maggoty, saltburnt, sunburnt, dun, pink, poorly split, round-tailed, blacknaped, bloodstained, inadequately washed, broken, and roughly handled. Cleanliness, as many reformers suggested, was essential. (TRPAD, VA 15b-24.11.)

Interior of fish stage in Labrador, 22 August 1893. (TRPAD, VA 152-171, Eliot Curwen fonds.)

Man culling dried fish. Culling was a contentious process between fishers and merchants, determining prices paid and supplies received. (TRPAD, VA 6-77.)

Bauline on the Avalon Peninsula: flakes with fish drying, spread and in piles. Making fish was the process of removing fish from water and water from fish. The latter was accomplished by both drying and piling. (TRPAD, VA 151-54.6.)

Women and men working on flakes, The Battery, St. John's. (MUNA, COLL-137, 03 07 003.)

PART III ∽ WATER OUT OF FISH

When you got some spearing they're hung out to dry,
It'll take all your time to brush off the flies;
To keep off the flies it is more than you'll do,
Then out comes the sun and she all splits in two.

And then next comes the merchant to see your supply,
The fine side of fishing you'll see by and by;
Seven dollars for large, and four-fifty for small,
You pick out your West Indies and you've nothing at all.

5

IMPROVING QUALITY

With the economy reeling from the Great Depression and democracy temporarily suspended in Newfoundland in February 1934, the newly instituted Commission of Government published a short memorandum reflecting on its initial achievements and charting the general policy to be followed going forward.[1] In the memorandum, the Commission noted that Newfoundland almost completely depended on a single industry, prosecuted in a highly individualistic manner. "The roots of the trouble," the meeting concluded, "are to be found in the difficulties experienced by the main industry in adjusting itself to modern methods and modern circumstances."[2] Using traditional methods, and organized by the credit system, the country's saltfish was placed on a world market "in competition with other food stuffs the result of a mass production."[3] In order to modernize Newfoundland's fishing industry, the Commission argued, the trade must produce and export a top-quality product. High quality and modernity were linked; so, too, were poor quality and the credit system.

To produce top-grade saltfish — "extra thick, light amber colour, even surface, thoroughly clean on both back and face, not showing blood stains, clots, liver or gut; well split and not showing excessive salt on the face"[4] — was difficult. As we saw in Chapter 2, the potential pitfalls in the production of saltfish were extensive: slimy, sour, maggoty, saltburnt, sunburnt, dun, pink, poorly split, round-tailed, *blacknaped*, bloodstained, inadequately washed, broken, and roughly handled. By the end of the nineteenth century, Newfoundland was losing its hold of the foreign markets. It was being outcompeted by the higher-quality saltfish produced by Norway, France, and Iceland. "Surely there must be something radically wrong here," argued "Practical Experience" in a letter to the editor of the *Evening Telegram*, "and it is very evident it lies in the cure of our fish."[5] This chapter examines attempts to modernize and rationalize saltfish processing techniques and to improve the quality of the country's chief export.

I.

Adolph Nielsen's first years as Newfoundland's Superintendent of Fisheries were busy. Alongside artificial propagation, the reorganization of the bait supply, and the production of "accurate knowledge" correlating fish abundance with ocean temperature, the Norwegian fisheries expert sought to apply scientific principles to improve the cure of saltfish following his appointment in April 1887. Initially preoccupied with building and operating his cod hatchery on Dildo Island, Nielsen turned his attention in the early spring of 1890 to the question of improving Newfoundland's cure, publishing a 78-page report entitled *Report on the Cure of Codfish and Herring*.[6] In this document, Nielsen made two claims regarding the problem with Newfoundland's cure, one moral and one economic. First, he stated that fish curers on both sides of the Atlantic faced the same problems, and that the means by which Newfoundland's competitors solved those problems were relatively simple: "It may be pronounced in one single word, namely: Carefulness."[7] Care in fish-making, for Nielsen, was a moral quality, dependent on the character, honesty, and industriousness of the fisher.

Nielsen identified a second reason for the country's problem with curing fish: the social division of labour. In Norway, he noted, catching and curing fish were separate endeavours. This allowed fish catchers to spend more time and energy on securing large catches, and allowed fish-makers to cure top-quality saltfish. In order to improve the cure of Newfoundland's saltfish, Nielsen called for the separation of fishing and curing and the exclusion of women's labour.[8]

In his annual report for 1894, written in the wake of the bank crisis of 1894, Nielsen refined his analysis, shifting blame for Newfoundland's inferior cure from carelessness and the division of labour to the credit system as a whole. For Nielsen, "Black Monday" proved that "something has been wrong for many years back in the way of maintaining and prosecuting [the fishing] industry."[9] The credit system, he argued, sapped the energy and independence of fishers, because fishers were perpetually in debt, exacerbated by the high prices charged by merchants to limit risk. "The credit and supplying system," he concluded, "proves clearly in the long run to have turned out one of the greatest curses that ever fell upon this country and its people."[10] In addition, the spatially diffuse and highly variegated nature of production frustrated efforts at culling fish, which led to ever-more dealers turning to the practice of *talqual* purchasing, or taking the "fish as they get it from the fishermen, no matter whether it is good or bad *at a fixed valuation.*"[11] This eliminated the price incentive for fishers to produce top-quality saltfish, "so that ultimately he adopts the policy of his careless, indifferent neighbour, and gets it off his hands with as little labour and as green as possible."[12]

Predating Hope Simpson's analysis in his letter to his son by 50 years, Nielsen proposed a revolutionary reorganization of the fishing industry, whereby fish would be bought *green* (unprocessed) from fishers *for cash*, to be cured in large, centralized processing facilities controlled by merchants.[13] A cash-based economy, Nielsen concluded, would "greatly lessen the risks of the trade, bring about a better cure of fish, and enable us to compete successfully with our rivals in foreign markets."[14] The cash system, he argued, would also affect a revolution in the moral character of Newfoundland's fishers, replacing the "extravagance, luxury, carelessness, recklessness regarding the future, want of energy, laziness and dependence"[15] encouraged by the credit system with "enterprise, energy, and a desire of independence."[16] Nielsen posited a relationship between the production of high-quality saltfish and the accurate measurement of *quality* through grading and *value* through a cash-based system of trade.

With Newfoundland's speedy return to the economic status quo following the bank crash, boosted by a good sealing season in the winter of 1895, and followed by a profitable cod season, the political-economic conditions for radical change in the organization of the saltfish industry evaporated.[17] Nielsen retired as Superintendent of Fisheries in 1896, returning to Norway to convalesce from a severe asthma attack.[18] In 1897, a Conservative government was formed under J.S. Winter, marking a shift in government policy. Winter's government set about pruning and reorganizing the civil service, creating the Department of Marine and Fisheries (DMF) in 1898.[19] The government, however, did not replace Nielsen with an equally qualified or ambitious fisheries expert, instead adopting a more *laissez-faire* approach to the industry. Blame for Newfoundland's inferior cure was placed primarily on carelessness — an individual issue, and thus not the proper domain of government. "It is hoped," the new government proclaimed in its response to the Governor's throne speech, "that those engaged in the trade will see the wisdom of devoting more attention to this important matter, for our fish, with proper care and attention, should hold the first place in the markets of the world."[20]

The first half-decade of the twentieth century witnessed a rare period of prosperity in Newfoundland. The country enjoyed a modest boom with the successful development of forestry and mining industries and witnessed a series of remunerative fishing seasons with large catches and high prices.[21] In this context of prosperity, rather than pushing for structural transformations in the fishery, reforming fishers' behaviour and attitudes by encouraging cleanliness and care was the principal method for improving the country's cure. In 1902, the DMF reminded fishers of their "primary duty" to produce top-quality saltfish. "Utmost cleanliness should therefore be observed in the primary operations of splitting, washing from the knife and dry-salting."[22] A 1903 pamphlet, produced by the major merchant firms, made a similar point: "It is not necessary to tell you what makes bad fish . . . with the exception of continuous bad weather, it can all be put into one word 'carelessness.'"[23] The Governor, H.E. McCallum, summed up the era's paternalistic ethos in a note to the newly appointed

Superintendent of Fisheries, E.C. Watson, a merchant and politician, not a fisheries scientist: "if our people will not improve their cure by invitation and example they should be treated as children and made to do so."[24]

Encouraged by "seven fat years"[25] and noting the combination of depleted fisheries elsewhere and the increasing scale and prosperity of the consuming markets, Governor William MacGregor, appointed in 1904, stated in his 1906 report on the country's economic prospects: "Indeed the market for fishery products would seem to have a bright prospect before it in the not far distant future."[26] The following two seasons, however, disproved MacGregor's prediction. Despite large catches in 1907 and 1908, rushed shipments to overstocked markets and a poor cull led to complaints in the foreign markets and low prices received. Prices dropped slightly in 1907 and collapsed by 50 per cent in 1908.[27] The economic crisis was particularly egregious because it was not the result of a poor catch or careless curing. As Governor MacGregor noted in his Throne Speech, "The result of last season's fishing operations was, on the whole, as regards the catch, more than an average."[28] Rather, as one politician pointed out, the 1907–08 crisis was the result of attempting to unload as much saltfish as possible, as quickly as possible, on a glutted market. "The commercial law of demand and supply," he concluded, "seems to be entirely eliminated from our calculations."[29]

Alongside reinvigorating calls for scientific investigation described in the previous chapter, the economic crisis repoliticized the organization of the fish trade by highlighting the industry's systemic problems. Rather than simply blaming downturns on the exigencies of an unpredictable maritime environment, or fishers' carelessness, attention was refocused on the culling and marketing practices of the exporting merchant firms and the government's role in regulating the industry.[30] The 1911 annual report drives home this point:

> It is useless for the merchants to circularize the fishermen, asking for better attention in the handling and curing of fish, and then stultify themselves by competing one

> against the other when purchasing from the fishermen, buying talqual, regardless of damp, giving bonuses, paying freight, and, generally by their own actions, putting a premium on poorer fish and encouraging a lower standard. Such a policy is suicidal, is admitted to be so, but no combined action is taken to remedy matters.[31]

The 1907–08 price slump had a profound impact on the country's political and economic complexion. Unionist, farmer, and telegraph operator W.F. Coaker used the anger caused by what he called the "Black Fall of 1908" to found the Fishermen's Protective Union (FPU) in November 1908.[32] "Last year, particularly in the Fall," wrote Coaker in 1909, "fish was a despised article of food, and the manner in which our fishermen were treated by fish exporters will not soon be forgotten."[33] Coaker sought to organize fishers through the FPU to more fairly redistribute the wealth created by fishers and appropriated by merchants, summarized in the Union's rather peculiarly individualistic motto: "To each his own."[34]

Coaker proposed a wide-ranging set of social and political reforms intended to help the "toiling masses in Newfoundland," including the collection of fishing information described earlier.[35] Coaker's most galvanizing proposals for reform, however, concerned the industrial organization of the fishing industry. He sought to modernize and standardize the industry by proposing a system of government grading, performed by government-employed cullers and regulated by government inspectors. "Reckless buying, without cull, is surely but slowly ruining the dry fish markets," he concluded at the FPU's third annual convention in 1911, "and the cure will not be improved until the man who sells good fish is paid a good price, and the man who sells bad is punished by receiving a low price."[36]

Occurring in the midst of an election, the 1908 crisis motivated opposition to the ruling party, Robert Bond's Liberal Party, and led to the formation of a new government under E.P. Morris's People's Party in May 1909.[37] Morris, recognizing the widespread dismay caused by the crisis, campaigned with calls for a standard cull and a system of government cullers, alongside a number of other populist measures.[38] Morris complained that Newfoundland's cull was dictated by the market, not abstract standards, varying with the price of fish or the shortage of the catch.[39] "An honest, bona fide attempt," he argued, "should be made to systematize that which at present has no system or method."[40]

Rather than act with legislation, however, the new government sought to improve the industry by encouraging the merchant class to organize itself with the formation of a Newfoundland Board of Trade, with members privately referring to one another as the "Knights of the leather chairs."[41] On 12 June 1909, the Board of Trade was incorporated, but without the regulatory power over the cull outlined in the initial proposal.[42] Denied full authority over the cull, the Board of Trade appointed Mr. Thomas Mundy as Inspector of Fish to offer voluntary inspection and certification for fish exports.[43] Voluntary inspection, however, failed to inspire confidence in foreign buyers and quickly devolved, being "treated with ridicule and contempt" as early as 1915.[44]

The formation of the FPU in 1908 and the Newfoundland Board of Trade in 1909 sharpened the class divisions between fishers and merchants. Following the formation of the Board of Trade, which he described as "the Merchants' Union of Newfoundland,"[45] Coaker warned fishers that the Board "must now be carefully watched by us. We must see that it don't use its powers to take the fishermen's dollar."[46] Similarly, the mercantile elite rejected the FPU's new role in the economy — which included the incorporation of the Fishermen's Union Trading Company (FUTC), the union's commercial arm, in 1911 — regarding them as unnecessary and meddlesome intrusions.[47] "I can see nothing but disaster likely to attend to the FISHERMEN," wrote G.C. Fearn, the Board of Trade's first secretary, "if they try to invade the MERCHANTS domain."[48]

Morris, perhaps recognizing the highly contentious nature of the issue in the context of a sharpened class division between fisher and merchant, continued to *promise* a standardized cull, but consistently failed to implement any actual legislation to accomplish it.[49] Coaker later stated that the Morris administration, with its oblique feints towards reform, "struggled by scratching the surface to ensure prosperity."[50] Morris's failure to enact his promised fishery reform soured his relation with Coaker, and in response the FPU decided to enter the political realm in 1913.[51] Noting Morris's failure to standardize fish culling, the FPU saw "no other course open to us except that of securing the return of sufficient Union members of the House of Assembly to ensure recognition of our just requests."[52] The FPU's political platform, known as the "Bonavista Platform," was comprehensive and radical, calling for a variety of reforms, including free education, improved outport health care, and anti-corruption laws. Reflecting the importance attributed to the issue, the Union's first demand was for the standardization of fish, with a new system of culling and inspection.[53]

The 1913 general election returned Morris to power with a majority, but highlighted the new political might of the FPU's political party, which won eight seats, one more than Bond's long-established Liberal Party. "The result of the election," stated Coaker in his fifth annual address to the FPU's Supreme Council, "has proved without doubt the power and influence of our Union."[54] The FPU was unable to pass any legislation, even when tacitly supported by Morris's party, due to opposition by the merchant-dominated Legislative Council.[55] However, with Prime Minister Morris alienating the Water Street merchants through his branch-line railway construction, taxes, and deepening debt, and recognizing the real threat posed by the FPU in upcoming elections, the government tried courting FPU support by taking its first real steps towards implementing fisheries reform.[56]

A 15-member joint committee was asked to investigate and report on the main issues facing the industry, including the question of standardization, grading, and conservation measures, in addition to the call for scientific research described in Chapter 4. This Commission on Fishery Matters submitted its final report on 1 May 1915.[57] Regarding the question of improving and standardizing the cure, the Commission stated that this was one of the country's most pressing problems. "It is not too much to say that as a general tendency, this evil — the deterioration in the cure of fish — is threatening the very existence of the Colony."[58] Yet, the Commission was reluctant to make any definite recommendations, "owing to the divergent opinions" and "decided lack of interest" in the merchant community.[59] They concluded, however, that the issue could not be left alone to private initiative, and made a few tentative suggestions, such as "compulsory or voluntary" inspection, the abolishment of talqual buying and strict culling, the "general disassociation" of curing and catching, and the formation of a fish inspection board to implement those changes.[60]

The report was brief, equivocal, and ultimately ineffectual. None of its suggestions were ever acted on. Although in part reflecting the lack of initiative on the part of the government and industry, the report failed to gain any traction because it was delivered in the midst of a scandal in the sealing industry, with 251 sealers dying in two separate calamities.[61] The growing likelihood of a European war throughout the spring and summer of 1914 further upset political calculations and dissolved the will for implementing reforms for the standardization and culling of saltfish. The question of a standardized, uniform cull had been thrust into the centre of the political discussion over the future of the fishery with the emergence of the FPU and the Board of Trade. Although the war offered a brief respite, a more contracted battle over the process of measuring quality awaited the country with the cessation of conflict.

II.

The outbreak of the Great War, "which paralyzed banking, upset exchange and dislocated trade," caused a worrisome, though brief, economic crisis in the country.[62] Fish prices plummeted, exchange rates were thrown into chaos, and increased freight insurance rates discouraged shippers from exporting fish.[63] Trade conditions, however, quickly improved, with rising fish prices and decreased foreign competition from both closed fisheries and requisitioned trawlers.[64] "Splendid returns from all branches of the fisheries," concluded the DMF in 1918, allowed Newfoundlanders to survive the war "with less deprivation and greater profit than probably any other self contained and self dependent people anywhere in the Empire."[65]

Fishers and merchants invested heavily in the fishery throughout the war, financed by increased borrowing against securities tied to fisheries commodities. "There has been," stated John Harvey, a merchant and member of the unelected Legislative Council, "an unhesitating and free reinvestment of existing capital, of profits made, and of money borrowed upon the security of these."[66] With both fishers and merchants seeking to profit from the abnormally favourable trade conditions, these conditions led to what historian Ian McDonald describes as a "speculative euphoria."[67] With the markets cornered, foreign buyers and consumers had little recourse to question the price or quality of Newfoundland's saltfish. The quality problems of Newfoundland saltfish were, for a time, forgotten for a simple reason: "the foreign markets are practically without fish and the people there are looking for fish."[68]

The wartime boom exacerbated the industry's pre-war quality problems, setting the stage for a brutal recession and a pitched battle over the question of government regulation following the cessation of conflict. The threat of renewed competition, exchange difficulties, and low prices, the DMF wrote in 1918, "will demand the very best thought and management of the whole community."[69] The time was ripe for the government to play a more active role in regulating the fish trade, as Newfoundland's experience with the war had changed perceptions regarding the proper role of government. "It is time," wrote Governor C.A. Harris, "to remove the reproach recorded in the Journals of the Assembly . . . 'We have done nothing in the past but talk.'"[70]

The post-war recession, and the struggle over government regulation, threatened Newfoundland even before the signing of the armistice in November 1918. An enormous order by Italian importers from September 1918, for 940,000 quintals at very high prices, encouraged Newfoundland producers to cure the fish as quickly as possible as they raced to send fish to fill the order.[71] However, in October 1918, the Italian government, reeling from a wartime profiteering scandal by saltfish importers, placed the industry under strict control, forming the Consorzio per l'Importazione e la Distribuzione dei Merluzzi e Stoccofissi.[72] The Italian government used the Consorzio to force the price of fish down by acting as a single buyer for the entire market. The Consorzio refused to pay the prices promised in September 1918, and the large stocks of fish reserved for the Italian market, representing 20 per cent of the year's fish exports, began accumulating and deteriorating in Italian ports. Tensions were high. The banks dreaded losing the money tied up in Italian cargoes, and exporters feared that unsold Italian fish would be diverted to other markets, causing a widespread price collapse.

In January 1919, after much debate with panicked exporters, the Newfoundland government appointed a four-person committee, chaired by merchant and Minister of Shipping J.C. Crosbie (whose grandson would later announce the 1992 cod moratorium as Canadian Minister of Fisheries and Oceans). The committee was formed to negotiate with the Consorzio and exert control over the distribution and sale of Newfoundland fish.[73] The Crosbie committee was given wide-ranging and unprecedented powers to fix the terms of sale, declare minimum prices, and detain shipments, in order to limit panic selling by Newfoundland exporters. The committee succeeded in preventing "a very violent collapse of markets, with all its attendant evils and disastrous results,"[74] further proving the benefit of government intervention and co-operative and systematic marketing. Despite these initial returns, the government refused to reconvene the Crosbie committee for the 1919 season in order to limit the discussions over fishery policy, which favoured the FPU, in the upcoming election.

The next season, the Consorzio imposed a low price and new purchasing arrangements that disadvantaged Newfoundland shippers.[75] The banks, still wary from the previous season, tightened credit, and tensions mounted yet again. Three days after taking office, and with a crisis threatening, FPU-founder William Coaker — now Minister of Marine and Fisheries and Deputy Prime Minister in the newly elected coalition with Richard Squires's Liberal Reform Party — issued a Proclamation, under the "Imports and Exports (Restriction) Act 1918," that imposed a set of legal restrictions on the export of codfish. Seeing that Crosbie "tried to work by persuasion, but failed,"[76] exporters now required a licence — subject to forfeiture upon violation of terms — issued by the Minister of Marine and Fisheries, a permit for each shipment from the minister that confirmed its sale and price, and an affidavit stating the quality and grade of each shipment. Coaker also instituted a small committee of exporters to act as an advisory board.[77]

Coaker's regulations were, in many ways, less extensive than those given to Crosbie the previous season. Unlike Crosbie, Coaker could neither detain shipments nor fix the price for each sale; he could merely set a minimum price for shipments, in consultation with an advisory board composed of exporters. Some merchants, however, unmoved by the co-operative spirit of the Great War, objected to Coaker's intervention in the economy, labelling him both a "Kaiser" and a "Bolshevist."[78] When Coaker refused to issue a permit to a dissenting firm with close ties to the Consorzio,[79] the firm sued the government in the Supreme Court and succeeded in having the law deemed unconstitutional. In response, the government reimposed the regulations under the War Measures Act (1914), still in effect 14 months after the armistice.

Despite opposition from a few vocal merchants, the Board of Trade initially supported Coaker's regulations.[80] The new marketing arrangements had some early success, with one fish broker negotiating a sale of 200,000 quintals with the Consorzio at satisfactory prices and under better terms: "sold on the basis of full cash and exchange for documents in London."[81] Coaker, buoyed by his support from the trade and finally in a position of power in a majority government, proposed three pieces of legislation, all passed on 13 July 1920, that completely restructured the culling, marketing, and selling of saltfish: "An Act to regulate the Exportation of Salt Codfish," "An Act to provide for the better obtaining of information respecting the Codfishery," and "An Act to provide for the Standardization of Codfish."[82] Coaker's regulations finally implemented the FPU's long-standing demand for a standard cull and the abolishment of talqual buying. It also created the machinery for regulating shipping by establishing a Codfish Exportation Board that issued licences and determined the conditions and terms of sale, minimum prices, and maximum quantities for each market.[83]

Conditions in the autumn of 1920, however, began to strain the delicate political balance that opened the possibility of exporting regulations. Anxiety mounted when 100,000 quintals of Labrador fish glutted St. John's in mid-November. With Italy a large consumer of Labrador fish and negotiations with the Consorzio uncertain, financiers and exporters were extremely apprehensive of a general price collapse. In December, the exporters nominated W.A. Munn, a vocal opponent to the regulations, to take over the negotiations with the Consorzio from Coaker-supporter George Hawes.[84] With supplies of French, Norwegian, and Icelandic saltfish entering Italy, many exporters began predicting the collapse of merchant co-operation and the end of the regulations.[85]

These suspicions were confirmed three days later, when it was reported that A.E. Hickman, a merchant and vocal critic of regulation, had shipped 28,000 quintals to Italy below regulation prices.[86] "Let us thank God we have a man amongst us of the calibre of A.E. Hickman," proclaimed "Citizen" in a letter to the *Evening Telegram*, "who has the pluck and manliness to fight the 'Mad Mullah' of Port Union [Coaker]."[87] By 29 December 1920, rumours began swirling in St. John's after two additional sales by Crosbie and Munn that the exporters' association had voted to abandon the regulations.[88] On 3 May 1921, Coaker moved in the House of Assembly to have the Exportation Act repealed, and on 5 July 1921 the export regulations were abolished by a one-sentence Act. Government control over the culling and marketing of saltfish had ended in failure.

The Coaker Regulations attempted to introduce new forms of measuring quality to reform the processing, distribution, and consumption of saltfish, alongside the collection of fisheries statistics (Chapter 4). It was believed that, through the institution of accurate grading standards, fishers would be encouraged to produce uniformly high-quality saltfish in order to expand consumption in Southern Europe. Opponents claimed that the regulations were doomed to fail, as price fixing was an economic violation against the inexorable laws of supply and demand. "Economic laws," stated W.G. Gosling, Bermuda-born merchant and mayor of St. John's, the capital city, "are infallible in their working and it is useless to try and dodge them. . . . It is as futile for one to stick a pin in his barometer by way of influencing the weather."[89] Coaker, in contrast, maintained that his regulations were sound, but were undermined by a lack of merchant co-operation and confidence. "Had political partisanship not entered into this great vital national issue last year," he stated, "Italy would have purchased at least 150,000 quintals of our fish at a price that entailed no loss, and our exporters would have been many hundreds of thousands of dollars in pocket."[90]

With Newfoundland's domestic political situation precluding reform — especially after the election of the conservative merchant government of W.S. Monroe in 1924 — the saltfish industry continued to lose markets throughout the 1920s. Mechanization, standardization, and government regulation in the Scandinavian fishing industries, as well as the development of Southern European fishing fleets, forced Newfoundland exporters to turn to markets in Latin America and the West Indies.[91] Rushed shipments, talqual buying, glutted markets, and low prices — exacerbated by currency exchange problems and the "pernicious individualism of the exporter"[92] — characterized this period. Moreover, the repeal of the regulations discouraged attempts at reform from other actors for fear that they, too, would be treated like a "political football."[93] In 1923, the Board of Trade concluded, "it is generally agreed among shippers that the idea of a joint marketing of the whole catch is merely an utopian ideal which is quite incapable of fulfillment, and that any interference by the Government in connection with the marketing, is certain to result detrimentally."[94] These conditions, however, would not survive the onslaught of the Great Depression, which brought about a tectonic shift in the relationship of government, industry, and regulation.

III.

Although exchange and fish prices stabilized by the mid-1920s, and increased foreign investment in the forestry and mining industries stimulated a brief period of prosperity, the country was in a very poor position to deal with the onset of the Great Depression. The country's public debt — caused primarily by the cost of World War I, the mismanaged railway, and the financing of infrastructure concessions to lure foreign investment — continued to rise, reaching stunning heights by 1933: from 35.9 per cent of current revenue in 1929–30 to a "breathtaking" 63.2 per cent by 1932–33.[95] When prices for Newfoundland's main export commodities — saltfish, newsprint, iron ore, lead, and zinc — dropped precipitously in late 1929, the country lost its main sources of revenue. Collapsing export markets had a double effect on the country's coffers: reduced incomes for labourers meant increased spending for "able-bodied relief" *and* decreased revenue from tariffs on imported goods.[96]

The extraordinary economic conditions caused by the Great Depression overcame social inertia and mercantile conservatism, yet again inspiring action in Newfoundland for standardized production and organized marketing. For example, in 1931, the government succeeded in passing the "Act Relating to Salt Codfish."[97] However, in the debate over the bill, an optional membership clause was inserted by the House, which the trade felt "defeated the main objects of the measure"[98] and thus rendered the bill inoperative. In 1933, this Act was amended, to give the power to appoint members of the Exportation Board to the Governor, which gradually extended the government's control over the trade.[99]

Alongside legislation that aimed to organize marketing, tentatively overcoming social inertia and mercantile conservatism, the government had a new weapon to fight declining quality: the Fisheries Research Commission (FRC). Formed in 1931, the FRC returned attention to curing methods, rather than marketing practices, as an important avenue for improving quality. As fish broker George Hawes noted in 1936 in a memorandum on the saltfish industry, although exporters often blamed marketing practices as the cause of the recession, "it will have become apparent that they are mainly the result of defective grading." "This, in turn," he continued, "is largely caused by defective curing."[100] In addition to the more basic research surveys of the country's oceanography and maritime fauna described in Chapter 4, the FRC focused significant attention on applied research aimed at standardizing saltfish-processing methods.[101] "The second and equally important work requiring attention," wrote Harold Thompson in his proposal for the establishment of the FRC, "is that of attempting to find improved and more remunerative methods of placing sea-foods on the market."[102] This involved, as the Kent Commission suggested in 1937, scientific research into ascertaining the "best formula" for curing the different varieties of saltfish.[103]

In 1931, the FRC developed a three-pronged "line of attack" to reform and standardize saltfish curing. First, the FRC concentrated on publicly disseminating already existing scientific knowledge regarding the processing of saltfish and the prevention of the common diseases (pink and dun) that bedevilled the industry. Second, the FRC conducted investigations into the optimal quantity and type of salt to use for curing. Third, the FRC experimented with the artificial drying of saltfish to overcome the problems posed by Newfoundland's variable weather.[104] The FRC devoted considerable attention to asserting scientific control over the quantity and quality of salt applied and over the climatic conditions during drying. This applied research, alongside the promotion of scrupulous cleanliness by fishers during curing, promised to improve the overall quality and uniformity of the country's saltfish output.

Regardless of the promise of economic renewal via new legislation and scientific research, the country's financial position remained fragile.[105] Continued loans from the Bank of Montreal, Bank of Nova Scotia, Royal Bank of Canada, and Canadian Bank of Commerce helped Newfoundland avoid default, but the banks grew reluctant to continue financing the country's debt by May 1931. With a default looming for 30 June 1931, Newfoundland succeeded in receiving another $2 million by promising to adhere to the banks' strict terms.[106] With the House dissolved due to a political scandal over misappropriation of funds, an election was called for June 1932. F.C. Alderdice, businessman and cousin of former Conservative Prime Minister W.S. Monroe, formed the United Newfoundland Party, which promised to form a committee to investigate the "desirability and feasibility of placing the country under a form of commission government for a period of years."[107]

With the country's credit exhausted and no further retrenchment possible, recently elected Prime Minister Alderdice agreed to the appointment of a mixed Royal Commission, comprised of British, Canadian, and Newfoundland members, to examine the country's finances in exchange for a loan to delay default on the public debt. On 17 February 1933, the Newfoundland Royal Commission was appointed, and by late November the Commission submitted what is known as the Amulree Report. They proposed a radical set of constitutional and financial recommendations to deal with the country's debt crisis. Finding the people demoralized and the politicians debased, the Royal Commission proposed a "rest from politics for a period of years"[108] through the replacement of the existing Legislature and Executive Council with "a system of 'Government by Commission.'"[109] Without an effective legislative opposition, and reflecting widespread opinions *within* Newfoundland,[110] the Amulree Report's suggestions were accepted and implemented, with Newfoundland surrendering Dominion status on 16 February 1934.

The suspension of democracy in Newfoundland offered novel possibilities for reforming all facets of Newfoundland's political and economic life. It was viewed as an opportunity to introduce administrative efficiency into each government department. In addition to the Governor, six commissioners, three nominated by Britain and three by Newfoundland, administered the country's affair, which were divided into six departments: Finance, Natural Resources, Public Utilities, Home Affairs and Education, Justice, and Public Health and Welfare. John Hope Simpson, a British civil servant with 25 years of service in the Indian Civil Service, was appointed as the first Commissioner of Natural Resources.[111] The Department of Natural Resources (DNR) had a very broad mandate, dealing with all aspects of the country's fisheries, including catching, curing, grading, inspection, standardization, and by-products, as well as Crown lands and surveying, timber lands, pulp and paper mills, forest fires, mineral resources, agriculture, livestock, wild game and fruits, even "sheep preservation and dog control."[112]

The unyielding world depression continued to place pressure on the country's fishing industry. The DNR, under Hope Simpson, reacted to the continued trade depression in three ways. First, in June 1935, it returned yet again to the question of co-operative, organized marketing with the "Act for the Better Organization of the Trade in Salt Codfish."[113] The Act proposed the creation of a Board that could create rules and regulations to control exporting, including issuing licences for export, setting the terms of sale, and refusing shipments. Hope Simpson blamed the disorganized marketing and intense competitiveness of the merchant class for the trouble in the fishery, proposing co-operation as a fruitful alternative. Second, the Commission of Government called a commission of inquiry into the conditions in the fishery, chaired by James Kent, in November 1935.[114] Third, Thompson's fisheries research organization, now part of Hope Simpson's Department of Natural Resources, continued its tripartite line of attack under the Commission of Government.

Under the DNR, the Fisheries Research Commission communicated its research findings in the press and through the publication of annual reports and substantive research reports.[115] Technical research focused on determining the optimal conditions and methods for the production of top-quality saltfish, including "the effect of the variation in the amount of salt used and of the temperature and humidity conditions under which the salting process is carried out."[116] The FRC investigated and disseminated the "data covering possible formulae for the various classes of cure."[117]

Artificial drying emerged as a central preoccupation, as it offered the greatest possibility of reforming the industry.[118] "The effective standardization of a product," stated Thompson in the FRC's first annual report, "involves its production under uniform conditions." "Some degree of control," he continued, "is essential."[119] The FRC scientists wished to overcome the uncertainty of Newfoundland's variable weather, and artificial drying promised control over the temperature, humidity, and wind conditions. The "uncertainties" of fish drying, the acting director, W.F. Hampton, wrote, are "due to the fact that, almost invariably the drying is carried on outdoors by rule-of-thumb methods so that no control can be maintained over the variables which influence the drying mechanism."[120] As the *Evening Telegram* outlined in 1925, if artificial drying was adopted:

> the quality of the cure would no longer be dependent upon weather conditions; the fishing season could be considerably extended; the frequent delay between the time of catching and curing fish would not occur; the carelessness in curing, in the anxiety to get back to the fishing grounds would cease; the fisherman's work would be on a cash basis, and in consequence the supply system would become to a great extent unnecessary, and by the establishment of these centralized depots, a standardized cure would be assured.[121]

This single technical innovation promised to radically transform the entire organization of saltfish production in Newfoundland.

Yet, as the FRC scientists soon discovered, like the many people who attempted it before them, the invention of a successful artificial drying chamber was rather difficult.[122] Artificially dried fish was often *case hardened* — that is, dry on the outside, but still wet on the inside.[123] The surface of fish was often described as uneven and "stringy."[124] Furthermore, it was difficult to achieve the yellow tinge that characterized "the hallmark of the Newfoundland shore fish."[125] Artificial drying, it was discovered, could not perfectly reproduce top-quality saltfish. Nevertheless, proponents argued that it could increase the amount of second-class saltfish by reducing the amount of lowest quality produced.[126]

Despite these governmental measures and scientific research, the 1935 season was almost disastrous due to problems in the European markets and the actions of Newfoundland exporters who continued to undercut one another, even after being organized into a purportedly co-operative association.[127] In April 1936, the Commission of Government responded by creating the Newfoundland Fisheries Board (NFB). Fish broker George

Hawes advocated more drastic measures to deal with merchant individualism: "Sir John [Hope Simpson] said to me: 'What can we do with people like that? What's the remedy?' I said: 'Sir John the remedy is a firing squad at dawn — the most drastic steps.'"[128]

Following the regulatory responses of other North Atlantic fishing nations, such as Norway, Iceland, and the Faroe Islands, to uncertain trade conditions caused by the Great Depression, the NFB placed the industry firmly under government control.[129] Hope Simpson branded the creation of the NFB as "mussolinizing the fishing industry."[130] He described the board as a "dictatorial body deliberately designed to dragoon an unruly crowd of merchants, each of whom has, of course, only his pocket to consider."[131] The NFB was comprised of three officials, appointed by the government, empowered to make rules and regulations for all aspects of the country's fishing industry.[132] Over the next 12 years, the NFB continued extending control over the export of fish, aided by the co-operative spirit brought about by the communal response to World War II, and by expanding the inspection service, introducing culling standards, and creating statistical services to provide "up-to-date information on conditions in Newfoundland, in the markets, and in the competitive countries."[133] In 1947, the NFB, following the recommendations of the Fisheries Post-War Planning Committee, instituted single-desk selling by granting the exclusive right to a single, central marketing organization, Newfoundland Associated Fish Exporters Limited (NAFEL).[134] "Step by step," concluded NFB chairman Raymond Gushue, "the vigorous and often predatory, individualistic competition in our export trade has been brought within the control of cooperative marketing groups."[135]

IV.

In 1935, the Commission of Government argued that the source of Newfoundland's troubles — laid bare by the Great Depression but rooted in the longer history of the credit system — was its failure to adopt modern methods and adjust to "modern circumstances."[136] Making fish was no longer to be governed by embodied, rule-of-thumb methods but by abstract formulae, overcoming the problem of qualitative fluctuation by plugging in values for the key variables of wind velocity, temperature, humidity, salt potency, and time. Fishers were instructed to invest in thermometers and hygrometers, and to base their drying decisions on their readings of temperature and relative humidity.[137] Fishers previously had to rely on their experience and embodied knowledge in making decisions regarding making fish, which entailed guesswork. "Now, as a result of studies carried out at the Fishery Research Institute," announced one circular, "it is possible by means of proper instruments, to tell definitely if a doubtful day is really suitable and to check on what appear to be excellent drying days."[138]

First proposed by Nielsen in the 1890s, the introduction of abstract, precise measures into the processing, culling, and distribution of saltfish was a messy, contingent project that spanned almost 50 years. Reformers focused efforts on improving the *quality* of saltfish exported, rather than simply increasing the quantity of saltfish exported. They sought to coax more value out of the ocean through novel fish-processing technologies. Ironically, this occurred just before a new set of socio-technical innovations — organized around industrial trawlers, mechanized processing facilities, and the distribution of frozen fish products — disrupted the historical saltfish trade.[139]

Improving and developing new by-products is a common strategy for improving returns in resource industries. The saltfish industry was no exception. Saltfish was not the only valuable product that emerged after taking fish from water. As we will see in the following chapter, collecting, processing, and refining cod livers into cod liver oil was an important, valuable, and equally *unpredictable* trade. Similar dynamics were at play in this secondary post-extraction process.

6

DISCOVERING QUALITY

"The cod," nineteenth-century Newfoundland boosters Joseph Hatton and Moses Harvey noted with pride, "is the most useful of all fish. No part is valueless."[1] Heads, tongues, cheeks, and sounds, they stated, were (and are) delicious articles of food. The head, along with the intestines, could be converted into manure. Norwegians and Icelanders fed the head and bones to their cows to increase milk output. The offal and bones could be steamed, dried, and ground into a "fish guano, which is almost equal as a fertilizer to the Peruvian guano."[2] The roe was exported to France and used as bait for the sardine fishery. Isinglass was made from the swimming bladder, which was used by confectioners before the commercial production of gelatin and by brewers in the fining (clarification) of beer. Hatton and Harvey, in their panegyric to the many uses of the cod, however, fail to mention the most important historical by-product: the oil produced by rendering the liver.

Unlike oily fish, such as salmon, herring, sardine, and mackerel, cod flesh is very lean. As argued in Chapter 2, this is one of the species' most important biophysical characteristics: cod flesh's low fat content limits lipid oxidation, making it particularly amenable to preservation.[3] This characteristic has a second effect. In contrast to the even distribution of fat content throughout the muscle of oily fish, fat in cod is concentrated in the liver. This made the separation, collection, and rendering of cod livers into cod oil or *train oil* possible during the production of saltfish.[4] The production of cod oil was the first by-product industry in the Newfoundland saltfish trade, emerging alongside it. For example, although the earliest cargoes brought back from Newfoundland after Cabot's "discovery" of Newfoundland in 1497 remain unknown, the historical record shows that Sir Francis Drake took several Portuguese vessels "freighted with fish and oil" as early as the sixteenth century.[5] Perhaps the ubiquity and commercial importance of cod liver oil production in Newfoundland explains why Hatton and Harvey failed to mention it in their discussion of cod by-products. The oil extracted from cod livers was too valuable, and too important, to be lumped with "waste" in any sense.

Yet even the most useful fish can always become *more* useful. As Marx notes in the *Grundrisse*, this is a constant drive under capitalist social relations. "The exploration of the earth in all directions, to discover new things of use as well as new useful qualities of the old; . . . the development, hence, of the natural sciences to their highest point; likewise the discovery, creation and satisfaction of new needs arising from society itself . . . is likewise a condition of production founded on capital."[6] Colonial exploration, scientific research, and the creation of new wants, needs, and desires — in addition to exploitation in production — are basic tendencies under capitalism. This chapter examines these dynamics in Newfoundland's cod liver oil industry by tracing the changing markers of quality and their effects on this important by-product industry.

I.

Cod liver oil had two primary historical uses. First, crude cod oil had a number of early commercial and industrial applications. It was used in leather production, soap-making, and industrial lubrication, as well as being used, along with seal and whale oils, as fuel for lamps and early streetlights.[7] Second, cod liver oil was widely recognized as having medicinal properties. Although the reasons for cod liver oil's curative properties were unknown, "it has proved its merits by results."[8] For example, Eber's

Papyrus, an Egyptian medical treatise written sometime between 1600 and 1500 BCE, cites the use of animal livers to cure night-blindness.[9] Hippocrates and Pliny mention the use of fish oils in medicine, both applied externally and ingested.[10]

For centuries, northern peoples and fishing families employed fish liver oils as a medicine, long before it was recognized by the medical profession. "In each country," wrote professor of pediatrics R.A. Guy, "the experience was the same: Cod liver oil was used by the fishing people and peasantry; then accidentally observed by some physician, tried by him, and so made known generally to the profession."[11] Cod liver oil was entered into the British Pharmacopeia in 1771, and was used to treat "chronic rheumatism" at the Manchester Infirmary by 1789. The use of cod liver oil by the medical profession spread across Europe throughout the eighteenth and nineteenth centuries, recognized in Holland and Germany by 1822, and in France by 1836.[12]

The earliest method of producing oil from cod livers was known as the "rotting process," whereby livers were collected in a receptacle and left to rot in the heat.[13] As putrefaction set in, the walls of the livers' hepatic cells burst, yielding oil, which rose to the top and could be drawn off. In this method, the fat-splitting enzymes (lipases) were not destroyed, which gave rise to foul odours and tastes, and degraded material (referred to as *blubber*) contaminated and darkened the oil. The lighter fractions were used medicinally, whereas the darker fractions were used for technical purposes.[14] As one can easily imagine, the resulting product was "an evil smelling rancid brown oil that was a torture, and can be called nothing else than an abomination."[15] The experience of taking cod liver oil, especially for children, was considered almost traumatic.[16]

Not only was the oil disagreeable to the palate, it was also intensely irritating to the stomach. After digestion, it became "unspeakably abominable."[17] At the time, its experiential qualities were secondary to its medicinal effects. Norwegian cod liver oil producer F.P. Møller described the experience of ingesting "rotted" oil in 1895. After the oil reaches the stomach, he stated, it "sets up eructation and brings the taste up to the mouth, where it asserts its unwelcome favours, not only once, but again and again, till the unhappy patient may be completely upset and firmly convinced that if it is to be at the expense of taking cod-liver oil, life is not worth living."[18] Nevertheless, Møller noted:

> many people did take it, and the only reasonably explanation is that the oil must have given strikingly favourable results; otherwise, medicinal men would not have been justified in prescribing it, nor could their patients have been induced to use it.[19]

Cod liver oil was an important and effective, but often detested, medicine.

Three technical developments between 1848 and 1903 radically altered the question of quality and palatability in the cod liver oil industry. The introduction of the indirect steam process in 1848, the removal of stearine by freezing in 1885, and the introduction of the direct steam process in 1903 were all aimed at improving the experiential qualities, and thus value, of cod liver oil. Although often attributed to Møller in 1853, the first use of the indirect steam process can be traced to Newfoundland in 1848 by English chemist Charles Fox.[20] Fox's method — a "long and tedious process"[21] — involved using two heavy tin pans: the smaller one filled with about 80 gallons of cod livers and placed inside the larger one, with a space of two to three inches to be filled with water. The water was kept boiling, and the livers were stirred constantly for roughly four hours, with the oil dipped off as it rose to the surface. Fox's second important innovation was insisting on only using "sweet fresh cream-coloured livers."[22] Any lean or diseased livers were discarded, and remaining livers were separated from any offal or gall bladders and cleaned thoroughly.[23]

Fox's method required larger fixed capital investments, but was also more lucrative and efficient, yielding a larger quantity of first-grade cod liver oil. Fox's success led to the proliferation of indirect steam method cod liver oil factories across Newfoundland and an increased export of refined cod liver oil.[24] With the indirect steam process, Fox produced a "bright yellow" oil that was more agreeable in taste and odour than the darker oils.[25] The medical profession and consumers, however, did not immediately take up this new product. Møller noted that steam-refined oil was so different from common cod oil "that there was no small difficulty, at first, in getting people to believe that it was cod liver oil at all."[26] Despite the initial prejudice in favour of the older, darker oils, steam-refined cod liver oil eventually won the market, with its lighter colour and more agreeable taste and smell.

Once the paler oils were accepted as superior, lightness in colour and transparency became important quality markers in the medicinal cod liver oil industry. This led to the second innovation: the removal of stearine by the freezing method.[27] First developed in Norway in 1885, the production of "non-freezing" or "frost-proof" cod liver oil was introduced to Newfoundland in 1888 by Superintendent of Fisheries Adolph Nielsen.[28] By the 1880s, consumers demanded perfectly clear steam-refined cod liver oil, but the product tended to congeal and turn cloudy at low temperatures, which was viewed as unappealing.[29] Turbidity in steam-refined cod liver oil was caused by the presence of solid fats, referred to "technically, but erroneously" as "stearine."[30] These fats were liquid at higher temperatures, but solidified at lower temperatures.[31] Stearine not only "made the oil look very unattractive to patients," it also "turned the oil rancid very quickly, which made it almost worthless as a medicine for a delicate stomach."[32]

The Norwegians developed a technique to remove stearine by freezing, filtering, and pressing refined cod liver oil.[33] Cod liver oil was placed in the cold storage room in cooling tanks until congealed, and then strained through fine calico bags. Under this "gentle natural pressure," the oil would drip through the bags and the so-called stearine could be separated out.[34] This process was expensive and time-consuming, but it produced an oil that was "beautifully bright and clear"[35] and "sparkling,"[36] and that remained liquid and transparent at all temperatures.

The third technical innovation was the introduction of the direct steam refining method. It was first introduced in Newfoundland at John Snow's cod liver oil factory in Quidi Vidi in 1903, following a visit by

Charles Fowler of the American firm Messrs. Scott & Browne.[37] In this method, livers were placed in an open boiling pan with a conical bottom, varying in size from 60 to over 100 gallons. The pan was connected to a boiler that produced steam between 75 and 80 lbs. of pressure, which churned up the livers and yielded a high-quality oil after only 30 to 40 minutes. The contents were left to settle, and the oil was dipped out and strained to remove all sediment. The residue was then pressed to extract more oil, which could be sold as lower-grade cod oil.[38] The direct steam method not only produced a superior oil, but "made for economy in labour" by eliminating the need for a worker to stir the blubber and shortening the extraction process from over four hours to only 30–40 minutes.[39]

These three technical innovations — the indirect steam process, the removal of stearine, and the direct steam process — radically reworked the question of quality in the cod liver oil industry. Buyers and consumers emphasized palatability, appearance, and uniformity, demanding "water white, sweet, nutty flavoured Cod Liver Oil."[40] Without a quantitative method of determining medicinal potency, the quality of cod liver oil was determined by more phenomenological criteria: colour, taste and smell.[41] It was no longer an abomination, a tonic that made one question whether the cure was worse than the disease. The new emphasis on quality was summed up in one 1880s advertising tagline: "Palatable as milk."[42] However these technical innovations offered the possibility of producing high-quality cod liver oil, Newfoundland refiners had to confront a more intractable problem: the biological and social drivers of low quality emerging from the spatial organization of saltfish production.

II.

Like the production of saltfish, the production of medicinal cod liver oil was beset by the multi-dimensional problem of fluctuation. The quantity and quality of cod liver oil production were subject to profound seasonal and annual variation, frustrating desires for uniformity. On top of the aggregate quantity of livers, the *quality* of the liver played an important role in determining the amount of oil produced. Lean livers yielded much less oil than healthy, well-fed livers. The average production ratio was three gallons of livers to one gallon of cod liver oil, but could rise as high as ten to one with lean livers.[43] In the early part of the season (June to July), cod migrated inshore with their livers in poor condition after spawning. The quality of their livers, however, improved over the course of the season as they feasted on caplin and squid, thus yielding more oil in August and September.[44] "Even the best oil," concluded biochemist C.E. Bills, "is subject to considerable variation in composition, the result of seasonal, sexual, nutritional, or other differences in the fish or mode of rendering."[45]

In addition to biological flux, the spatial division of labour and the methods of production shaped the quantity and quality of cod liver oil. Newfoundland's population was spread diffusely across the island's many bays and coves. This afforded certain advantages. As the majority of fishing was carried on within one or two miles of the shore using traps, cod were taken ashore in a very fresh condition, and the livers could be collected and refined within a few hours of harvesting.[46] Moreover, as the catch was almost exclusively cod, the "adulteration" of the cod liver oil with fish livers of different species was a non-issue, in contrast to certain regions of Norway.[47] Norwegian cod liver oil producers' "ideas as to what constitutes cod liver," noted nineteenth-century manufacturer Peter Møller, "are not unlike the rule laid down by the railway porter regarding dogs: 'Cats is dogs, and rabbits is dogs, and a parrot is a dog.'"[48]

But the spatial division of labour also presented certain obstacles. With most of the island's capital tied up in the credit system, the investment in fixed capital required to produce non-freezing medicinal oil (boilers, pans, tin-lined barrels, cold storage room, etc.) was comparatively rare. Moreover, with inadequate transportation facilities, factories could only collect cod livers from nearby communities, precluding economies of scale. As one British pharmaceutical company noted succinctly, "The conditions in Newfoundland, so far as we know, do not make large production possible."[49] With production spread across a number of small-scale, decentralized facilities, and with considerable biological variation between seasons and years, uniformity was difficult to ensure. These problems were further exacerbated by the "violent fluctuations in price,"[50] due to competition from Norway, and the cod liver oil's more limited demand in comparison to other fishery products, being used primarily in Great Britain and the United States.

Although the introduction of the freezing process and the direct steam method increased the yield and quality of Newfoundland medicinal cod liver oil, it remained a distant second to Norwegian cod liver oil over the first decade of the twentieth century. Norway's cod liver oil exhibited greater uniformity and attractiveness, which over time led consumers to favour the Norwegian product for a more intangible reason: its reputation. Newfoundland exporters often complained of the "prejudice" against their cod liver oil, "strong enough to cause them [English importers] to pay a much higher price for it [Norwegian oil] than is demanded for Oil of Newfoundland manufacture."[51]

Deemed "one of our great resources that must be developed to a larger extent in the near future," the Newfoundland government sought to establish the country's position on the world market by increasing the quality, quantity, and uniformity of the island's cod liver oil. The DMF noted that Norway's production of medicinal cod liver oil exceeded Newfoundland's *combined* output of medicinal and common cod liver oil, despite exporting less saltfish than Newfoundland.[52] Fishers and merchants, thus, did not utilize all the livers obtainable, nor did they refine the livers as efficiently as possible.[53] "If scientifically cared for," the department promised, "the quality of our oil will surpass anything that Norway can produce."[54] In 1910, they hired an expert to inspect and instruct the island's refiners.[55]

The following year, the DMF, with the help of the Board of Trade, secured the services of expert Norwegian manufacturer M.B. Simonsen to improve the production of cod liver oil in Newfoundland.[56] Arriving in St. John's on 13 June 1911, Simonsen departed for his first inspection trip on 10 July 1911, visiting over 20 communities in Trinity and Conception bays and the on Avalon Peninsula.[57] On his tour, he handed out rules for the proper method of refining cod liver oil, inspected the cleanliness and condition of the factories and the cod liver oil produced, offered advice on how to improve the factory's output, and supervised and assisted a number of boils.[58]

In his report to A.W. Piccott, the Minister of Marine and Fisheries, Simonsen stressed the need for regular inspection, encouraged the spread of the direct steam method, and recommended the use of tin-lined barrels for the transportation of cod liver oil instead of the "abnoxious [*sic*] puncheons."[59] Simonsen, strongly supported by the Board of Trade, also stressed the need for the licensing of cod liver oil factories in order to regulate and improve the industry by enabling punitive measures against careless refiners, and the erection of a model factory in St. John's for the "practical demonstration" of best practices in cod liver oil production that would resolve the problem faced by the country's diffuse nature of settlement.[60] Despite recurrent calls for licensing, Prime Minister E.P. Morris — mirroring his reluctance to enact standardization legislation described in the previous chapter — remained skeptical. He favoured "moral suasion" to official legislation.[61]

The outbreak of World War I changed the Prime Minister's perspective. The necessity of inspection and standardization in the cod liver oil industry could no longer be ignored. "Probably at no other time," wrote Fisheries Minister Piccott in 1915, "has there been a better outlook for the oil products of the Newfoundland fisheries."[62] With a large portion of Norway's production sold to Germany for military purposes, as well as increased global demand of cod oil for military and munitions requirements, demand and prices paid for Newfoundland cod oil advanced steadily.[63] Moreover, the war highlighted and exacerbated problems of malnutrition in Europe. Medical examinations of volunteers and conscripts, and fitness tests for women entering the industrial workforce, revealed staggering rates of malnutrition.[64] These problems only worsened with wartime disruptions in food provisioning systems.

During the war, Newfoundland began exporting cod liver oil, both refined and common, to new markets, expanding beyond the US, UK, Canada, and the British West Indies to India, Australia, New Zealand, China, Southern Europe, and Latin America.[65] To retain these new markets, Newfoundland producers had to maintain a high standard of production, "equel [*sic*] in colour, taste, and smell" to Norwegian oils.[66] The high prices paid for oil, however, encouraged inexperienced and even dishonest producers to enter the trade, seeking to maximize sales regardless of quality.[67] To standardize output and bring all factories under control via inspection, "it is considered necessary that all factories be licensed."[68]

On 4 May 1916, in time for the start of the next cod liver oil season, the Newfoundland government passed "An Act Respecting the Refining of Cod Liver Oil," an outcome that proved difficult for saltfish production.[69] This bill required all cod liver oil factories, after 1 June 1916, to obtain a licence from the DMF, to follow the rules and regulations for the proper manufacture of cod liver oil, and to have all cod liver oil inspected and branded before export, with strict pecuniary penalties for any infractions.[70] Simonsen, who had recently returned from Norway after a period of convalescence, and E.J. Coyell were appointed as inspectors.[71]

This rigid system of inspection stressed the need for cleanliness, the use of modern equipment, and the boiling of only the finest livers. It also required each manufacturer to brand every barrel exported, in order to make each product traceable and each producer liable for any quality deficiencies. "In this way," noted N.L. Macpherson, a biochemist working for the FRC, "producers are kept up to the scratch, so that the quality of their products may be of the best."[72] The 1916 legislation had almost immediate effects, raising the country's output of refined cod liver oil.[73] The industry received a further boost in 1917–18 when Wyndham Dunstan, a professor of chemistry and director of the Imperial Institute in London, published a report stating that Newfoundland and Norwegian cod liver oils were of equal "therapeutical value."[74] Despite the new licensing regulations and improved product quality, Newfoundland medicinal cod liver oil faced a steep cut in export volume and value after the end of the Great War.

Shortly thereafter, however, the industry was transformed and revitalized by the discovery of a new facet of quality: vitamin potency. As Newfoundland cod liver oil producer W.A. Munn pointed out in 1917, cod liver oil's medicinal value had long been known by fishing peoples and physicians, but "the most enlightened chemist has never been able to state definitely what constituted the remedy for the diseased body, that is found in the oil rendered from the livers of cod fish."[75] However, over the first two decades of the twentieth century, scientific research into the question of nutrition and optimal human diet had isolated the presence of a new substance — referred to as "accessory food factors" or "vitamines" — which were essential to human growth and health.

The discovery of vitamins transformed the industry, as the traditional markers of quality — colour, taste, and odour — were no longer adequate to define "first-grade" medicinal cod liver oil. This upset the traditional calculations of value and price and represented a profound shift in the measurement of quality. As Sir Walter Fletcher, secretary of Britain's Medical Research Council, noted, "From a medical point of view it has been proved that the market price of cod liver oil has no relation to its value for the only purposes for which it is bought."[76] The science of vitamins made more refined and precise metrical technologies possible, and opened new realms for the extraction of oil and value from cod livers.

III.

Although the relationship between diet and a number of diseases, such as scurvy, rickets, and beriberi, had been established by the nineteenth century, the precise biochemical nature of the relationship remained a mystery. For example, the anti-scorbutic properties of citrus juices had been discussed in German physician Johann Georg Heinrich Kramer's *Medicina Castrensis* (1720) and Scottish physician James Lind's 1753 treatise on scurvy.[77] The British Navy first issued compulsory rations of lemon juice in 1804.[78] The first definitive case histories of rickets cured by cod liver oil date to 1824 and the work of German physician D. Schütte.[79] In 1885, Japanese naval physician Kanehiro Takaki radically reduced the prevalence of beriberi in Japanese sailors by adding barley, meat, and fruit to their diet of polished white rice.[80] But precisely *why* these interventions worked remained puzzling.

By the late 1800s, with the work of German physiologist Gustav von Bunge and his students at the University of Dorpat, Nicolai Lunin and Carl Socin, evidence began pointing to an additional substance (or substances) required for optimal human health beyond what were believed to be the four essential human requirements in food: proteins, fats, carbohydrates, and mineral salts.[81] The absence of any or all of these substances, in turn, was correlated to a range of nutritional deficiencies, such as avian polyneuritis by Dutch army surgeon Christian Eijkman and his student Gerrit Grijns, beri-beri by Dutch physician M.D.J. Hulshoff-Pol, and scurvy by Norwegian bacteriologist Axel Holst and pediatrician Theodor Frölich.[82] This realization, in part, was delayed by the predominant germ theory of disease, which attributed disease to positive agents rather than nutritional deficiencies.[83] By 1906, the English biochemist and first chair of Biochemistry at Cambridge, Frederick Gowland Hopkins, reported, "no animal can live upon a mixture of pure protein, fat, and carbohydrate and even when the necessary inorganic material is carefully supplied, the animal still cannot flourish."[84]

In 1912, Polish biochemist Casimir Funk, who was working at the Lister Institute of Preventive Medicine, made the brilliant, if slightly premature, conceptual move of linking disease and nutrition research into a single paradigm by articulating the "deficiency theory of diseases." He posited that scurvy, beriberi, rickets, and pellagra were not the result of a positive germ agent, but the result of "vitamine" deficiencies.[85] Serving as a "catchword which meant something even to the uninitiated,"[86] Funk coined the word "vitamine" to "indicate that the substance in question was an amine essential to life or bearing special relationship to vitality."[87] However, as many detractors pointed out, "vitamines" were important, but by no means the only substance necessary for a healthy life and vitality, and they were certainly not all amines. F.G. Hopkins, who won the Nobel Prize in 1929 for his pioneering work in vitamin research, preferred the term "accessory food factor."[88] American biochemists E.V. McCollum and Marguerite Davis proposed the substances be known by alphabetical designations, qualified by their solubilities: thus "fat-soluble A" or "water-soluble B."[89] In 1920, English biochemist J.C. Drummond proposed a compromise between the two systems, retaining the alphabetical designation, and dropping the "e" — as this eliminated the amine confusion and corresponded to the standard nomenclature of the Chemical Society, "which permits a neutral substance of undefined composition to bear a name ending in '-in'."[90] Drummond's system, whereby the substances were called vitamin A, B, C, etc. (obviously) caught on.

Following the publication of Funk's important paper, research into the nature and role of vitamins was taken up by American biochemists such as Thomas Osborne, Lafayette Mendel, E.V. McCollum, and Marguerite Davis, who conducted feeding experiments on rats.[91] They demonstrated that young rats could not survive when fed artificial diets of pure protein, fat, carbohydrates, and mineral salts, but could survive with the addition of milk, butter, eggs, or cod liver oil.[92] In 1919, English physiologist Edward Mellanby identified a second vitamin in cod liver oil, responsible for the lipid's anti-rachitic properties, by demonstrating that oxidized cod liver oil could not cure xerophthalmia, a vitamin A deficiency, but remained an effective cure for experimental rickets in puppies.[93] The discovery of vitamins A and D finally offered a scientific explanation for the origins of cod liver oil's well-known medicinal value.

Cod liver oil producers and boosters in Newfoundland and abroad immediately latched onto the idea, hoping to capitalize on the recent scientific discovery. "Whatever 'Vitamin' may be and scientists will tell all about it in a few periods, there is nothing like knowing that the colony has it in bulk, and is prepared to fill any orders in quantity and quality."[94] Some commentators even likened the discovery of vitamins in cod liver oil to a gold rush: "Here in Newfoundland we have something of far greater value than gold, diamonds, or pearls which scientists from the greatest universities of Great Britain and America have described as many times more valuable for building up healthy children than it is possible to obtain from any similar product in any other part of the world."[95] "Gold, diamonds, and pearls," the article continued, "have their uses but all fade into insignificance in comparison to healthy children."[96]

With the development of quantitative assays of vitamin potency, the industry was further encouraged because it was scientifically proven, through accurate measurement, that cod liver oil was an extraordinarily potent source of vitamins.[97] S.S. Zilva and Masataru Miura, biochemists from the Lister Institute, for example, noted that one sample of unrefined cod liver oil was 250 times more potent than an average sample of butter.[98] More importantly, Zilva and Miura pointed out that producers, seeking to minimize the oil's taste, colour, and smell, often employed means that "conduce to the partial or even total destruction of the accessory factor" through exposure to oxygen and ozone.[99]

Building on these early studies, the British Medical Research Council (MRC) funded Zilva and J.C. Drummond, a professor of physiological chemistry at the University of London, to investigate the impact of modern cod liver oil production methods on the final product's vitamin potency.[100] They visited Norway in the early summer of 1921, travelling to the main cod-fishing regions of Lofoten and Finnmarken accompanied by legendary fisheries scientist Johan Hjort.[101] After examining the different methods of cod liver oil manufacture, they determined that modern processing methods had little effect on vitamin potency, barring the "bleaching" of dark oils by exposure to light or air.[102] They concluded that variations in vitamin potency were rooted in biological, seasonal, and dietary fluctuations in the fish, not production methods. In 1922, they continued these investigations in Newfoundland, reaching the same conclusions.[103]

Newfoundland cod liver oil producers felt that Drummond, Zilva, and Graham's work on the causes of fluctuations in vitamin potency would lead to "splendid possibilities" for the country's cod liver oil trade.[104] The correlation of vitamin potency with the biological condition of fish, not production methods, opened the possibility of *regional* advantages in the vitamin potency of cod liver oil, rooted in the organization of production.[105] Norway's winter fishery coincided with the cod's spawning season in March and April, whereas Newfoundland's fishery occurred exclusively post-spawning. This offered Newfoundland a competitive advantage, as cod livers "yield oils with a diminished vitamin content during the spawning period."[106] "Dr. Drummond explained to me," wrote local producer W.A. Munn, "that if his theory worked out, that it would be a great thing for Newfoundland."[107]

The science of vitamins finally provided a lever through which Newfoundland cod liver oil could differentiate itself from Norwegian cod liver oil and *prove* its superiority, scientifically and conclusively. It was hoped that this knowledge, alongside rigid government inspection and technical improvements in production, could finally overcome the prejudice in England for the Norwegian product.[108] "Having vivid memories of his childhood," reported the *Evening Telegram*, summarizing Acting High Commissioner Victor Gordon's response to a lecture by Zilva at a meeting of the Society of Chemical Industry in London, "he never thought he could become enthusiastic about cod-liver oil, but Dr. Zilva and his colleague, Dr. J.C. Drummond, had so stimulated interest in this commodity that one could not help being enthused."[109]

This enthusiasm extended to American firms, which began demonstrating significant interest in the possibility of investing capital in Newfoundland — a development that proved so difficult in other industries, such as manufacturing, mining, forestry, and the development of cold storage.[110] In 1923, E.M. Johnson and Dr. J.J. Quilligan, of Mead Johnson & Co., visited Newfoundland to investigate the vitamin potency of Newfoundland cod liver oil and its potential as an ingredient for the company's line of baby food.[111] Impressed by their initial findings, Johnson and Quilligan returned the following year, with Dr. C.E. Bills of Johns Hopkins (and a former student of E.V. McCollum) and Mildred Weinstock to conduct further experiments.[112] They concluded that Newfoundland cod liver oil showed the "greatest anti-rachitic activity on experimental rats," which they hypothesized was due to the fact that Newfoundland's fishing season occurred post-spawning, and because the spatial division of labour ensured the processing of cod livers in the freshest state.[113] In addition, the rigid government inspection and instruction ensured the production of high-quality and standardized medicinal cod liver oil.[114] This research convinced Mead Johnson & Co.

to focus on purchasing Newfoundland cod liver oil, and to pay higher prices for it than for the Norwegian product.[115]

Following Mead Johnson & Co., a number of American and Canadian firms began investigating Newfoundland cod liver oil: Dr. Emmet, from the research department of Parke-Davis Co., visited in 1924; the principal members of the firm Ayers, McKenna, and Harrison Ltd. visited in 1925; and J.C. Lewis, of Messrs. E.R. Squibb and Sons of New York, and James Patch, of E.L. Patch Co., visited in 1926.[116] The public and private research on cod liver oil and vitamin potencies led to the industry's strongest period of growth, tripling between 1924 and 1926. The DMF noted that the construction of factories "has been general in all directions," demonstrating that refiners are confident in "investing money in buildings and property with the intention of continuing permanent work."[117]

The industry's "marked progress" even fostered diversification into other by-product industries, such as the commercial production of fishmeal for livestock feeding at Munn's Harbour Grace factory in 1926, fish guano or fertilizer, and lower-grade poultry oil in 1929.[118] Fishmeal exports grew rapidly, from 337,500 lbs. in 1926–27 to 764,917 lbs. in 1928–29.[119] These new products increased the profitability of cod liver oil production by finding remunerative uses for previously wasted products, such as the liver residue left after oil extraction. "Refiners have taken little notice of this residue in the past years," the DMF noted, "but they are now giving it very careful attention."[120]

The discovery of vitamins and the importance of cod liver oil as a source of vitamins created a new lever of accumulation in Newfoundland's oil refining industry. Variations in vitamin potency, rendered visible by new scientific techniques of measurement, generated new opportunities for the extraction of value. The science of vitamins reformulated the question of quality, spurred foreign investment, and led to diversification in production.

It also created the conditions that eventually undermined cod liver oil's place as a source of vitamins.

IV.

With the initial research into regional variation in vitamin potencies suggesting the superiority of Newfoundland cod liver oil, attention was turned "to enlarg[ing] the trade for Newfoundland cod liver oil in the British Isles by a vigorous advertising campaign there."[121] Newfoundland refiners remained fixated on overcoming the consumer preference for Norwegian cod liver oil in Great Britain, despite the growing importance of the North American market. As George J. Saunders, of Doremus & Co. advertising company, wrote in a letter soliciting a contract with the Newfoundland Board of Trade, this involved changing women's attitudes:

> Today, however, when a woman goes into a drug store she finds the bottle on the counter labelled "Genuine Norwegian": as a result she has been adduced to think that the Norwegian Cod Liver Oil is the only kind she should buy. At a very little expense to us we could easily change this attitude by advertising the qualities of Newfoundland Cod Liver Oil . . . .[122]

The question of advertising became even more important as of 1 January 1926, when the Norwegian government instituted a small export tax on cod liver oil to finance the advertising of Norwegian oils in foreign markets.[123]

In 1925, P.T. McGrath, Newfoundland's representative on the recently formed Imperial Economic Committee (IEC), suggested applying to the new institution for funds to advertise Newfoundland cod liver oil.[124] Formed in 1925, the IEC sought to increase the British consumption of Empire products, creating the Empire Marketing Board (EMB), its advertising and scientific research wing, in 1926. In September 1927, this goal was encouraged following a visit by Oxford geographer Halford Mackinder, chairman of the IEC, who promised to advertise Newfoundland cod liver oil widely in Great Britain if local refiners could prove that the country could produce sufficient supply to meet imperial demand, and if they could maintain high-quality standards through a government brand.[125] Mackinder's promise, however, remained unfulfilled, because the IEC claimed that cod liver oil was a medicine, not food, and therefore did not fall under the institution's remit.[126]

Despite the refusal to advertise the merits of Newfoundland cod liver oil, the IEC recognized the importance of cod liver oil, noting that it was the richest *and cheapest* source of vitamins available. In their *Report on Fish*, they stated, "If efforts are made to increase the quantity of these vitamins in the ordinary diet or in case of illness, it seems probably therefore that the source from which they will be sought will be cod liver oil."[127] With this in mind, the IEC recommended the scientific investigation, through the EMB, of "the nature of the variations in the vitamin content of cod liver oils produced from fish from various sources and a study of the underlying causes of such variations."[128]

In early 1928, Dr. Drummond and Dr. T.P. Hilditch, the Campbell Brown chair of Industrial Chemistry at Liverpool University, began a "comprehensive study of the composition of cod liver oil, its manufacture and its medicinal value" on behalf of the EMB.[129] The stated goal of their study was to compare the vitamin potencies of cod liver oils from different Empire and foreign sources. They requested samples of cod liver oils from British producers in the Moray Firth and the North Sea, and foreign producers in Norway, Iceland, and Newfoundland, from the summer, autumn, and winter catches of 1928 and 1929. In addition to these samples, they conducted two research voyages on the F.R.S. *Explorer* in July–September 1928 and spent three weeks in Newfoundland in July and August 1929, visiting factories and taking samples of different oils.[130]

Drummond and Hilditch sought to accurately measure and compare the vitamin A and vitamin D potencies of the different oils. This posed a technical challenge. The most common method, biological assay, presented "almost insuperable practical difficulties."[131] First, it was only "roughly quantitative," due to "the variations in response shown by individual animals."[132] Second, it was very time-consuming, and thus impractical for an experiment to analyze hundreds of different samples. After developing a novel colorimetric assay technique for vitamin A potency, they concluded that there were wide variations in potency in the oils from different regions, and ranked Newfoundland oils as the most potent in both vitamin A and vitamin D.[133] They also noticed a "definite parallel" between the depth of yellow colouration and vitamin A potency, challenging the consumer preference for pale oils.[134]

In their conclusion, they summed up their findings concisely: "Of the oils from the important cod areas studied, those from Newfoundland were found to be of richest vitamin potency."[135]

Such a pronouncement, naturally, was received with much excitement by manufacturers and boosters in Newfoundland, even with the steep cut in exports in 1930 following the onset of the Great Depression, down from a record high of 364,239 gallons in 1929 to 163,864 gallons in 1930.[136] Local producers, nevertheless, were optimistic for the future, and pleased with the results of the Drummond-Hilditch report: "It is very favourable to us and our oil is getting a great deal of publicity."[137] With the seemingly conclusive scientific proof of Newfoundland's superiority, local producers returned to the problem of marketing Newfoundland cod liver oil in Great Britain.[138] Newfoundland producers wished to overcome the pharmaceutical and consumer preference for Norwegian oil. This was in part related to the traditional markers of quality of taste, smell, and colour, as consumers still preferred the paler Norwegian oil to the "straw coloured" Newfoundland oil, despite the correlation between colouration and vitamin potency.[139] Ultimately, however, in the context of the Great Depression, "the entire problem . . . resolves itself into a question of price."[140]

In contrast to Norway, the dispersed nature of settlement and saltfish production in Newfoundland, and the requirement for perfectly fresh livers, precluded economies of scale in cod liver oil production, raising production costs and the price of Newfoundland cod liver oil.[141] Barring the large-scale transformation of Newfoundland's social geography, Newfoundland producers employed different tactics to resolve the price issue. First, the Newfoundland government began pressuring the British government for tariffs against non-Empire sources of cod liver oil.[142] Second, they sought to advertise the superior vitamin potency of Newfoundland cod liver oil to reframe the consumer's calculation between price and value. "Our work in England must be devoted to make consumers realize that they are not buying cod liver oil *but buying vitamins*."[143] For example, Munn argued that if consumers could be "made to believe" that one drop of Newfoundland cod liver oil has the same vitamin potency, and thus medicinal benefit, as two drops of Norwegian — which he believed the Drummond-Hilditch report demonstrated with scientific authority — then "it should be easy to sell Newfoundland cod liver oil at 5/- against Norwegian at 3/7d."[144]

"With such strong endorsement regarding the merits of Newfoundland cod liver oil," Munn complained, "we expected that our troubles would vanish, and our efforts to get some good advertising would soon be accomplished."[145] These expectations, however, continued to be frustrated by the IEC's refusal to define cod liver oil as a food. This deeply frustrated Munn: "I have always believed in British Fair Play, but whoever instigated that recommendation is an insidious expert, who was trying to block us again."[146] Munn could not understand the recurrent rejection to fund the advertising of Newfoundland cod liver oil, noting:

> You can see large posters tacked up in our Board of Trade Rooms sent us by the British Marketing Board, to advertise Asbestos from Cyprus and Egyptian Cotton, also Sisal from East Africa for making rope. Who can call these articles Food Products? But these outside places are getting every preference for advertising their products over the most LOYAL COUNTRY in the whole BRITISH EMPIRE.[147]

"These men," concluded Munn, "are choc full of prejudice to the throat against our Newfoundland oil."[148]

Despite the failure to secure IEC funds for advertising in the UK, the governments of Great Britain, Canada, Newfoundland, South Africa,

India, Southern Rhodesia, New Zealand, and Australia did succeed in negotiating a 1/4d. tariff on imports on non-Empire cod liver oil to Great Britain at the 1932 Imperial Economic Conference in Ottawa, Canada.[149] With this tariff, wrote Newfoundland's senior diplomat in the UK, "we may be able to beat the Norwegian cod liver oil in price."[150] While successfully reducing Norwegian exports of cod liver oil to Great Britain, this tariff had an unexpected consequence: rather than shifting consumption to Newfoundland oil, it increased home consumption and intra-Empire exports of *British-made* cod liver oil.[151]

With the formation of the Fishery Research Commission (FRC) in April 1931, Newfoundland had its own dedicated scientific authority to investigate and improve the production of cod liver oil. Harold Thompson, head of the FRC, envisioned the Bay Bulls laboratory assisting the cod liver oil industry in three ways: first, to ascertain the highest feasible standard of oil that can be produced; second, to assist in the standardization of the oil and to offer authoritative analyses of vitamin potencies; and, third, to experiment on other preparations (such as emulsions) as "accessories" to the bottled cod liver oil trade.[152] Through this work, Thompson sought to make the industry more profitable and to expand the market for Newfoundland cod liver oil in Great Britain.[153] He assigned Norman L. Macpherson, the FRC's biochemist, to study the cod liver oil industry.[154]

In 1933, Macpherson published an important study in the prestigious journal *Nature* that examined the cause of fluctuations in vitamin A potency in cod liver oil.[155] Drummond and Hilditch had hypothesized the vitamin A potency was a function of the food supply and oil content of the liver.[156] Macpherson upset this theory by conclusively demonstrating that vitamin A potency "depends upon the growth rates and ages of the cod at those sources."[157] He also established a definite relationship among vitamin A potency, the age of the cod, and the colour of the liver oil, yet again proving the superiority of Newfoundland's tawnier oil. This discovery, however, undermined Newfoundland's claims to regional superiority in vitamin potency: "It would be a very dangerous thing to boost Newfoundland oil as the finest oil in the world," he stated in his testimony to the Kent Commission, "because it may be that the older stocks would fall away in a few years and the young stocks would give a low oil. . . . Next year we may have to eat our words owing to the average age of the catch being less."[158]

Macpherson's hunch proved correct. Continued research into the vitamin potencies of different fish liver oils had isolated new, highly potent sources of vitamin D, such as halibut, swordfish, menhaden, and tuna liver oils.[159] "The fishermen of the world soon had a bonanza," wrote biochemist C.E. Bills. "Livers formerly regarded as offal were in such demand that in some species they sold for more than the rest of the fish."[160] Newfoundland, in contrast, complained H.G.R. Mews, the secretary-treasurer of Newfoundland's Board of Trade, "has merely rested on her laurels, with the result that today Norway has a more potent oil on the market, and the very few special customers that Newfoundland had are inclined to switch over to Norwegian oil."[161]

The discovery of more potent sources of vitamins in different species challenged another one of Newfoundland's structural advantages: the long-held belief that the exclusive use of cod livers was a marker of quality, producing "purer" cod liver oils.[162] "No other than cod fish livers," wrote Minister of Marine and Fisheries H.B.C. Lake to the British Embassy in Washington, "are allowed to be used for medicinal cod liver oil."[163] Newfoundland's former advantage became a barrier to expansion and ensured higher prices. "The principal reason that a larger output does not come from that country," argued cod liver oil producer W.A. Munn, "is because [of] its extensive coast line, its limited and scattered population."[164] As Macpherson noted, "some form of centralized production designed to eliminate overhead and to curtail transportation costs is essential."[165]

Although cod liver oil production remained the most economically viable liver oil industry, the discovery of more potent sources of vitamins allowed the possibility of mixing different fish liver oils to maximize and optimize the vitamin potencies of cod liver oil.[166] Potency superseded purity in the schema of quality, and producers competed to place the most potent source of vitamins on the market. The shift towards potency, moreover, opened the possibility of fortifying and optimizing cod liver oil through *artificial* sources of vitamins. This possibility emerged with the isolation of the chemical structure and the artificial synthesis of different vitamins in the 1930s.[167] Irradiated ergosterol, for example, was a more potent source of vitamin D than cod liver oil by several orders of magnitude.[168] Produced in a laboratory, irradiated ergosterol was a boon to the food-processing sector, making vitamin fortification commercially viable.

Artificial sources of vitamins were "the final triumph of chemistry," offering "emancipation from the fish that swim in the ocean and the vegetation that grows on the land."[169] By the mid-1930s, Newfoundland's competitive advantage in the vitamin potency of the country's cod liver oil had evaporated through the emergence of mixed oils to optimize vitamin potency and artificial sources of vitamins. Scientific research and technical sophistication initially enhanced, but eventually undermined, cod liver oil's role as a source of vitamins.

When the FRC's Bay Bulls laboratory burned down in April 1937, Newfoundland's cod liver oil industry faced an uncertain future. Rigid government inspection and supervision after 1916 had successfully raised the quality of cod liver oil exported, creating a more standardized and uniform commodity that satisfied the traditional markers of quality: taste, smell, and colour. Scientific research into human nutrition had isolated a new quality, vitamin potency, which offered the country an initial competitive advantage in the 1920s, due to the structural organization of production. However, this advantage faded over time, as the question of vitamin potency was better understood and as foreign competitors increased the vitamin potency of their products.

Two novel forms of measure — government inspection and the quantitative vitamin potency assays — fundamentally restructured the cod liver oil industry in Newfoundland. Rendering oil from cod livers emerged historically alongside the production of saltfish, and was always an important source of value for fishers and merchants. Penny-pinching opportunists were keen to make sure that Hatton and Harvey's panegyric to the cod was truer than ever: "The cod is the most useful of all fish. No part is valueless."[170] They sought to overcome biophysical fluctuations in cod liver oil quality, and created novel opportunities for firms to compete over the extraction of value from cod livers. Innovations in scientific knowledge, government regulation, and technology eventually offered the possibility to extract *more* value from cod livers and to develop *new* products from previously wasted materials, like poultry oil, fishmeal, and fertilizer. The discovery of new qualities, such as palatability, and the production of new needs, such as vitamin potency, opened new realms over which capitalists can compete to extract surplus value. As Marx argued in the *Grundrisse*, the discovery and creation of new qualities or use-values within already existing commodities through colonial exploration and the development of science are thus a "condition of production founded on capital."[171]

PART IV ∽ BREAKING COLLAR

So the best thing to do is to work with a will,
When it's all over and we're hauled on the hill;
And we're hauled on the hill, and put down in the cold,
And you're dead in your grave, but you're still in the hole.

FROM DORY TO DESK

When Hope Simpson sat down at his writing desk to write a letter to his son, Ian, in early March 1936, he was exasperated and he was exhausted.[1] "I have had a busy and difficult week," he exclaimed. The Italian market situation was deteriorating. Mussolini's fascist government was instituting a system of import controls in response to being sanctioned by the League of Nations after its invasion of Ethiopia. Diverted saltfish glutted the other markets, and the local merchants were left with large piles of saltfish deteriorating in their stores, "which they consider that the government should take over at a price remunerative to the merchants and of which it should dispose otherwhere than in the market – i.e. the sea!, which is of course absurd." Hope Simpson was frustrated with both the ruthlessly individualistic merchants, who had "no interest whatever in the general welfare," and with the demoralized fishers, whose average standard of life he described as deplorable.

A later letter to his second daughter, Greta, caught Hope Simpson in a more contemplative, appreciative mood. Perhaps reflecting his relationship with his daughter, perhaps reflecting the relief he felt knowing that he would soon be released from his stressful duties by a qualified replacement ("He has the same mentality and training as I have . . ."), Hope Simpson struck a different tone.

> It is 6.15 a.m. The foghorn is mooing at the Narrows, but it is clear on the water, and the mist is on the hilltops. Indeed, the sun is trying to come through. I am sitting in my office room in the hotel. You know that I have a little private office there, next to our bedroom. The window is on my left as I face the writing-desk, and the schooners that have come in for salt and for supplies for the fishery are sailing down the Narrows, one after another, such a pretty sight.[2]

But John's wistful musings did not last long. His mind quickly reverted to the main problem that occupied his time as Commissioner of Natural Resources: the organization of the saltfishery by the credit system. "Forgive my lecture," he apologized, after a perceptive synopsis of the credit system, "which is on a subject which forms my daily bread! I am thinking of the problem all the time and all the time devising some way or ways to get around or over it." His mind churned over the issues at hand. It was in this context that he developed and proposed his curious solution — the "knowledge of arithmetic and the application of a little common sense" — as the basis upon which to reorganize the production and marketing of saltfish in Newfoundland.

Although he thought his diagnosis was novel, it had deeper roots than he realized. This book has traced the roots and development of the knowledge of arithmetic in Newfoundland over 50 years, starting with the inception of the Fisheries Commission, under Norwegian fisheries expert Adolph Nielsen in April 1887, and ending with various policies and practices of the Commission of Government's Department of Natural Resources, under Hope Simpson in the late 1930s. And so to conclude and to finish disputes, this chapter refracts the book's main argument and reflects on its strengths and weaknesses through a close reading of a painting by English artist Rhoda Dawson. It then broadens the analysis to point towards how the separation between the knowledge of fishing and the knowledge of arithmetic might be overcome.

I.

Born in Chiswick, England, in 1897, the eldest daughter of artists Nelson and Edith Dawson, Rhoda Dawson was a perceptive observer of Newfoundland society. Inspired by her father's passion for the sea and sailing crafts, and driven by her girlhood dream to "paint the little coloured houses" she had read about in Grenfell's books, she joined the Grenfell Mission in 1930. In total, she spent six years in Labrador and northern Newfoundland, three working with the Mission's Industrial Department and three simply painting.[3] "Newfoundland is a country about which very little is known in England," she wrote in a draft of her unpublished memoir. "I shared the general ignorance when I first went out."[4] She quickly corrected that ignorance. Dawson was in awe of the people and place: "A Newfoundland fishing family in comfortable circumstances is quite remarkable — spotlessly clean, good cooks, house-proud, they spin & knit their own woolens, even the men's underwear. The floors are gay with bright rugs; the walls brightly painted or papered."[5] Her experience inspired her to study anthropology at the London School of Economics, with Bronislaw Malinowski, one of the discipline's founders. She began, but never finished, a thesis on life in Labrador.[6] Newfoundland studies is poorer for that loss.

After finishing her spell with the Grenfell Association, Dawson spent nine months in St. John's prior to returning to England.[7] During this brief period in the country's commercial and political capital, the same year that Hope Simpson wrote that letter to Ian, she painted a watercolour cartoon of Newfoundland society, which she described as "a wry comment from someone on the spot, enjoying a bit of doodling."[8] Despite her bashful description, it was far more radical. We can get a sense of the political tensions behind it from the response of a Memorial University College professor to whom she showed the painting at the time. She described him as "very anxious, in fact terrified, of anyone seeing it." She said that he "begged" her not to show it to anyone else.[9]

Rhoda Dawson's "doodle" depicting Newfoundland society, 1936. (Collection of Peter Neary and Hilary Bates Neary.)

Structured in a "Dante-esque fashion," Dawson's doodle depicts a rigidly hierarchical society, divided in six groups and arranged vertically.[10] At the top of the painting, the Governor and his wife float above the fray, projecting a sense of colonial authority over the country's different classes. Next come the mercantile and professional elite, gossiping and fighting among themselves, with one merchant carelessly tossing his papers about. Below them, the clergy, schoolmasters, and Memorial academics — "soaring only in the empyrean of abstract thought"[11] — watch over and lecture the plebeians below. The working class is split between the more successful fishers, lumbermen, and miners on top, and the struggling population, crushed under debt and sustained by the dole, below. Divided by a line of playing cards, the difference between successful and struggling working peoples is framed as a cruel game of chance — most likely Auction forty-fives, or its regional variant *growl* or *120s*, Newfoundland's "national card game."[12] Finally, at the bottom sitting at and standing by desks marked "H.M.G" (His Majesty's Government), are the Commissioners, the civil servants charged with governing Newfoundland's affairs: prodded by demons, drowning in neatly stacked papers, legs bound by ball and chain.

Rigidly striated and governed by chance, Dawson's painting documents a country riven by class and colonial differences. She made visible striations, planar fractures, and fault lines rooted in the tectonic displacements of European settlement in Newfoundland. But what made her "doodling" so brilliant, and so radical, is that she identified a nascent, emergent form of power and knowledge, *desk-bound reason*, an emergent form on the verge of turning Newfoundland society — the society that she found so fascinating and admirable, and that she visually depicted so perceptively — upside down.

Dawson was correct in highlighting the important role of chance in Newfoundland society by emphasizing playing cards in her cartoon. "A fisherman," notes political scientist S.J.R. Noel, "is of necessity a gambler and an optimist: he must have faith in tomorrow's catch, even if today his nets are empty."[13] Both Hope Simpson and his wife, Quita, agreed. As she notes, the credit system "has affected the morale of the people, as it is such an uncertain trade that the gambling instinct [has been] encouraged."[14] But, as her husband concluded, "it is the sport of the thing, I suppose, and the gamble, that appeal to them."[15]

Whether framed as chance, providence, or chaos, fishers and merchants, as argued in Chapter 2, confronted *the problem of fluctuation* when producing saltfish. Fish are migratory, and their populations can surge and collapse wildly between years. They respond to subtle environmental changes in the ocean that alter their behaviour and movement over the course of a single fishing season and between seasons. Finding and extracting fish was defined by uncertainty. The problem of fluctuation, however, was not resolved by removing fish from water. The process of making fish entailed both removing fish from water and water (and oil) from fish. Fishers, merchants, and brokers confronted fluctuating biophysical processes post-extraction, such as autolytic and bacterial decay, fungal infections, and the social biology of human consumption. The quality of saltfish, market conditions, and consumer preferences — like the biogeophysical characteristics of fish and the ocean — were profoundly dynamic. The problem of fluctuation, in sum, had both quantitative and qualitative dimensions that shaped all moments in the circulation of saltfish and capital.

Over the course of the nineteenth century, the credit system had emerged to confront and overcome the problem of fluctuation inherent in extracting and distributing fish across the globe, organized around the embodied, practical knowledge of fishing. It was an ingenious solution. It ensured shipments of large volumes of highly differentiated saltfish by spreading risk across space in Newfoundland to overcome regional catch failures, and by using credit to suture the seasonal and spatial disjuncture between production in Newfoundland and realization in the consuming markets. This had an effect on the metrical mindsets and social lives of fishers and merchants. As merchant, politician, and social critic James Murray reminded fishers, after the bank crash of 1894 they were "an average member of a System that dealt in averages."[16] And, as Rhoda Dawson wrote 40 years later, "The fact that a man may be tied to his merchant by an overwhelming debt, although disheartening, is ameliorated by the fact that *his time is his own & his work in his own hands.* . . . Lack of discipline is the constant complaint of industrial powers, who find all their men missing on a fine day, gone off to pick berries in the hills."[17]

This system was breaking down over the period of this study, due to structural shifts in the economic geography of the global saltfish industry. New consumer demands for quality, emerging competition from Norway, Iceland, and France, the development of steam transport, and the spread of talqual buying all led to a perceived crisis of accumulation in Newfoundland. Starting in April 1887, with the formation of the country's first Fisheries Commission, politicians, merchants, fishers, and imported experts in fisheries science and management sought to overcome these fluctuations through the development and application of the knowledge of arithmetic, in Hope Simpson's telling language. Parts II and III were tasked with detailed, granular examinations of these processes at work at different moments in the commodity chain. Part II investigated attempts to introduce novel fishing measures *pre*-extraction to improve and control the *quantity* of saltfish exported, through artificial propagation, reforming bait supply, and fisheries science. Part III examined the introduction of fishing measures *post*-extraction that sought to improve and control the *quality* of saltfish exported, through standardization, inspection, and innovation. Cod reproduction, predation, migration, maturation, decomposition, and vitamin potency, in sum, were all subject to new forms of scientific measurement and government intervention, subject to novel fishing measures.

Herein lies the book's strengths and weaknesses. If it succeeds, it does so in two ways. First, this book is an attempt to recover the Marxist critique of science. Inspired by two largely forgotten left-wing scientific movements — the Red Scientists of the 1930s and the *Radical Science Journal* collective of the 1970s[18] — it is an attempt to ground the history of science in material conditions and practical activity, that is, in the social relations of capitalism, broadly conceived. This may be dismissed as economically deterministic, but following Lukács, this implies that the object of science is independent of the social relations that produce it. My contention is simply that science is a practical activity that occurs under specific material conditions. It is immanent to its social context, and *assuming capitalism exists*, value relations are thus relevant to our analysis. Science and technology studies (STS) have much to offer, but the micro-scale studies of laboratory life often ignore "how the laboratory's macro-scale relationship to society was being re-engineered all around them, not to mention the shift in those paying for all those DNA sequencers and inscription devices."[19] Scientists may appear to float in the empyrean of abstract thought, but they, too, live in the material world of money and power.

Building on this, the second contribution is situating Newfoundland's credit system in the history and logic of global capitalism. Following Marx's expansive definition of production in the *Grundrisse*, it pushes the political-economic analysis of "fishing" beyond the extractive moment to include circulation, realization, and distribution. Getting water out of fish was just as important as getting fish out of the water. This scales the analysis up from the outport and the lived experience of fishers and merchants to offer a spatial and ecological reading of the credit system. It shows how the system was shaped by the materiality of fish and ocean-space, and how those characteristics offered opportunities to be reshaped in the image of capital. This perspective challenges the accepted periodization of the industrialization of Newfoundland's fishery. The roots of the post-World War II industrialization, I have argued, stretch back to the late nineteenth century in the ideological shifts I describe, in the institutionalization of the knowledge of arithmetic between the 1880s and 1930s.

But the limitations should be even clearer. Readers who do not subscribe to the materialist reading of history (if you have made it this far) will be left unsatisfied. The temporal and spatial scale of the analysis is vast, and it necessarily blurs or sweeps over the granular details. Lastly, it reproduces many of the lacunae and omissions of Newfoundland historiography writ large: it assumes the credit system as dominant and structuring in the social lives of outport people; it mostly ignores Labrador; and it is profoundly settler-centric. All of these factors are critical, and I hope they do not detract from the overall contribution of the book. Marx described his method as rising from the abstract to the concrete. *Fishing Measures* might be too abstract for some, but what I hope it offers is a different starting point — immanent, dialectical, and materialist — for analyzing and understanding the historical-geographical "concrete" of Newfoundland's saltfishery.

If, in Rhoda Dawson's "doodle," the merchant on the top left, carelessly discarding his papers, overlooking the rows of fishers governed by playing cards, represents the credit system's disregard for precision and calculation, the Commissioners at the bottom, flooded by neatly stacked papers, represent the new system of government framed around the knowledge of arithmetic. In modern states, as historian of South Africa Adam Ashforth reminds us, "The real seat of power is the bureau, the locus of writing."[20] Ashforth's work highlights the *bureau*cratic and administrative techniques of government that constitute modern states. Dawson's depiction of desk-bound technocrats, thus, visually represents the epochal transformation in the relationship of knowledge production, the environment, and capitalism in the global fishing industry.

But as Timothy Mitchell points out in his examination of surveying and mapmaking in Egypt, these new forms of abstract calculation did not succeed in producing more accurate knowledge, or even *more* knowledge; rather, they represented "a reformatted knowledge, information that has been translated, moved, shrunk, simplified, redrawn." "What is new," Mitchell concludes, "is the site, and the forms of calculation and decision that can take place at this new site."[21] By the late 1930s, despite the false starts and pyrrhic victories over the previous 50 years, the locus of authority and expertise had shifted from practical fishers on the water, in the dory, governed by colonial authority, to desk-bound experts in the bowels of the Colonial Building.

Hope Simpson reflected on this shift in a letter to his daughter, Greta. The freshly arrived Governor of Newfoundland, Vice-Admiral Sir Humphrey T. Walwyn, he noted, was gradually realizing that he had less power than he was accustomed to, having only one vote in seven. "He began not only by saying what he was going to do," Hope Simpson stated:

> but by writing memoranda to the Commission containing such expressions as, "I have decided that, &c.," until he learnt that he, of himself, can do just nothing, and that he may decide what he likes but that the decision

> has no effect whatever unless it is also the decision of the six obstructionists who form the Commission. I thoroughly sympathize with the feelings of an active, somewhat unintelligent and irascible naval officer who discovers, for the first time in his life, that he cannot give an order, and is fundamentally impotent. Fortunately, I have lots of tact, and he is not too old to learn.[22]

In 1936, Hope Simpson's call for fisheries policy structured around the "knowledge of arithmetic" may have seemed novel, but a mere two decades later, fisheries management and policy was defined by it. Desk-bound technocrats and experts — based in St. John's and Ottawa, and versed in the "knowledge of arithmetic"— replaced the British-appointed Governor as the locus of authority governing society and replaced fishers as the locus of expertise governing fishing practices in Newfoundland.

This was a profound rupture in the logic of power governing Newfoundland society, from colonial authority to managerial calculation, and Dawson's "bit of doodling" captured it. This is what made her drawing so radical and so terrifying for that unnamed professor. But she captured it in an inverted form. Like Marx's reading of Hegel's idealist dialectic, "It must be inverted, in order to discover the rational kernel within the mystical shell."[23] The Governor may have been floating above the fray, but the desk-bound technocrats, drowning in neatly stacked piles of paper, took control over decision-making. And out of their desks evolved grotesque ideas, ideas that led to the near-annihilation of one of the world's most fecund resources, ideas that — as we'll see in the following section — might yet lead to a livable and liberated future, if freed from the destructive sway of self-valorizing value.

II.

For Hope Simpson, the problems plaguing Newfoundland's saltfish industry were neither complicated nor confusing. Their resolution required simply a little common sense. But as Italian Marxist Antonio Gramsci points out in his *Prison Notebooks*, common sense (*senso comune*) should be understood as more than simply the taken-for-granted, dictionary definition of sound, practical judgment. For Gramsci, it is the culturally and historically specific ensemble of ideas and beliefs that people encounter as already existing and self-evident. He did not assert there are no truths in common sense, but rather that "common sense is an ambiguous, contradictory and multiform concept, and that to refer to common sense as a confirmation of truth is a nonsense."[24]

Hope Simpson's opposition between the knowledge of fishing and the knowledge of arithmetic, as he wrote to Ian, *was* common sense, but in the Gramscian sense: a culturally specific "chaotic aggregate of disparate conceptions,"[25] rooted in a particular time and place, but framed as timeless and placeless. His common sense was common to historically and geographically specific groups of people, with a particular form of knowledge: modern, rational, calculative, predictive, mathematical, or simply put, the knowledge of arithmetic. He opposed this mindset to the knowledge of fishing: rule of thumb, embodied, generational, practical, sensuously engaged with the marine environment. As I argued in the first chapter of this book, this opposition between the knowledge of fishing and arithmetic is one of the clearest articulations of the antimonies of bourgeois thought and practice. Building on the subterranean strand of Marxist form analysis, I asserted that this opposition is rooted in the contradictory commodity-form. It is an outcome of the unfolding of the contradiction between use-value and value.

How, then, *can* the opposition between fishing and arithmetic, between the dory and the desk, be overcome? How can we negate the antinomies of essence/appearance, object/subject, thing/relation, body/mind that structure bourgeois consciousness? Marx offers a somewhat paradoxical answer, and thus for him, paradigmatic. As he noted in a parenthetical aside to his confidant Kugelmann, "(you see, I always move in dialectical contradictions)."[26] For Marx, the answer was in the *development*, not the abolition, of science.

Science played an ambiguous role in Marx's thinking. On the one hand, he was fully aware of its incorporation and subsumption by capital into the productive process, and its role in the development of machinery that degraded, deskilled, and replaced workers. "It is, firstly," he wrote in the *Grundrisse*, "the analysis and application of mechanical and chemical laws, arising directly out of science, which enables the machine to perform the same labour as that previously performed by the worker."[27] At high levels of technical sophistication, he argued, "Invention then becomes a business, and the application of science to direct production itself becomes a prospect which determines and solicits it."[28]

But, on the other hand, Marx was fully committed to science's liberatory and emancipatory potential. It offered the possibilities for the fullest possible flourishing of society and flowering of creative potential. The development of science for the creation of new needs and new forms of surplus time, he argued:

> [for the] cultivation of all the qualities of the social human being, . . . in a form as rich as possible in needs, because rich in qualities and relations — production of this being as the most total and universal possible social product, for, in order to take gratification in a many-sided way, he must be capable of many pleasures, hence cultured to a high degree — is *likewise a condition of production founded on capital.*[29]

Science, for Marx, offered the tools for both class exploitation and human liberation. It was a source of both material wealth and revolutionary consciousness.

The development of science and technology for the use-values of human liberation, freedom, and curiosity, for the reduction of necessary labour-time to a minimum, "which then corresponds to the artistic or scientific development of the individuals in the time set free, and with the means created, for all of them,"[30] is a worthwhile endeavour. But this would *necessarily* mean the breakdown of production based on exchange-value that structures capitalist social relations, dictated by the expansionary law of value: accumulation for accumulation's sake. "Only when the forces of production finally cast off the shell of private appropriation surrounding them," concludes Belgian Marxist economist Ernest Mandel, "will the revolutionary powers which are still for the most part slumbering in contemporary science be able to be fully utilized to serve the liberation of labour and the liberation of humanity."[31] Only then would it offer the possibilities for a liberated society of free, fulfilled, creative individuals, sensuously engaged in the reproduction of their social lives. We must live in hopes, supposing we dies in despair.

Coda: Breaking Collar

The *Dictionary of Newfoundland English* documents an unusual use of the word "collar" in the Newfoundland dialect. Derived from the nautical term for a type of knot, being *on the collar* referred to the location where a boat was anchored.

> 1977 BURSEY 136 Our boats were on the collar.

But the word extended to the dorymen, not just the dories. To *go in collar* or *come to collar* was to sign on as member of a fishing or sealing crew. To *break collar* was to come to the end of one's period of employment.

> 1974 SQUIRE 17–18 Preparations for the Labrador fishery generally began around May 1 each year. That was when the various crews came in collar.... Fishermen broke collar about the end of October and the schooner was moored for the winter.

Reaching back further in the depths of English language and consciousness, the *Oxford English Dictionary* lists 17 definitions and 32 separate compound words for the noun "collar." They are divided into two main categories: "something worn about the neck" and "transferred or technical terms," including from the more familiar definition of the part of a garment that encircles the neck:

> *c.* 1405, G. Chaucer *Miller's Tale* (Hengwrt) (2003) l. 79 A brooch she baar vp on hir loue coler.

to an ornamental band worn around the neck to denote an office:

> *c.* 1485, W. Caxton tr. *Paris & Vienne* (1957) 24 Thenne they took the colyer and the whyte baner of vyenne.

to the literal band of iron placed around the neck of a prisoner or the figurative meaning of being placed under arrest:

> *c.* 1865 *Leaves from Diary Celebrated Burglar* 151/1 His intended judy, Mary Ann, had the "collar" put on her.

In brief, the word "collar" is rich in meanings and evocations. Work, yoke, knot, crime, and hierarchy were semantically knotted together. To sign on as a member of a fishing crew, as a worker under the strict discipline of a skipper, was, like a boat moored to a stage, to be *on the collar*, to sacrifice the freedom and movement of subsistence and petty commodity production, however partial, to the dictates of the law of value. Removing the yoke of work was to *break collar*, to return to the "quality of life lived in unredeemed time."[32]

In 1919, the American socialist author Upton Sinclair added another etymological wrinkle to the word "collar" in his largely forgotten book, *The Brass Check*. Better remembered for *The Jungle* — his novelistic exposé of the Chicago meatpacking industry and its exploitation of immigrant workers, which shocked the American public and led to the Meat Inspection Act of 1906 — Sinclair's *The Brass Check* was a full-throated attack on the American commercial press. In it, he wrote:

> It is a fact with which every union workingman is familiar that his most bitter despisers are the petty underlings of the business world, the poor office-clerks, who are often

> the worst exploited of proletarians, but who, *because they are allowed to wear a white collar* and to work in the office with the boss, regard themselves as members of the capitalist class.[33]

There were antecedents, dating to 1909–10, but Sinclair popularized the distinction between white and blue collars, between cotton dress shirts and denim work shirts, as a symbol of the difference between mental and manual labour.

Both, he reminds us, were exploited by capital. "The blue-collar blues is no more bitterly sung than the white-collar moan," writes Studs Terkel, in his magisterial oral history of work in America. He continues:

> "I'm a machine," says the spot welder. "I'm caged," says the bank teller, and echoes the hotel clerk. "I'm a mule," says the steelworker. "A monkey can do what I do," says the receptionist. "I'm less than a farm implement," says the migrant worker. "I'm an object," says the high-fashion model. Blue collar and white call upon the identical phrase: "I'm a robot."[34]

Both were dominated by that which they produced, dominated by value metamorphized into capital, by "value, i.e. past labour in its objectified and lifeless form, . . . which can perform its own valorization process, *an animated monster* which begins to 'work' 'as if its body were by love possessed.'"[35] Both felt the freedom of removing the yoke of work, of loosening their collars. Both dreamed of breaking collar.

~ ~ ~

What would happen if desk-bound reason *broke collar*? What would happen if it overcame the opposition between blue and white collars, between mental and manual labour, between fishing and arithmetic? What *would* a liberated fisheries science look like? One oriented towards emancipation, not exploitation; one oriented towards developing the vital potentialities of the global collective worker, not the vampiric compulsions of capital; one oriented towards the flourishing free, sensuous, creative human activity, not the bleak expansion of alienated, empty activity?

It is hard to predict. But, in the end, that might be the point.

NOTES

Chapter 1

1. John Hope Simpson to Betty, 16 June 1935, in P. Neary, *White Tie and Decorations: Sir John and Lady Hope Simpson in Newfoundland, 1934–1936* (Toronto: University of Toronto Press, 1996), 170. For a short biography, see *Newfoundland Quarterly* 33, no. 4 (1934): 24.
2. J.H.S. to Ian Hope Simpson, 8 Mar. 1936, in Neary, *White Tie*, 275–77. Unless indicated otherwise, all subsequent quotes in this section are from this letter.
3. Historically, the "credit system," "truck system," and "supply system" are all used interchangeably. I prefer the term *credit system* as it emphasizes the political-economic dynamics of credit debt that organized Newfoundland's saltfish economy.
4. J. Moreton, *Life and Work in Newfoundland: Reminiscences of Thirteen Years Spent There* (London: Rivingtons, 1863), 40. For an analysis, see G. Sider, *Between History and Tomorrow: Making and Breaking Everyday Life in Rural Newfoundland* (Peterborough, ON: Broadview Press, 2003 [1986]), ch. 9.
5. J.H.S to Greta, 13 May 1943, in Neary, *White Tie*, 86.
6. Ironically, given his paternalistic tone, he miscalculates this figure in the original document. Historian Peter Neary corrects his "simple" arithmetical exercise in *White Tie*. So much for the rule of experts.
7. T.H. Huxley, *Inaugural Meeting of the Fishery Congress: Address Delivered June 18, 1883* (London: William Clowes and Sons Limited, 1883), 14. For

histories of fishing crises, see D.H. Cushing, *The Provident Sea* (Cambridge: University of Cambridge Press, 1988); H.M. Rozwadowski, *The Sea Knows No Boundaries: A Century of Marine Science under ICES* (Seattle: University of Washington Press, 2002); T.D. Smith, *Scaling Fisheries: The Science of Measuring the Effects of Fishing 1855–1955* (Cambridge: University of Cambridge Press, 1994).

8. For an overview of marine fisheries crises, see Smith, *Scaling Fisheries*. For specific national histories, see D.C. Allard, "Spencer Fullerton Baird and the Foundations of American Marine Science," *Marine Fisheries Review* 50, no. 4 (1988): 124–29; W. Garstang, "The Impoverishment of the Sea: A Critical Summary of the Experimental and Statistical Evidence bearing upon the Alleged Depletion of the Trawling Grounds," *Journal of the Marine Biological Association of the United Kingdom* 6, no. 1 (1900): 1–69; J.M. Hubbard, *A Science on the Scales: The Rise of Canadian Atlantic Fisheries Biology, 1898–1939* (Toronto: University of Toronto Press, 2006); A.F. McEvoy, *The Fisherman's Problem: Ecology and Law in the California Fisheries, 1850–1980* (Cambridge: University of Cambridge Press, 1986); V. Schwach, "The Sea around Norway: Science, Resource Management, and Environmental Concerns, 1860–1970," *Environmental History* 18, no. 1 (2012): 101–10.
9. Smith, *Scaling Fisheries*, 38–69.
10. J.E. Taylor, "Burning the Candle at Both Ends: Historicizing Overfishing in Oregon's Nineteenth-Century Salmon Fisheries," *Environmental History* 4, no. 1 (1999): 54–79.
11. C. Finley, *All the Fish in the Sea: Maximum Sustainable Yield and the Failure of Fisheries Management* (Chicago: University of Chicago Press, 2011); S.B. Longo, R. Clausen, and B. Clark, *The Tragedy of the Commodity: Oceans, Fisheries, and Aquaculture* (New Brunswick, NJ: Rutgers University Press, 2015); R. Rogers, *The Oceans Are Emptying: Fish Wars and Sustainability* (Montreal: Black Rose Books, 1995); Smith, *Scaling Fisheries.*
12. Marx, *Capital, Vol. 1*, 165.
13. Ibid.
14. E. Mandel, *The Formation of the Economic Thought of Karl Marx: 1843 to Capital* (London: Verso, 2015 [1967]), 101.
15. Quoted in Mandel, *The Formation*, 101. See also R. Bellofiore, G. Starosta, and P.D. Thomas, *In Marx's Laboratory: Critical Interpretations of the Grundrisse* (Leiden: Brill, 2013).

16. R. Bellofiore and T. Redolfi Riva, "The Neue Marx-Lektüre. Putting the Critique of Political Economy Back into the Critique of Society," *Radical Philosophy* 189 (2015): 24–36; W. Bonefeld, *Critical Theory and the Critique of Political Economy: On Subversion and Negative Reason* (London: Bloomsbury, 2014); W. Bonefeld, R. Gunn, and K. Psychopedis, eds., *Open Marxism: Dialectics and History* (London: Pluto Press, 1991); J.I. Carrera, *El Capital: Razón Histórica, Sujeto Revolucionario y Conciencia* (Buenos Aires: Imago Mundi, 2013 [2003]); E. Dussel, *Towards an Unknown Marx: A Commentary on the Manuscripts of 1861–63*, trans. Y. Angulo (London: Routledge, 2001 [1988]); G. Lukács, "Reification and the Consciousness of the Proletariat," in Lukács, *History and Class Consciousness: Studies in Marxist Dialectics*, trans. R. Livingstone (Cambridge, MA: MIT Press, 1971); M. Postone, *Time, Labor, and Social Domination: A Reinterpretation of Marx's Critical Theory* (Cambridge: Cambridge University Press, 1993); G. Starosta, *Marx's Capital, Method and Revolutionary Subjectivity* (Leiden: Brill, 2015).
17. M. Arboleda, *Planetary Mine: Territories of Extraction under Late Capitalism* (London: Verso, 2020).
18. Lukács, "Reification," 83.
19. Ibid., 170.
20. I.I. Rubin, *Essays on Marx's Theory of Value*, trans. M. Samardźija and F. Perlman (Detroit: Black and Red, 1973), 2.
21. The full flowering of this perspective is beyond the scope of this book. Form analysis offers a number of profound insights that reshape our understanding of capitalism, in terms of: its temporality; its character of domination; the nature of unfreedom and consciousness; class struggle and revolutionary subjectivity; the state; and the grounds for capitalism's historical negation. It also has limitations in terms of its limited engagement with race and gender as fetishized forms of exploitation, but I hope that this work might inspire further interrogation along these lines. Early articulations of this perspective (esp. Lukács's "standpoint of the proletariat") inspired feminist "standpoint" approaches. See S. Harding, "Stronger Objectivity for Sciences from Below," *Em Construção* 5 (2019): 175. This approach also offers a new set of resonances to Martin Luther King Jr.'s famous "Beyond Vietnam" address, delivered at New York City's Riverside Church on 4 April 1967: "I am convinced that if we are to get on the right side of the world revolution, we as a nation must undergo a radical revolution of values. *We must rapidly*

begin the shift from a thing-oriented society to a person-oriented society. When machines and computers, profit motives and property rights are considered more important than people, the giant triplets of racism, extreme materialism and militarism are incapable of being conquered" (emphasis added). Or Franz Fanon: "As soon as I *desire* I am asking to be considered. I am not merely here-and-now, *sealed into thingness.*" Fanon, *Black Skin, White Masks*, trans. C.L. Markman (London: Pluto Press, 1986), 218 (emphasis added).

22. Marx, *Capital, Vol. 1*, 163.
23. Ibid.
24. Ibid., 127.
25. Ibid., 128.
26. Ibid., 163–64. This is one of the most important images in Marx's oeuvre, as it demonstrates his overarching method so perfectly. Marxist critics and critics of Marxism are more familiar with a similar image in relation to his appropriation of Hegel's dialectics. He writes: "My dialectical method is, in its foundations, not only different from the Hegelian, but exactly opposite to it. . . . With *him it is standing on its head.* It must be inverted, in order to discover the rational kernel within the mystical shell" (emphasis added). Marx, "Postface to the Second Edition," in *Capital, Vol. 1*, 102–03. See also J.I. Carrera, "Dialectics on Its Feet, or the Form of the Consciousness of the Working Class as Historical Subject," in Fred Moseley and Tony Smith, eds., *Marx's Capital and Hegel's Logic* (Leiden: Brill, 2014), 64. Marx wrote that he skimmed Hegel's *Science of Logic* as preparation to work on the *Grundrisse.* J.I. Carrera, "Method: From the Grundrisse to Capital," in R. Bellofiore, G. Starosta, and P.D. Thomas, eds., *In Marx's Laboratory: Critical Interpretations of the Grundrisse* (Leiden: Brill, 2013), 47; Mandel, *The Formation*, 102.
27. Marx, *Capital, Vol. 1*, 138. Marx's category of abstract labour is complex, problematic, and a source of textual argument. The ontology of abstract labour is very much open to debate. Confusingly, his first definition of it seems to indicate its physiological nature, but in subsequent work it refers more to an immaterial, social substratum. See W. Bonefeld, "Abstract Labour: Against Its Nature and on Its Time," *Capital & Class* 34, no. 2 (2010): 257–76; Postone, *Time*, 144–48.
28. Postone, *Time*, 139.
29. Lukács, "Reification," 83.

30. G. Starosta, "The Commodity-Form and the Dialectical Method: On the Structure of Marx's Exposition in Chapter 1 of *Capital*," *Science & Society*, 72, no. 3 (2008): 295–318; G. Starosta, "The Role and Place of 'Commodity Fetishism' in Marx's Systematic-Dialectical Exposition in Capital," *Historical Materialism* 25, no. 3 (2017): 101–39.
31. Quoted in Carrera, "Method," 44.
32. E. Mandel, *Late Capitalism* (London: Verso, 1978 [1972]), 15.
33. As a Hegelian, Marx's interest in essences and appearances is shot right through his oeuvre, dating back to his 1841 doctoral dissertation, *The Difference between the Democritean and Epicurean Philosophy of Nature.*
34. K. Kosik, *Dialectics of the Concrete: A Study on Problems of Man and World* (Boston: D. Reidel Publishing Company, 1976), 15. Cf. Mandel, *Late Capitalism*, 16.
35. K. Marx, *Grundrisse: Foundations of the Critique of Political Economy*, trans. M. Nicolaus (Harmondsworth: Penguin, 1973), 83. See Carrera, "Method," 44.
36. Marx, *Capital, Vol. 1*, 125.
37. Postone, *Time*, 141.
38. Marx, "Postface to the Second Edition," in *Capital, Vol. 1*, 102. See also Postone, *Time*, 140–41.
39. "What is certain is that I, *I* am not a Marxist." Engels reports this conversation in a November 1882 letter to Eduard Bernstein. Quoted in S.E. Liedman, *A World to Win: The Life and Works of Karl Marx* (London: Verso Books, 2018), 521.
40. Marx, *Capital, Vol. 1*, 169.
41. Kosik, *Dialectics*, 1.
42. Lukács, "Reification," 154.
43. Ibid.
44. N. Smith, *Uneven Development: Nature, Capital and the Production of Space*, 3rd ed. (Athens: University of Georgia Press, 2008 [1984]), 135.
45. Lukács, "Reification," 110.
46. Postone, *Time*, 174.
47. S. Shapin and S. Schaffer, *Leviathan and the Air-Pump: Hobbes, Boyle, and the Experimental Life* (Princeton, NJ: Princeton University Press, 1985).
48. L. Daston, "Objectivity and the Escape from Perspective," *Social Studies of Science* 22, no. 4 (1992): 597–618; P. Dear, "From Truth to Disinterestedness in the Seventeenth Century," *Social Studies of Science* 22, no. 4 (1992): 619–31;

T.M. Porter, "Quantification and the Accounting Ideal in Science," *Social Studies of Science* 22, no. 4 (1992): 633–51.

49. W. Kula, *Measures and Men*, trans. R. Szreter (Princeton, NJ: Princeton University Press, 1986), 13.
50. Ibid.
51. Ibid., 15.
52. Ibid.
53. S. Kern, *The Culture of Time and Space 1880–1918*, 2nd ed. (Cambridge, MA: Harvard University Press, 2003).
54. Regarding task-orientation, see E.P. Thompson, "Time, Work-Discipline, and Industrial Capitalism," *Past & Present* 38 (1967): 59. "Measured clank" comes from L. Mumford, *Technics and Civilization* (Chicago: University of Chicago Press, 2010 [1934]), 20.
55. Kula, *Measures,* 25–30.
56. Ibid. See also J.C. Scott, *Seeing Like a State: How Certain Schemes to Improve the Human Condition Have Failed* (New Haven: Yale University Press, 1998), 25–29.
57. Moreton, *Life and Work*, 30.
58. Ibid., 37.
59. Mumford, *Technics*, passim. See also A. Crosby, *The Measure of Reality: Quantification and Western Society, 1250–1600* (Cambridge: Cambridge University Press, 1997); Kern, *Culture,* passim; M. Poovey, *A History of the Modern Fact: Problems of Knowledge in the Sciences of Wealth and Society* (Chicago: University of Chicago Press, 1998), passim; T.M. Porter, *Trust in Numbers: The Pursuit of Objectivity in Science and Public Life* (Princeton, NJ: Princeton University Press, 1995), passim; Scott, *Seeing*, 30–33. The "character of calculability" comes from G. Simmel, "The Metropolis and Mental Life," in G. Bridge and S. Watson, eds., *The Blackwell City Reader* (Oxford and Malden, MA: Wiley-Blackwell, 2002 [1903]), 13.
60. Thompson, "Time," 80; Porter, *Trust in Numbers*, 25.
61. P. Mirowski, *The Effortless Economy of Science?* (Durham, NC: Duke University Press, 2004), 150.
62. Mumford, *Technics,* 14.
63. Ibid., 15.
64. Newton, *Principia*, quoted in Postone, *Time*, 202.
65. Ibid.
66. Ibid, 203.

67. Ibid., 200–16.
68. Ibid., 206. For example, various forms of water clocks in Hellenistic and Roman society used a uniform process, the flow of water, to represent variable hours. Complicated technical mechanisms were developed to translate a continuous, regular flow of water into a variable, seasonal understanding of time. For Postone, this was not technologically determined: temporal variability was, in fact, more technically challenging to accomplish. The reasons were social and cultural: "variable hours apparently were significant, whereas equal hours were not." Similarly, medieval China had both a conception of constant hours and higher level of technical development than Europe, yet did not revolutionize and regulate its society to the Newtonian clank of the mechanical clock. Even after the widespread introduction of mechanical clocks to China in the late sixteenth century by Jesuit missionary Matteo Ricci, they did not revolutionize society. They were primarily regarded and used as toys. See, Postone, *Time*, 200–16.
69. K. Marx, *A Contribution to the Critique of Political Economy*, trans. N.I. Stone (Chicago: Charles H. Kerr & Company, 1904), 11–12.
70. K. Marx, *The German Ideology* (New York: International Publishers Co., 1970), 47, quoted in Smith, *Uneven Development*, 55.
71. Smith, *Uneven Development*, 63.
72. D. Harvey, *The Limits to Capital* (London: Verso, 2006 [1982]), 98–136.
73. Marx, *Capital, Vol. 1*, 799.
74. A. Sohn-Rethel, *Intellectual and Manual Labour: A Critique of Epistemology* (London: Macmillan, 1978), 113.
75. Ibid., 35.
76. I have neither the experience nor expertise to fully articulate this point, but I am raising it here to acknowledge the critically important work aimed at decolonizing fisheries science and histories of fishing. I hope that this adds some grist to the mill. See, for example, D. Hoogeveen, "Fish-hood: Environmental Assessment, Critical Indigenous Studies, and Posthumanism at Fish Lake (Teztan Biny), Tsilhqot'in Territory," *Environment and Planning D: Society and Space* 34, no. 2 (2016): 355–70; A.J. Reid, L.E. Eckert, J.F. Lane, N. Young, S.G. Hinch, C.T. Darimont, S.J. Cooke, N.C. Ban, and A. Marshall, "'Two-Eyed Seeing': An Indigenous Framework to Transform Fisheries Research and Management," *Fish and Fisheries* OnlineFirst (2020): 1–19; Z. Todd, "Fish Pluralities: Human–Animal Relations and Sites of

Engagement in Paulatuuq, Arctic Canada," *Études/Inuit/Studies* 38, nos. 1–2 (2014): 217–38; Z. Todd, "Refracting the State through Human–Fish Relations: Fishing, Indigenous Legal Orders and Colonialism in North/Western Canada," *Decolonization: Indigeneity, Education & Society* 7, no. 1 (2018): 60–75.

77. G. Coulthard and L.B. Simpson, "Grounded Normativity/Place-based Solidarity," *American Quarterly* 68, no. 2 (2016): 249–55. See also G. Coulthard, *Red Skin, White Masks: Rejecting the Colonial Politics of Recognition* (Minneapolis: University of Minnesota Press, 2014); R.W. Kimmerer, *Braiding Sweetgrass: Indigenous Wisdom, Scientific Knowledge and the Teachings of Plants* (Minneapolis: Milkweed Editions, 2013); L.B. Simpson, *Dancing on Our Turtle's Back: Stories of Nishnaabeg Re-creation, Resurgence, and a New Emergence* (Winnipeg: Arbeiter Ring, 2011). For a Latin American perspective, see H. Cleaver, "The Zapatistas and the Electronic Fabric of Struggle," in John Holloway and Eloísa Peláez, eds., *Zapatista! Reinventing Revolution in Mexico* (London: Pluto Press, 1998), 81–103; A. García Linera, *Hacia el gran ayllu universal: Pensar el mundo desde Los Andes* (Santiago: Editorial Arcis, 2014); M. Gonzalez, *In the Red Corner. The Marxism of José Carlos Mariátegui* (Chicago: Haymarket Books, 2019); José Carlos Mariátegui, "The Problem of Land," in *Seven Interpretive Essays on Peruvian Reality*, trans. M. Urquidi (Austin: University of Texas Press, 1988), 31–76. R. Solnit, *Hope in the Dark: Untold Histories, Wild Possibilities* (Chicago: Haymarket Books, 2016), 40–45.

78. L.B. Simpson, "Land as Pedagogy: Nishnaabeg Intelligence and Rebellious Transformation," *Decolonization: Indigeneity, Education & Society* 3, no. 3 (2014): 1–25.

79. Quoted in Lukács, "Reification," 92.

80. Sohn-Rethel, *Intellectual*, 39.

81. Lukács, "Reification," 110–11.

82. Q.H.S. to Ian and Sheila, 20 Feb. 1934, in Neary, *White Tie*, 34.

83. D. Cullen, "Race, Debt and Empire: Racialising the Newfoundland Financial Crisis of 1933," *Transactions of the Institute of British Geographers* 43, no. 4 (2018): 1–14.

84. J.H.S. to Betty, 1 June 1936, in Neary, *White Tie*, 306.

85. N. Bukharin et al., *Science at the Crossroads*, 2nd ed. (London: Frank Cass & Co., 1971 [1931]), 174.

86. W. Cronon, *Nature's Metropolis: Chicago and the Great West* (New York: W.W. Norton, 1991), 310.
87. Ibid.
88. The Rooms Provincial Archives Division (TRPAD), MG 73, Box 17, File 9, Hugh Haneberg to Aaron Stone, 24 Jan. 1925.

Chapter 2

1. TRPAD, MG 73, Box 17, File 9, Hugh Haneberg to Aaron Stone, 30 Dec. 1924.
2. Ibid., Translation of certified appraisal of shipment, no. 2253, n.d.
3. Ibid.
4. Ibid., Haneberg to Stone, 24 Jan. 1925.
5. Ibid., Haneberg to Stone, 14 Apr. 1925.
6. Ibid., Haneberg to Stone, 24 Jan. 1925.
7. G.A. Rose, *Cod: The Ecological History of the North Atlantic Fisheries* (St. John's: Breakwater Books, 2007), 26–27. For a critical geographer's perspective, see P.E. Steinberg, "Of Other Seas: Metaphors and Materialities in Maritime Regions," *Atlantic Studies* 10, no. 2 (2013): 156–69; Steinberg and K. Peters, "Wet Ontologies, Fluid Spaces: Giving Depth to Volume through Oceanic Thinking," *Environment and Planning D: Society and Space* 33, no. 2 (2015): 247–64.
8. R. Carson, *The Sea Around Us* (Oxford: Oxford University Press, 2003 [1950]), 174–75; Rose, *Cod*, 26–27.
9. *Evening Telegram (ET)*, "The Ocean Around Newfoundland," 10 Feb. 1925, 4; H. King, *The Marketing of Fishery Products in Newfoundland*, Economic Bulletin No. 2 (St. John's: Department of Natural Resources, 1937), 3; M. Kurlansky, *Cod: A Biography of the Fish That Changed the World* (London: Vintage, 1999), 137–38; TRPAD, MG 73, Box 9, File 5 (1918), E.A. Payn to A. Percival Love, 16 July 1918. Newfoundland historian Shannon Ryan points out that the use of "fish" as a synonym for cod extends beyond the English language. For example, Norwegians called their dried cod *torrfisk* (dried fish); the French referred to the cod dried on St. Pierre and Miquelon as *poisson de côte*. Shannon Ryan, *Fish Out of Water: The Newfoundland Saltfish Trade 1814–1914* (St. John's: Breakwater Books, 1986), 29. For an etymological analysis for the other set of words commonly used to refer to preserved cod — *bacalao* (Spanish), *bacallá* (Catalan), *bachalao* (Italian), *bacalhau*

(Portuguese), *kabeljou* (Swedish) and *kabeljauw* (Dutch) — see M. Schuyler, "The Etymology of the Dutch Word Kabeljauw," *Journal of Germanic Philology* 4, no. 1 (1902): 55–57.

10. D. Bavington, *Managed Annihilation: An Unnatural History of the Newfoundland Cod Collapse* (Vancouver: University of British Columbia Press, 2010), 1; C. Roberts, *The Unnatural History of the Sea* (Washington: Island Press/Shearwater Books, 2007), 32–43.
11. Bolster, *The Mortal Sea* (Cambridge, MA: Harvard University Press, 2012), 40.
12. Rose, *Cod*, 68.
13. A.E. Ghaly, D. Dave, S. Budge, and M.S. Brooks, "Fish Spoilage Mechanisms and Preservation Techniques," *American Journal of Applied Sciences* 7, no. 7 (2010): 859–77.
14. N.L. Macpherson, *The Dried Codfish Industry*, Service Bulletin No. 1 (St. John's: Fishery Research Commission, 1935), 16. See also Ghaly et al., "Fish," 861; M.K. Mukundan, P.D. Antony, and M.R. Nair, "A Review on Autolysis in Fish," *Fisheries Research* 4, nos. 3–4 (1986): 259–69.
15. Macpherson, *Dried Codfish Industry*, 18.
16. J.J. Waterman, *The Cod*, Torry Advisory Note No. 33 (Rome: Food and Agriculture Organization, 2001), at http://www.fao.org/wairdocs/tan/x5911e/x5911e00.htm. Accessed 7 Aug. 2018.
17. Ghaly et al., "Fish," 861.
18. Department of Marine and Fisheries (DMF), *Annual Report*, 1905, 8.
19. Kurlansky, *Cod*, 34.
20. Unlike the blander *stockfish* (dried, but not salted), salt preserves fish flesh enough "for enzymes of both fish and harmless salt-tolerant bacteria to break down flavourless proteins and fats into savoury fragments, which then react further to create flavours of great complexity." H. McGee, *On Food and Cooking: The Science and Lore of the Kitchen* (New York: Simon and Schuster, 2004), 232.
21. Marx, *Capital, Vol. 1*, 915.
22. As one reviewer rightly pointed out, variability and uncertainty are not the same. Variability can be deterministic or stochastic, determined by specific parameters or possessing some inherent randomness with high or low degrees of confidence. I use the term "fluctuation" to encompass all forms of variability and uncertainty, as well as more experiential notions of providence, chance, and supernatural mischief.

23. J. Hjort, "Fluctuations in the Great Fisheries of Northern Europe Viewed in the Light of Biological Research," *Rapports et Procès-Verbaux des Réunions du Conseil International pour l'Exploration de la Mer* 20 (1914): 1.
24. C. Finley, *All the Fish in the Sea: Maximum Sustainable Yield and the Failure of Fisheries Management* (Chicago: University of Chicago Press, 2011), 5–6.
25. P.A. Larkin, "Fisheries Management: An Essay for Ecologists," *Annual Review of Ecology and Systematics* 9 (1978): 60.
26. D. Harvey, "Resources, and the Ideology of Science," *Economic Geography* 50, no. 3 (1974): 272.
27. M.A. Lever, O. Rouxel, J.C. Alt, N. Shimizu, S. Ono, R.M. Coggon, W.C. Shanks, L. Lapham, M. Elvert, X. Prieto-Mollar, and K.U. Hinrichs, "Evidence for Microbial Carbon and Sulfur Cycling in Deeply Buried Ridge Flank Basalt," *Science* 339, no. 6125 (2013): 1305–08.
28. M. Arboleda and D. Banoub, "Market Monstrosity in Industrial Fishing: Capital as Subject and the Urbanization of Nature," *Social & Cultural Geography* 19, no. 1 (2018): 120–38.
29. A. Muszynski, *Cheap Wage Labour: Race and Gender in the Fisheries of British Columbia* (Montreal and Kingston: McGill-Queen's University Press, 1996), 3–4.
30. The gender dichotomy in fishing labour is captured nicely in Newfoundland's most famous folksong, "I'se The B'y": "I'se the b'y that builds the boat / And I'se the b'y that sails her / I'se the b'y that catches the fish / And brings them home to Liza."
31. Muszynski, *Cheap Wage Labour*, 4.
32. J. Faris, *Cat Harbour: A Newfoundland Fishing Settlement*, Newfoundland Social and Economic Studies No. 3 (St. John's: ISER Books, 1973); M. Firestone, *Brothers and Rivals: Patrilocality in Savage Cove*, Newfoundland Social and Economic Studies no. 5 (St. John's: ISER Books, 1967).
33. Sider, *Between History and Tomorrow*, 80. For more elaboration on the distinction between "fixed capital" and "circulating capital," see Harvey, *The Limits to Capital*, 206–08.
34. Newfoundland, *Report of the Commission of Enquiry investigating the Sea-fisheries of Newfoundland and Labrador other than the Sealfishery*, Economic Bulletin No. 3 (St. John's: Department of Natural Resources, 1937), 68–69.
35. W. Keough, "'Good Looks Don't Boil the Pot': Irish-Newfoundland Women as Fish(-Producing) Wives," *Signs: Journal of Women in Culture and So-*

ciety 37, no. 3 (2012): 536–44; M. Porter, "'She Was Skipper of the Shore-Crew': Notes on the History of the Sexual Division of Labour in Newfoundland," *Labour/Le Travail* 15 (1985): 105–23.

36. J.H.S. to Betty, 25 Sept. 1935, in Neary, *White Tie*, 222.
37. Fisheries Research Commission (FRC), *Annual Report*, 1936–37, 6–8; T. Lodge, *Dictatorship in Newfoundland* (London: Cassell & Co. 1939), 51; Newfoundland, *Report of the Commission of Enquiry*, 29.
38. S. Cadigan, *Hope and Deception in Conception Bay: Merchant–Settler Relations in Newfoundland, 1785–1855* (Toronto: University of Toronto Press, 1995), 25; Ryan, *Fish Out of Water*, 55.
39. Great Britain, *Newfoundland Royal Report: Presented by the Secretary of State for Dominion Affairs to Parliament by Command of His Majesty, November, 1933*, Cmd. 4480 (London: His Majesty's Stationery Office, 1933), 97.
40. Salt bulk (n): split, washed, and salted codfish placed not yet dried in a fishing stage or aboard a vessel. Green (a): codfish, split, salted, but not dried.
41. Macpherson, *Dried Codfish Industry*, 5.
42. D. Alexander, *The Decay of Trade: An Economic History of the Newfoundland Saltfish Trade 1935–1965* (St. John's: ISER Books, 1977), 45.
43. Macpherson, *Dried Codfish Industry, 5.*
44. DMF, *Annual Report*, 1894, 19.
45. Ibid., 51.
46. Lodge, *Dictatorship*, 53.
47. Stage head (n): End of a fishing stage that extends over the water where fish is landed.
48. L.A. Anspach, *A History of Newfoundland* (London: Sherwood, Gilbert and Piper, 1819), 431.
49. S.A. Beatty and G. Fougère, *The Processing of Dried Salted Fish*, Bulletin No. 112 (Ottawa: Fisheries Research Board of Canada, 1957), 4; A.G. Huntsman, *Method of Handling Fish: I. The Processing of Dried Fish*, Bulletin No. IX (Ottawa: F.A. Acland, 1927), 6–7; TRPAD, File GN 2.15.25, Suggestions for improving the cure of codfish, 8 Apr. 1903, 2.
50. W.F. Hampton, *Approved Methods of Handling Codfish for Salting and Drying*, Service Bulletin No. 9 (St. John's: Department of Natural Resources, 1938), 10–11; TRPAD, GN 73, Box 70, File 3, "Directions," n.d.
51. Huntsman, *Method*, 9-10.
52. Beatty and Fougère, *Processing*, 15–16.

53. M.E. Ferguson, "Making Fish: Salt-Cod Processing on the East Coast of Newfoundland — A Study in Historic Occupational Folklife," MA thesis (Department of Folklore, MUN, 1996), 107; Huntsman, *Method*, 10; Macpherson, *Dried Codfish Industry*, 38.
54. Hampton, *Approved Methods*, 12; Macpherson, *Dried Codfish Industry*, 24–28.
55. TRPAD, GN 127, Box 1, "Evidence: Dr. Norman L. Macpherson," 26 May 1936.
56. Beatty and Fougère, *Processing*, 16; Ferguson, "Making Fish," 137.
57. Hampton, *Approved Methods*, 14.
58 Ferguson, "Making Fish," 143.
59. Huntsman, *Method*, 13.
60. Flake (n): a platform built on poles and spread with boughs.
61. Lodge, *Dictatorship*, 53.
62. A. Nielsen, *Report on the Cure of Codfish and Herring* (St. John's: Evening Herald Office, 1890), 6.
63. FRC, *Annual Report*, 1932, 8; Huntsman, *Method*, 10.
64. N.L. Macpherson, *Technical Investigations of the Dried Codfish Industry* (St. John's: Fishery Research Commission, 1932), 12.
65. Ferguson, "Making Fish," 159; Huntsman, *Method*, 12.
66. C.L. Cutting, *Fish Saving: A History of Fish Processing from Ancient to Modern Times* (New York: Philosophical Library, 1956), 176; Macpherson, *Dried Fish Industry*, 38.
67. A. Shea, *Newfoundland: Its Fisheries and General Resources in 1883* (n.p., 1883), 4.
68. TRPAD, MG 73, Box 17, File 9, Translation of certified appraisal of shipment, no. 2253, n.d.
69. Ibid.
70. K. Marx, *Capital: A Critique of Political Economy, Vol. 2*, trans. B. Fowkes (London: Penguin, 1992 [1885]), 229.
71. Ibid.
72. Newfoundland, *Report of the Commission of Enquiry*, 54.
73. J.K. Hiller, "The Newfoundland Credit System: An Interpretation," in R. Ommer, ed., *Merchant Credit and Labour Strategies in Historical Perspective* (Fredericton, NB: Acadiensis Press, 1990), 87.
74. TRPAD, MG 73, Box 34, File 17, Harold Earle to H.T. Renouf, 17 May 1938.
75. Ibid., Box 23, File 11, James Strong to E.A. Payn, 9 Mar. 1931.
76. DMF, *Annual Report*, 1910, 18.
77. TRPAD, GN 127, Box 1, "Evidence: George Hawes," 28 Mar. 1936.

78. Fishers, for example, could change their curing method to produce a heavier, very white fish that could deceive the culler, but would deteriorate rapidly in transit "so that, for example, that which was originally purchased as Maderia [*sic*] would have to be sold at a loss as West India." See Ryan, *Fish Out of Water*, 43. The pecuniary motivation for merchants to under-grade fish is self-evident.
79. TRPAD, MG 73, Box 11, File 11, "Reports RE — Fish Export Regulations," Mr. Crosbie, 5 Feb. 1920, p. 5/27.
80. S. Ryan, "The Introduction of Steam Transport into the Newfoundland Saltfish Trade during the Latter Nineteenth Century," paper presented to the International Commission for Maritime History Conference: "Food for the World: Maritime Trade and Shipping of Foodstuff" (Madrid, 28–31 Aug. 1990): 9; I.D.H. McDonald, *"To Each His Own": William Coaker and the Fisherman's Protective Union in Newfoundland Politics, 1908–1925* (St. John's: ISER Books, 2008 [1987]), 7.
81. FRC, *Annual Report*, 1936–37, 21.
82. TRPAD, MG 73, Box 10, File 7, Consorzio to Editor of Trade Review, 6 Oct. 1919.
83. Ibid., GN 34/2, Box 146, File: Fish — Fish Labrador, 1921, R.B. Job to W.F. Coaker, 30 July 1921.
84. Newfoundland, *Report of the Commission of Enquiry*, 61; TRPAD, MG 73, Box 11, File 11, "Reports RE — Fish Export Regulations," Mr. Dunfield, 3 Feb. 1920, p. 3/38.
85. TRPAD, MG 73, Box 8, File 7, S.C. Coish to W.B. Grieve, 30 Mar. 1917. See also ibid., File 5, E.A. Payn to President, British Chambers of Commerce, Genoa, 17 May 1917; ibid., A.H. Murray and W.A. Munn to W.B. Grieve, 26 Apr. 1917; ibid., File 8, "Resolution passed by the Newfoundland Board of Trade on May 11th, 1917."
86. Newfoundland, *Report of the Commission of Enquiry*, 64.
87. TRPAD, MG 73, Box 11, File 11, "Reports RE — Fish Export Regulations," Mr. Barr, 3 Feb. 1920, p. 3/6.
88. Ibid., Mr. Brookes, 3 Feb. 1920, p. 3/30.
89. Ibid., Mr. Barr, 5 Feb. 1920, p. 5/42.
90. Marx, *Grundrisse*, 91.
91. TRPAD, GN 34/2, Box 146, File: Applications Various, W. Wainwright to H.B. Clyde Lake, 6 Oct. 1931. See also R.C. Hoffmann, "Frontier Foods for

Late Medieval Consumers: Culture, Economy, Ecology," *Environment and History* 7, no. 2 (2001): 145.

92. M. Harvey, *Newfoundland As It Was in 1894: A Hand-Book and Tourists' Guide* (St. John's: JW Withers, 1894), 147; TRPAD, MG 73, Box 3, File 6, Report on Labrador Cod-Fish, Patras, 14 Feb. 1911.
93. Alexander, *Decay of Trade*, 21; TRPAD, GN 34/2, Box 146, File: Applications Various, Wainwright to Lake, 6 Oct. 1931.
94. Ryan, *Fish Out of Water*, 78.
95. Cutting, *Fish Saving*, 154.
96. W.F. Coaker, *Twenty Years of the Fishermen's Protective Union of Newfoundland* (St. John's: Advocate Publishing Co., 1930), 384. See also TRPAD, MG 73, Box 15, File 1, Lt. Col. A.R. Bernard to Secretary, Board of Trade, 28 Mar. 1923.
97. Macpherson, *Dried Fish Industry*, 6.
98. Ferguson, "Making Fish," 229.
99. Ryan, *Fish Out of Water*, xxi.
100. Ibid., xxii.
101. D.J. Davies and A. Oldford, *Report of the Tour of Inspection which was made to the Newfoundland Foreign Fish Markets* (St. John's: Marine and Fisheries Department, 1933).
102. Quoted in P.E. Pope, *Fish into Wine: The Newfoundland Plantation in the Seventeenth Century* (Chapel Hill: University of North Carolina Press, 2004), 31.
103. Marx, *Capital, Vol. 1*, 247.
104. B. Riggs, "Currency," in J.R. Smallwood and R.D.W. Pitt, eds., *Encyclopedia of Newfoundland and Labrador, Volume 1* (St. John's: Newfoundland Book Publishers, 1981), 575.
105. Quoted in Ryan, *Fish Out of Water*, xxii.
106. Marx, *Capital, Vol. 1*, 251.
107. Newfoundland, *Report of the Commission of Enquiry*, 66.
108. G.L. Henderson, "Nature and Fictitious Capital: The Historical Geography of an Agrarian Question," *Antipode* 30, no. 2 (1998): 111.
109. This point emerged from my reading of the Annual Reports of the Department of Fisheries (in all of their various formations) from 1883 to 1937.
110. Ryan, *Fish Out of Water*, 274, n. 4.
111. TRPAD, GN 1/3/A, Box 60, Despatch 36, "Report on the Foreign Trade and Commerce of Newfoundland, 1905-06."

112. Macpherson, *Technical Investigations*, 6; Ryan, *Fish Out of Water*, xxiv.
113. TRPAD, MG 73, Box 23, File 1, John Bishop to Board of Trade, 22 Jan. 1931; *ET*, "Chairman of the Imperial Economic Committee Addressed the Board of Trade," 10 Sept. 1927, 7.
114. DF, *Annual Report*, 1895, 42; *ET*, "Reddening of Fish," 4 July 1922.
115. DMF, *Annual Report*, 1920, 6. See also TRPAD, GN 127, Box 1, "Evidence: Dr. Norman L. Macpherson," 26 May 1936.
116. TRPAD, MG 73, Box 1, File 7, "About Codfish" by C. Lays, Bergen, Sept. 1909.
117. *Proceedings of the Convention of Licensed Codfish Exporters (PCLCE)* (St. John's: Department of Marine and Fisheries, 1920), 75. Available at: CNS, MUN.
118. Alexander, *Decay of Trade*, 131.
119. TRPAD, GN 127, Box 1, "Evidence: George Hawes," 28 Mar. 1936.
120. Ryan, *Fish Out of Water*, 99.
121. Ibid., 90.
122. *Evening Mercury (EM)*, "How the Norwegians Beat Us in the Cure of Codfish," 4 Aug. 1887, 4; *EM*, "Cash versus Credit. Norway and Newfoundland Methods of Fishing," 5 Aug. 1887, 4; *EM*, "How the Norwegians Regulate Their Fisheries," 6 Aug. 1887, 4; *Daily News* (*DN*, St. John's), "United Effort Improves Iceland's Fishing Industry," 4 July 1933, 6.
123. DMF, *Annual Report*, 1910, 49.
124. Ryan, *Fish Out of Water*, 96.
125. TRPAD, MG 73, Box 5, File 6 (1914), W.A. Munn to E.A. Payn, 9 Apr. 1914.
126. Davies and Oldford, *Report*, 9.
127. DMF, *Annual Report*, 1910, 49.
128. TRPAD, MG 73, Box 27, File 9, "Regained. Thinks Nfld. Codfish Can Stage Comeback," press clipping, n.d. See also *ET*, "The Fisheries of Nfld. — Bait Depots," 15 Oct. 1923, 8; TRPAD, MG 73, Box 17, File 9, Valencia Oversea Trade Association to Board of Trade, 14 Apr. 1925
129. TRPAD, GN 34/2, Box 146, File: C Miscellaneous (2), Geo. Copland to H.B. Clyde Lake, 13 June 1931.
130. Ibid., GN 127, Box 1, "Evidence: Dr. Norman L. Macpherson," 26 May 1936.
131. Davies and Oldford, *Report*, 4; TRPAD, GN 34/2, Box 146, File: C Miscellaneous (2), Geo. Copland to H.B. Clyde Lake, 13 June 1931.
132. TRPAD, GN 34/2, Box 147, File: High Commissioners Office, 1930–31, Ian J. Fraser to D. James Davies, 13 Jan. 1931.

133. DMF, *Annual Report*, 1910, 49.
134. TRPAD, GN 34/2, Box 147, File: High Commissioners Office, 1930–31, Ian J. Fraser to D. James Davies, 13 Jan. 1931; ibid., MG 73, Box 23, File 11, H.F. Hoole to D. James Davies, 13 Jan. 1931; *ET*, "The Fishery and the Fish Markets," 2 Dec. 1908, 3.
135. Ryan, *Fish Out of Water*, 58.
136. Ryan, "The Introduction of Steam Transport," 12.
137. McDonald, *"To Each His Own"*, 9.
138. *Trade Review (TR)*, "Editorial Notes," 9 Sept. 1893, 1. Shannon Ryan, through an extensive analysis of marketing reports from 1814 to 1914, has shown that his perception was accurate. For example, in Leghorn, the first shipments in 1883 fetched 26 shillings per hundredweight, the next arrivals 21 and 19 shillings, and the last cargoes 13 and 14 shillings. See Ryan, "The Introduction of Steam Transport," 12.
139. TRPAD, GN 127, Box 1, "Evidence: George Hawes," 28 Mar. 1936.
140. *ET*, "Subject of Dry Codfish," 19 July 1897, 4.
141. Also defined as a "corruption of the French *tel quel*" in Great Britain, *Newfoundland Royal Report*, 104. See also S. Cadigan, *Newfoundland and Labrador: A History* (Toronto: University of Toronto Press, 2009), 149–50; McDonald, *"To Each His Own"*, 9; Ryan, *Fish Out of Water*, 44–46; Sider, *Between History and Tomorrow*, 168–70.
142. Great Britain, *Newfoundland Royal Report*, 105.
143. Ryan, *Fish Out of Water*, 45.
144. McDonald, *"To Each His Own"*, 11; Newfoundland, *Report of the Commission on Fishery Matters* (St. John's: The Evening Herald Print, 1915), 5; TRPAD, MG 73, Box 1, File 2, William Earle to G.C. Fearn, 7 Sept. 1909.
145. DF, *Annual Report*, 1894, 19; DF, *Annual Report*, 1896, 28.
146. *ET*, "Our Staple Product," 28 June 1897, 3. See also *EM*, "Symposium on 'What should be done in Newfoundland?' No. 3," 8 July 1887, 4; *EM*, "The Credit System; Its Evils and Its Cure," 8 July 1887, 4; *ET*, "Our Staple Product," 28 June 1897, 3; TRPAD, MG 73, Box 1, File 9, A. Solling to M.G. Winter, 21 Dec. 1909; TRPAD, MG 73, Box 10, File 5, "Memorandum on the Fisheries of Newfoundland," 18 Dec. 1918; *ET*, "The Fisheries of Nfld. — Bait Depots," 15 Oct. 1923, 8; TRPAD, MG 73, Box 23, File 1, John Bishop to Board of Trade, 22 Jan. 1931; ibid., GN 127, Box 1, "Evidence: Mr. Patrick Clancy," 16 Apr. 1936.

147. DMF, *Annual Report,* 1908, 8.
148. Alexander, *Decay of Trade*, 26.
149. *ET*, "Are We Slaves to an Accursed System?" 11 July 1925, 6; TRPAD, GN 127, Box 1, "Evidence: George Hawes," 28 Mar. 1936.
150. J.H.S. to Ian and Sheila, 8 Feb. 1934 in Neary, *White Tie*, 27.
151. EPR Kirby and Company, Management Consultants Group, Inc., *Historic and Cultural Significance of Dildo Island* (n.p., 1995). Available at CNS, MUN.
152. *DN*, "The Herring Fishery of Newfoundland: Practical Suggestions by a Practical Man," 26 Sept. 1914, 7.
153. TRPAD, GN 127, Box 1, "Evidence: Dr. Norman L. Macpherson," 26 May 1936.
154. Ibid.
155. Ibid. He went on: "He doesn't know that a hogshead of light salt and a hogshead of heavy salt are different things altogether. . . . He knows in a vague sort of way but he doesn't know properly. The difference between Torrevieja and Cadiz is five to seven."
156. *ET*, "The Fishery and the Fish Markets," 1 Dec. 1908, 3.
157. Ibid.
158. *ET*, "Subject of Dry Codfish," 19 July 1897, 4.
159. TRPAD, MG 73, Box 2, File 13, Assistant Collector to G.C. Fearn, 3 Nov. 1909.
160. E. Chappell, *Voyage of His Majesty's Ship Rosamond to Newfoundland and the Southern Coast of Labrador* (London: J. Mawman, 1818), 222.
161. Cadigan, *Hope*, 42; H. Innis, *The Cod Fishery: The History of an International Economy* (Toronto: University of Toronto Press, 1954), 306.
162. L.G. Small, "The Interrelationship of Work and Talk in a Newfoundland Fishing Community," PhD thesis (Department of Folklore and Anthropology, University of Pennsylvania, 1979), 166; Ryan, *Fish Out of Water*, 22.
163. Newfoundland, *Report of the Commission of Enquiry*, 67.
164. Ibid.
165. Crosby, *Measure of Reality*, 99–224; Poovey, *History of the Modern Fact*, 29–91.
166. J. Murray, *The Commercial Crisis in Newfoundland: Cause, Consequence and Cure* (St. John's: J.W. Withers, 1895), 4. For an analysis, see D. Banoub, "Black Monday, 1894: Saltfish, Credit, and the Ecology of Politics in Newfoundland," *Atlantic Studies* 17, no. 2 (2020): 227–43.
167. *ET*, "In Their Own Hands," 2 July 1920, 6.

168. Great Britain, *Newfoundland Royal Report*, 105.
169. TRPAD, GN 1/3/A, Box 44, Despatch 328, Robert Bond to Cavendish Boyle, 4 Mar. 1903.

Chapter 3

1. *ET*, "Fish Scale Studies," 7 Mar. 1919, 8.
2. Harvey, *Newfoundland As It Was*, 160.
3. *EM*, "Symposium on 'What should be done in Newfoundland?' No. 1," 4 July 1887, 4
4. M. Baker, A.B. Dickinson, and C.W. Sanger, "Adolph Nielsen: Norwegian Influence on Newfoundland Fisheries in the Late 19th-Early 20th Century," *Newfoundland Quarterly* 27, no. 2 (1992): 25–35; Harvey, *Newfoundland As It Was*, 160; Rose, *Cod*, 316-18; Ryan, *Fish Out of Water*, 70–74.
5. Fisheries Commission (FC), *Annual Report*, 1892, 5.
6. M. Harvey, "The Artificial Propagation of Marine Food Fishes and Edible Crustaceans," *Transactions of the Royal Society of Canada* 10, no. 4 (1892): 17–37; K. Hewitt, "The Newfoundland Fishery and State Intervention in the Nineteenth Century: The Fisheries Commission, 1888–1893," *Newfoundland Studies* 9, no. 1 (1993): 62.
7. J.A. Hutchings, B. Neis, and P. Ripley, "The 'Nature' of Cod, *Gadus morhua*," in R. Ommer, ed., *The Resilient Outport: Ecology, Economy, and Society in Rural Newfoundland* (St. John's: ISER Books, 2002), 149–52.
8. *EM*, "Necessity of Fish Hatching," 15 Sept. 1888, 4.
9. K. Hewitt, "Exploring Uncharted Waters: Government's Role in the Development of Newfoundland's Cod, Lobster and Herring Fisheries, 1888–1913," MA thesis (Department of History, MUN, 1992), 7.
10. Harvey, *Newfoundland As It Was*, 160.
11. *Journal of the House of Assembly of Newfoundland* (*JHA*), 1887, 109.
12. *JHA*, 1887, 153.
13. For his report, see *JHA*, 1877, 730–54.
14. FC, *Annual Report*, 1888, 5.
15. *EM*, "Hatching Codfish — A Superintendent Appointed," 15 Sept. 1888, 4.
16. FC, *Annual Report*, 1888, 7–18. The following discussion of the Fisheries Commission is indebted to Baker et al., "Adolph Nielsen"; Hewitt, "The Newfoundland Fishery"; and L. Whiteway, "Inception of the Newfoundland

Department of Fisheries," *Newfoundland Quarterly* 45, no. 2 (1956): 29–43. For information on Nielsen's visit to Newfoundland, with Inspector Jens D. Dahl, see *EM*, "A Visit of Norwegian Officials," 30 July 1887, 4.

17. *EM*, "The Science of Fish Culture, Second Article," 5 Mar. 1889, 4.
18. Department of Fisheries (DF), *Annual Report*, 1893, 41.
19. *EM*, "Artificial Hatching of Codfish," 1 Aug. 1887, 4.
20. Allard, "Spender Fullerton Baird"; Smith, *Scaling Fisheries*.
21. *EM*, "The Science of Fish Culture," 2 Mar. 1889, 4.
22. Harvey, "Artificial Propagation," 20.
23. C.E. Nash, *The History of Aquaculture* (Danvers, MA: Blackwell Publishing, 2011), 18–21; R.R. Stickney, *Aquaculture: An Introductory Text* (Wallingford: CABI, 2009), 6.
24. Harvey, "Artificial Propagation," 17. For a discussion of modern aquaculture, see D. Kinsey, "'Seeding the Water as the Earth': The Epicenter and Peripheries of a Western Aquacultural Revolution," *Environmental History* 11, no. 3 (2006): 527–66.
25. Harvey, "Artificial Propagation," 29–30; Nash, *History of Aquaculture*, 54–56.
26. Kinsey, "'Seeding the Water'," 531. Promising to permit the "seeding of the waters with fish, as one seeds the earth with grain," the processes gelled with the Emperor's imperialistic ideology of control over nature.
27. V. Schwach, "The Impact of Artificial Hatching of Cod on Marine Research," *Historisch-Meereskundliches Jahrbuch* 5 (1999): 27–47; P. Solemdal, E. Dahl, D.S. Danielssen, and E. Moksness, "The Cod Hatchery in Flodevigen — Background and Realities," in E. Dahl, D.S. Danielssen, E. Moksness, and P. Solemdal, eds., *The Propagation of Cod Gadus Morhua L* (Arendal: Institute of Marine Research Flødevigen Biological Station, 1984).
28. G.O. Sars, "Report of Practical and Scientific Investigations of the Cod Fisheries Near the Loffoden Islands, Made during the Years 1864–1869," in S.F. Baird, ed., *Report of the Commissioner for 1877, Part V* (Washington: Government Printing Office, 1879), 565–90. See also T.D. Smith, J. Gjøsæter, N.C. Stenseth, M.O. Kittilsen, D.S. Danielssen, and S. Tveite, "A Century of Manipulating Recruitment in Coastal Cod Populations: The Flødevigen Experience," *ICES Marine Science Symposia* 215 (2002): 402–15; T. Svåsand, T.S. Kristiansen, T. Pedersen, A. Salvanes, R. Engelsen, G. Nævdal, and M. Nødtvedt, "The Enhancement of Cod Stocks," *Fish and Fisheries* 1, no. 2 (2000): 173–205.

29. Sars, "Report," 576.
30. Ibid.
31. Ibid., 578.
32. Allard, "Spender Fullerton Baird"; W.S. March, *Some Piscatorial Notes and Suggestions* (St. John's: News Job Print, 1895).
33. Allard, "Spender Fullerton Baird;" *Boston Evening Transcript*, "How Cod Are Hatched," 18 Mar. 1896, 7
34. G.M. Dannevig, "Apparatus and Methods Employed at the Marine Fish Hatchery at Flödevig, Norway," *Bulletin of the Bureau of Fisheries* 28, no. 2 (1910): 799–810; G.M. Dannevig, "The Utility of Sea-Fish Hatching," *Bulletin of the Bureau of Fisheries* 28, no. 2 (1910): 811–16; Solemdal et al., "The Cod Hatchery."
35. For a more exhaustive history of the Dildo Island hatchery, see Baker et al., "Adolph Nielsen"; Hewitt, "The Newfoundland Fishery"; and Whiteway, "Inception."
36. *EM*, "Cod Hatching. Mr. Nielsen's Expected Arrival," 8 Jan. 1889, 4. Regarding Nielsen's difficulty securing his release from the Norwegian government, see *EM*, "Our New Superintendent of Fisheries. Mr. Adolphe Nielsen," 30 Nov. 1888, 4.
37. *JHA*, 1889, 618.
38. *EM*, "The Fisheries Commission — Mr. Nielsen's Report," 25 Mar. 1889, 4. For Nielsen's full report, see *ET*, "Report By Mr. Adolph Nielson [*sic*] of His Journey around the Heads of Conception, Trinity and Placentia Bays," 15 Apr. 1889, 3.
39. *ET*, "Report by Mr. Adolph Nielson," 15 Apr. 1889, 3.
40. Ibid.
41. *EM*, "Dildo Codfish Hatchery," 2 May 1889, 4.
42. FC, *Annual Report*, 1889, 5. See also TRPAD, GN 2/5/A, File 32-k, W.M. Macfarlane to A.W. Piccott, 29 Apr. 1911.
43. FC, *Annual Report*, 1889, 9–12.
44. Ibid., 1890, 5.
45. Ibid., 9.
46. Ibid., 1891, 16–17.
47. Ibid., 18; M. Harvey, "The Newfoundland Fisheries Commission," in D.W. Prowse, *A History of Newfoundland* (Portugal Cove-St. Philip's: Boulder Publications, 2007 [1895]), 648; Memorial University Archives (MUNA),

COLL-307, File 10.06.089, "Adolph Nielson, July 19, 1962." For a discussion of the Norwegian method, see Dannevig, "Apparatus."

48. FC, *Annual Report*, 1891, 18.
49. Ibid., 22.
50. Ibid.
51. DF, *Annual Report*, 1896, 18–19.
52. *Acts of the General Assembly of Newfoundland* (henceforth *Statutes*), 1893, 30–32.
53. DF, *Annual Report*, 1894, 5–6.
54. For an in-depth analysis, see Banoub, "Black Monday, 1894."
55. *DN*, "From The Daily News of Over Sixty Years Ago," 26 Oct. 1956, 5.
56. TRPAD, GN1/3/A, Box 25, File 1, George H. Emerson to Governor Terence O'Brien, 10 Dec. 1894.
57. MUNA, COLL-237, Box 23, File 9.01.042, "The Newfoundland Bank Trials," 565.
58. *ET*, "Week-end Notes," 19 May 1917, 4
59. EPR, "Historic," n.p. Available at CNS, MUN. This report contains three letters written by Nielsen to Dannevig, and translated by Knut A. Nygaard, dated 1 Nov. 1889, 24 Feb. 1890, and 22 July 1892. They do not provide the provenance of these letters.
60. *JHA*, 1889, 620; *The Daily Colonist,* "An Inconsistent Position," 26 Jan. 1891, 4. Regarding the "non-political" nature of the Fisheries Commission, see *EM*, "The 'Telegram' on the Fisheries Commission," 24 Aug. 1887, 4; *EM*, "The Fisheries Commission," 5 July 1889, 4; *EM*, "Cod Hatching Once More," 6 Aug. 1889, 4.
61. *EH*, "A Word of Advice to the 'Telegram,'" 30 Sept. 1890, 4
62. EPR, "Historic," n.p.
63. Ibid.
64. *Proceedings of the House of Assembly of Newfoundland* (*PHA*), 1914, 461.
65. DF, *Annual Report*, 1895, 16.
66. Ibid., 1896, 20.
67. *ET*, "Editorial Notes," 29 Apr. 1896, 4. Nielsen would return to Newfoundland the following year as principal investor and manager of a private Norwegian–Newfoundland owned whaling firm, the Cabot Steam Whaling Co. Ltd. See also *ET*, "Our Genial Friend," 10 May 1898, 4; *ET*, "Legislative Council Proceedings," 3 May 1902, 3. On 1 November 1903, Nielsen was found dead

from an asthma attack in his room at the Crosbie Hotel. *ET*, "Found Dead," 2 Nov. 1903, 4.

68. DF, *Annual Report*, 1897, 46; *ET*, "Our Fisheries Department," 24 Aug. 1896, 4.
69. *ET*, "Personal Notes," 8 June 1903, 3; *TR*, "Fish Hatchery," 13 Jan. 1906, 4.
70. TRPAD, GN2/5A, File 32-k, A.W. Piccott to R. Watson, 6 May 1911. See also *ET*, "Here and There," 1 July 1911, 4.
71. Ibid., GN 1/3/A, Box 59, Despatch 163, R.H. Anstruther to Wm. MacGregor, 20 Oct. 1906.
72. F.N. Clarke, *The Newfoundland Bait Service: Historical Notes on the Catching and Preservation of the Bait Fishes* (n.p., 1969); L.C. Outerbridge, *The Bait Supply: Observations and Suggestions Submitted to the Fishery Exporter's Association* (n.p., 1933). Both available at CNS, MUN. TRPAD, GN 34/2, Box 146, File: Fisheries — International and Scientific Investigation, 1931–1932, A.G. Huntsman to H.B. Clyde Lake, 29 Apr. 1932.
73. DF, *Annual Report*, 1904, 8. See also *DN*, "The Herring Fishery of Newfoundland: Practical Suggestions by a Practical Man," 26 Sept. 1914, 7.
74. *ET*, "Cold Storage," 8 Oct. 1903, 3
75. *ET*, "Cold Storage," 7 Oct. 1903, 3.
76. Ibid.
77. FRC, *Annual Report*, 1936–37, 10; TRPAD, MG 73, Box 9, File 4 (1918), E.A. Payn to Fred H. Hue, 20 May 1918.
78. *PHA*, 1922, 115.
79. Quoted in Rose, *Cod*, 150, n. 64.
80. Outerbridge, *Bait Supply*, 2.
81. Ibid., 4.
82. TRPAD, MG 73, Box 3, File 4, William C. Job to G.C. Fearn, 25 July 1911. See also *ET*, "Assurance of a Bait Supply," 4 Nov. 1933, 6.
83. *DN*, "The Herring Fishery of Newfoundland: Practical Suggestions by a Practical Man," 26 Sept. 1914, 7. Reprinted as W. Duff, *The Fisheries of Newfoundland: Lecture Delivered in St. John's by Mr. Walter Duff of the Fishery Board for Scotland* (St. John's: n.p., 1914). Available at CNS, MUN.
84. *ET*, "Editorial Notes," 4 June 1901, 4.
85. TRPAD, GN 34/2, Box 146, File: Cold Storage 1931 (2), James Nerge to H.B. Clyde Lake, 21 May 1931.
86. Ibid., MG 73, Box 5, File 4 (1914), Thos. Fitzpatrick to John S. Munn, 28 Jan. 1914.

87. FC, *Annual Report*, 1890, 22.
88. Ibid., 1891, 33–34.
89. Ibid.
90. DF, *Annual Report*, 1893, 248.
91. Hewitt, "Exploring Uncharted Waters," 48.
92. DMF, *Annual Report*, 1902, 10.
93. Ibid.
94. Ibid., 1904, 13.
95. Harvey, *Newfoundland As It Was*, 167–68. For more exhaustive accounts of the history of cold storage, see Hewitt, "Exploring," 191–222; R.G. Hong, "'An Agency for the Common Weal': The Newfoundland Board of Trade, 1909–1915," MA thesis (Department of History, Memorial University of Newfoundland, 1998), 107–16; W.G. Reeves, "'Our Yankee Cousins': Modernization and the Newfoundland–American Relationship, 1898–1910," PhD thesis (Department of History, University of Maine, Orono, 1987), 283–300.
96. DF, *Annual Report*, 1893, 17.
97. Ibid. For more on this method, see M.H.A. Charles Way's 1902 report on cold storage in DMF, *Annual Report*, 1902: Appendix, 7–13.
98. Harvey, *Newfoundland As It Was*, 167.
99. DF, *Annual Report*, 1894, 13.
100. *PHA*, 1914, 463.
101. Reeves, "'Our Yankee Cousins'," 284.
102. *JHA*, 1898, 103.
103. *ET*, "Freezing Fortune Bay Fish," 30 Nov. 1898, 4.
104. DMF, *Annual Report*, 1902, 10.
105. TRPAD, MG 73, Box 3, File 3, Alan Goodridge to G.C. Fearn, 5 Oct. 1911.
106. *ET*, "House of Assembly Proceedings," 9 July 1903, 3; TRPAD, GN 1/3/A, Box 51, Despatch 123, W.H. Horwood to Alfred Lyttelton, 23 May 1904; and TRPAD, GN 1/3/A, Box 51, Despatch 123 for a series of communications between Jas. Wright and Robert Bond regarding the contract, especially: Wright to Bond, 31 July 1903.
107. *ET*, "Legislative Council," 6 Apr. 1905, 3; *JHA*, 1904, 7–13; *Statutes*, 1904, 6–14.
108. TRPAD, GN 8.9, Folder 2, E.P. Morris to E.J. Greenstreet, 23 Nov. 1909.
109. E.P. Morris, "Cold Storage in Its Application to the Newfoundland Fisheries," *Newfoundland Quarterly* 22, no. 2 (1922): 30–31.

110. S.J.R. Noel, *Politics in Newfoundland* (Toronto: University of Toronto Press, 1971), 76.
111. For communications with J.J. Lane of Boston Cold Storage, see TRPAD, GN 8.9, Folder 1. His proposal is outlined in Lane to Morris, 27 Dec. 1909. For communications with cold storage expert E.J. Greenstreet, see ibid., Folder 2. His proposal is outlined in Greenstreet to Morris, 14 Oct. 1909. For more information on Greenstreet, see ibid., MG 73, Box 2, File 7, E.P. Morris to G.C. Fearn, 15 Oct. 1910; ibid., File 3, E.J. Greenstreet to G.C. Fearn, 9 Sept. 1910. For the 1911 Act to Encourage the Establishment of Cold Storage Plants in This Colony, see *Statutes*, 1911, 115–21.
112. *Statutes*, 1911, 115–21; TRPAD, GN 1/3/A, Box 74, Despatch 42, An Act to Encourage the Establishment of Cold Storage Plants in This Colony, 27 Dec. 1910. See also *Newfoundland's Fisheries; 'Richer by Far Than all the Gold Mines of Peru,' As Lord Bacon Declared Three Centuries Ago* (n.p., 1910), 13. Available at CNS, MUN.
113. The Bait Act of 1887 restricted the sale of bait from Newfoundland waters to foreign fishers, especially French Bank fishers. The 1904 Department of Fisheries *Annual Report* (p. 11) summarizes the Bait Act's geopolitical logic: "Newfoundland, so long as she controls the supply of bait fishes, has at her command an immensely powerful lever which can at any time be used, if necessary, against her rivals in North American waters to limit their catch." For legal opinions regarding whether the agreement contravened the Bait Act, see TRPAD, MG 73, Box 3, File 3, John Fenelon to W.G. Gosling, 25 Feb. 1911; ibid., File 6, James McGrath to W.G. Gosling, 25 Feb. 1911; ibid., File 7, E.P. Morris to W.G. Gosling, 18 Feb. 1911; ibid., GN 1/3/A, Box 74, Despatch 42, Ralph Williams to L.V. Harcourt, 16 Mar. 1911. For a general summary of the issue, see *ET*, "The Cold Storage Agreement and the Bait Act," 28 Feb. 1911, 4. Regarding the issue of concessions, see *ET*, "Fishermen, Take Warning," 17 Feb. 1911, 6.
114. Quoted in Hong, "An Agency," 113.
115. TRPAD, GN 8.57, Folder 1, E.P. Morris to unaddressed, 9 May 1912.
116. *ET*, "Bait and Ice for Americans," 2 July 1912, 4; *ET*, "Bait Concession to Foreigners," 2 July 1912, 4; *ET*, "Those Bait Concessions," 5 July 1912, 4; *ET*, "What About Those Concession to Americans?" 7 Oct. 1912, 4; *ET*, "Taken to Task," 1 Nov. 1912, 4;

117. *ET*, "Cold Storage Concession," 24 June 1912, 4.; *ET*, "Busy for the Americans," 26 July 1912, 8. For more information on the Booth Fisheries Co. experiments, see *ET*, "Booth Co. in Newfoundland," 12 Aug. 1912, 6; *ET*, "Booth Fisheries Co. Investigations," 28 Aug. 1912, 5; *ET*, "Notes and Comments," 20 May 1913, 4.
118. *ET*, "Some Morris Fizzles," 3 Sept. 1913, 4.
119. DMF, *Annual Report*, 1914, 15; Newfoundland, *Report of the Commission of Enquiry*, 24.
120. W.C. Stockwood, "Clouston, John William (1869–1956)," in J.R. Smallwood and R.D.W. Pitt, eds., *Encyclopedia of Newfoundland and Labrador, Volume 1* (St. John's: Newfoundland Book Publishers, 1981), 455.
121. Innis, *The Cod Fishery*, 465.
122. Newfoundland Board of Trade (BT), *Annual Report*, 1928, 21; Newfoundland, *Report of the Commission of Enquiry*, 24.
123. L.A. Parsons, "Bait Fish," in J.R. Smallwood and R.D.W. Pitt, eds., *Encyclopedia of Newfoundland and Labrador, Volume 1* (St. John's: Newfoundland Book Publishers, 1981), 115–16.
124. P. Neary, *Newfoundland in the North Atlantic World, 1929–1949* (Montreal and Kingston: McGill-Queen's University Press, 1988), 13.
125. Great Britain, *Newfoundland Royal Report.*
126. *Statutes*, 1933, 46–47 181–88.
127. Outerbridge, *Bait Supply*; T.R. Wingate, *A Study of the Newfoundland Bait Service, Volume 1* (n.p., 1971), 1. Available at CNS, MUN.
128. *ET*, "Assurance of a Bait Supply," 4 Nov. 1933, 6. See also Clarke, *The Newfoundland Bait Service*; Parsons, "Bait Fish."
129. Department of Natural Resources (DNR), *Annual Report*, 1934, 2. See also TRPAD, MG 73, Box 32, File 25, Secretary to Department of Natural Resources, 18 Nov. 1937.
130. Commission of Government (CG), *Annual Report*, 1937, 20.
131. DF, *Annual Report*, 1893, 41.
132. Smith et al., "A Century of Manipulating Recruitment," 403.
133. The quotation is from *DN*, "Great Success of Cod Hatching at Dildo," 16 June 1894, 4. See also DF, *Annual Report*, 1893, 5; DF, *Annual Report*, 1895, 10; Harvey, *Newfoundland As It Was*, 165; *Trade Review (TR)*, "Editorial Notes," 29 July 1893, 1; *DN*, "Codfish at Dildo," 5 July 1894, 4; *EH*, "Successful Operations in Lobster and Cod Hatchery. Mr. Nielsen's Report," 26 Sept.

1890, 4; *EH*, "Cod Hatchery at Dildo," 6 Aug. 1895, 4; TRPAD, GN 1/3/A, Box 29, Despatch 160, W.S. March to H.E. McCallum, 3 July 1899.

134. *EH*, "Cod Hatchery at Dildo," 6 Aug. 1895, 4.
135. Alexander, *Decay of Trade*; M. Wright, *A Fishery for Modern Times: The State and the Industrialization of the Newfoundland Fishery, 1934–1968* (Toronto: Oxford University Press, 2001).
136. DF, *Annual Report*, 1893, 41.
137. D. Harvey, *The Enigma of Capital and the Crises of Capitalism* (Oxford: Oxford University Press, 2010), 123.
138. Harvey, "Artificial Propagation," 20.
139. Ibid.

Chapter 4

1. *DN*, "Fire Destroys Bay Bulls Plant," 20 Apr. 1937, 3; *ET*, "Fire Destroys Fisheries Research Station at Bay Bulls," 24 Apr. 1937, 7.
2. *ET*, "Fire Destroys Fisheries Research Station at Bay Bulls," 24 Apr. 1937, 7.
3. *DN*, "Fire Destroys Bay Bulls Plant," 20 Apr. 1937, 3.
4. *ET*, "Fishery Station at Bay Bulls Destroyed by Fire Last Night," 20 Apr. 1937, 6; *ET*, "Fire at Bay Bulls Still Smouldering," 22 Apr. 1937, 5.
5. *ET*, "Fire Destroys Fisheries Research Station at Bay Bulls," 24 Apr. 1937, 7.
6. *DN*, "Cause of Fire Is Not Yet Known," 21 Apr. 1937, 3.
7. Ibid.
8. *ET*, "Bay Bulls Fire," 21 Apr. 1937, 4.
9. DF, *Annual Report*, 1895, 3.
10. Ibid. See also FC, *Annual Report*, 1893, 22.
11. FC, *Annual Report*, 1891, 12.
12. Ibid., 48.
13. Ibid., 47.
14. Baker et al., "Adolph Nielsen," 28–29; FC, *Annual Report*, 1892, 41; R. Rompkey, *Grenfell of Labrador: A Biography* (Toronto: University of Toronto Press, 1991), 46–47; *TR*, "Editorial Notes," 31 Oct. 1892, 1.
15. DF, *Annual Report*, 1894, 17.
16. Ibid., 1895, 67.

17. FC, *Annual Report*, 1892, 54–55.
18. Ibid., 1891, 55–56; ibid., 1892, 54–58.
19. Ibid., 1892, 57.
20. Ibid., 1891, 56.
21. DF, *Annual Report*, 1893, 21–22.
22. S. Elden, "Missing the Point: Globalization, Deterritorialization and the Space of the World," *Transactions of the Institute of British Geographers* 30, no. 1 (2005): 8–19.
23. FC, *Annual Report*, 1892, 43.
24. Ibid.
25. DMF, 1910, 47.
26. Baker et al., "Adolph Nielsen," 28. See also TRPAD, GN 34/2, Box 146, File: Colonial Secretary, 1930–1932, Deputy Minister to A. Barnes, 27 Jan. 1931.
27. DMF, 1914, 4.
28. *ET*, "The Fishery and the Fish Markets," 30 Nov. 1908, 5; Noel, *Politics*, 34.
29. Cadigan, *Newfoundland and Labrador*, 177; Hong, "Agency," 22-24; McDonald, *"To Each His Own"*, 155.
30. The quote is taken from Noel, *Politics*, 65. I will return to the formation of the FPU and the Board of Trade in more detail in Chapter 5.
31. Cadigan, *Newfoundland and Labrador*, 179–82; Coaker, *Twenty Years*, 44–63; Noel, *Politics*, 98–99; *Statutes*, 1909, 7. See also *ET*, "The Fishery and the Fish Markets," 30 Nov. 1908, 5.
32. *ET*, "Study Fish and the Fisheries," 27 Sept. 1910, 7.
33. *ET*, "Survey Ship Arrives," 4 July 1910, 6; *ET*, "Dr. Hjort Lectures," 5 Nov. 1914, 3; A. Selwyn-Brown, "The Atlantic Voyage of the 'Michael Sars,'" *Newfoundland Quarterly* 8, no. 1 (1913): 1–3. For more on Hjort, see J. Hubbard, "Johan Hjort: The Canadian Fisheries Expedition, International Scientific Networks, and the Challenge of Modernization," *ICES Journal of Marine Science* 71, no. 8 (2014): 2000–07; V. Schwach, "A Sea Change: Johan Hjort and the Natural Fluctuations in the Fish Stocks," *ICES Journal of Marine Science* 71, no. 8 (2014): 1993–99.
34. TRPAD, MG 73, Box 3, File 9, M.B. Simonsen to G.C. Fearn, 29 Aug. 1911; ibid., File 14, unaddressed mimeographed letter, 4 Sept. 1911. See also M. Baker and S. Ryan, "The Newfoundland Fishery Research Commission, 1930–1934," in J.E. Candow and C. Corbin, eds., *How Deep Is the Ocean? Historical Essays on Canada's Atlantic Fishery* (Sydney, NS: University College of Cape Breton

Press, 1997), 161; DMF, *Annual Report*, 1911, 35; A.N. Rygg, *Norwegians in New York, 1825–1925* (Brooklyn, NY: The Norwegian News Company, 1941).

35. Dominions Royal Commission (DRC), *Royal Commission on the Natural Resources, Trade, and Legislation of Certain Portions of His Majesty's Dominions Minutes of Evidence Taken in Newfoundland in 1914* (London: Eyre and Spottiswoode, 1915), 49; W.A. Munn, *The Cod Liver Oil Industry in Newfoundland* (St. John's: W.A. Munn, Manufacturers and Exporters, 1925), 11.

36. DMF, *Annual Report*, 1914, 11.

37. Duff, *The Fisheries of Newfoundland*. For reports of his lecture, see *DN*, "The Fisheries of Newfoundland: Last Night's Lecture by Mr. Duff," 26 Sept. 1914, 4; *DN*, "The Herring Fishery of Newfoundland: Practical Suggestions by a Practical Man," 26 Sept. 1914, 7.

38. Hjort, "Fluctuations," 1–228.

39. Hubbard, "Johan Hjort," 2005; Hubbard, *A Science on the Scales*, 75–78.

40. DMF, *Annual Report*, 1914, 4–6; *DN*, "Last Night's Lecture," 5 Nov. 1914, 3; *ET*, "Fish Expert Here," 3 Nov. 1914, 5; *ET*, "Dr. Hjort Lectures," 5 Nov. 1914, 3.

41. Newfoundland, *Report of the Commission on Fishery Matters*, 4.

42. Baker and Ryan, "The Newfoundland Fishery Research Commission," 162; BT, *Annual Report*, 1915, 6; TRPAD, MG 73, Box 6, File 6, W.A. Munn to W.S. Monroe, 7 June 1915.

43. Quotation from TRPAD, MG 73, Box 10, File 5, "Memorandum on the Fisheries of Newfoundland," 18 Dec. 1918, 6. See also DMF, *Annual Report*, 1916, 11; TRPAD, GN 8.58, "Memorandum On the Shortage of Fish and the Practicability of Obtaining a Supply from Newfoundland," Bowles and Sons, Printers, n.d; ibid., P. Gilmour to L.V. Harcourt, 11 Feb. 1915; ibid., GN 8.60, Frederick Foss & Son to E.P. Thomson, 20 Sept. 1917.

44. Ibid., MG 73, Box 10, File 5, "Memorandum on the Fisheries of Newfoundland," 18 Dec. 1918, 6. See also *ET*, "Newfoundland's Industries," 25 July 1923, 6.

45. TRPAD, MG 73, Box 10, File 5, "Memorandum on the Fisheries of Newfoundland," 18 Dec. 1918, 5. See also ibid., Henry L. Riseley to E.P. Morris, 9 Jan. 1919.

46. *ET*, "Fishermen Hold Demonstration," 14 Nov. 1922, 7. See also TRPAD, MG 73, Box 11, File 13, "Minute," 6 Mar. 1920.

47. I will return to the "Coaker Regulations" in more detail in the following chapter. For a detailed analysis, see McDonald, *"To Each His Own"*, 87–105.

48. *ET*, "Worthy of Support," 6 May 1920, 6.

49. TRPAD, MG 73, Box 11, File 11, "Reports RE — Fish Export Regulations," 3/11-3/20.
50. *ET*, "Fish Scale Studies," 7 Mar. 1919, 8.
51. A.G. Huntsman was one of Canada's leading fisheries biologists. He acted as curator (1911–19) and director (1919–34) of the St. Andrews Biological Research Station, and director of the Fisheries Experimental Station at Halifax from 1924 to 1928. He was also affiliated with University of Toronto, supervising a number of postgraduate students in the Department of Zoology. See J.M. Hubbard, "Home Sweet Home? A.G. Huntsman and the Homing Behaviour of Canadian Atlantic Salmon," *Acadiensis* 19, no. 2 (1990), 49–71.
52. Finley, *All the Fish in the Sea*, 84–87.
53. DMF, *Annual Report*, 1922, 33; S.S. Zilva, J.C. Drummond, and M. Graham, "The Relation of the Vitamin A Potency of the Liver Oil to the Sexual Condition and Age of the Cod," *Biochemical Journal* 18 (1924): 178–81. Dr. Zilva, a professor at the Lister Institute of Preventive Medicine, was an early pioneer in vitamin research. I will return to his work in Chapter 6. See also *ET*, "Appreciation of Dr. S.S. Zilva and Mr. Graham," 5 Sept. 1922, 8; TRPAD, MG 73, Box 13, File 10, Edgar Bowring to E.A. Payn, 5 July 1921; ibid., Edgar Bowring to E.A. Payn, 18 July 1921.
54. M. Graham, *Report to the Director of Fishery Investigations Comprising Observations on the Natural History of the Newfoundland Shore Cod* (Lowestoft: Fisheries Laboratory, 1922). See also Hutchings et al., "The 'Nature' of Cod," 154–55.
55. DMF, *Annual Report*, 1923, 23–24; *ET*, "The Ocean around Newfoundland," 10 Feb. 1925, 3. The results are published as A.G. Huntsman, *The Ocean around Newfoundland* (n.p., 1925).
56. J.M. Hubbard, "Mediating the North Atlantic Environment: Fisheries Biologists, Technology, and Marine Spaces," *Environmental History* 18, no. 1 (2013): 93; North American Council on Fishery Investigations (NACFI), *North American Council on Fishery Investigations Proceedings 1921–1930*, No. 1 (Ottawa: F.A. Acland, 1932), 3–4; Rozwadowski, *The Sea Knows No Boundaries*, 101.
57. NACFI, *Proceedings 1921–1930*, 4.
58. Huntsman, *The Ocean around Newfoundland*, 8.
59. Ibid., 10.
60. Ibid., 15.

61. Ibid., 17.
62. Ibid.
63. Graham, *Report*, 37.
64. For more on Davies's lecture, see *ET*, "Fish Scale Studies," 7 Mar. 1919, 8. For the lecture by Huntsman and Gardiner, see *DN*, "Board of Trade Hears Lecture on Fisheries Research," 19 Sept. 1923, 4. For Taylor's lecture, see J.A. Taylor, *A Report on the Development of the Fisheries of Newfoundland* (n.p., 1924); *ET*, "Address to the Board of Trade on Our Fisheries," 26 Aug. 1924, 4.
65. DMF, *Annual Report*, 1921, 18.
66. M. Macleod, *A Bridge Built Halfway: A History of Memorial University College, 1925–1950* (Montreal and Kingston: McGill-Queen's University Press, 1990), 22.
67. MUNA, President's Office, Box PO-9, file "Biology, JLP," Paton to Russell, n.d. Quoted in Baker and Ryan, "The Newfoundland Fishery Research Commission," 163.
68. Baker and Ryan, "The Newfoundland Fishery Research Commission," 165. For details of Weiss's career, see *Nature*, "News and Views," 156 (27 Oct. 1945): 500.
69. S. Cadigan, "Science, Industry, and Fishers in Fisheries Management: The Experience of Newfoundland and Labrador, 1890s–1990s," *Studia Atlantica* 13 (2009): 81–82; Macleod, *A Bridge Built Halfway*, 62; Rose, *Cod*, 338.
70. Macleod, *A Bridge Built Halfway*, 62; Rose, *Cod*, 338.
71. *Western Star (WS)*, "Scientist Accepts Professorship," 30 June 1926, 1.
72. Attendees included Dr. H.B. Bigelow of the Harvard Museum, Elmer Higgins and O.E. Sette of the US Fishery Bureau, Canadian Director of Fisheries Mr. W.A Found, and A.G. Huntsman. See NACFI, *North*, 5. *DN*, "North American Committee on Fishery Investigation," 10 July 1926, 4; TRPAD, MG 73, Box 18, File 2, A.G. Huntsman to D. James Davies, 21 June 1926.
73. DMF, *Annual Report*, 1926, 34.
74. *DN*, "Prof. Sleggs' Address to Rotary Club," 26 Oct. 1926, 7.
75. G.W. Jeffers, *Bulletin No 18: Observations on the Cod-fishery in the Strait of Belle Isle* (Toronto: Biological Board of Canada, 1931). See also *WS*, "Scientific Investigation of Nfld. Fisheries," 14 Aug. 1929, 1.
76. Quoted in Baker and Ryan, "The Newfoundland Fishery Research Commission," 165; Rose, *Cod*, 339.

77. I.M. Drummond, *British Economic Policy and the Empire, 1919–1939* (London: George Allen and Unwin, 1972), 65–67; L.C.A. Knowles and C.M. Knowles, *The Economic Development of the British Overseas Empire, Vol. II: Comparative View of Dominion Problems, Canada* (New York: Routledge, 2005 [1930]), 78–79. For the Newfoundland perspective, see *ET*, "Work of the Imperial Economic Committee," 29 May 1925, 12; TRPAD, MG 73, Box 17, File 6, W.A. Munn and John Clouston to Tasker Cook, 21 May 1925; ibid., GN 34/2, Box 146, File: Cod Liver Oil, W.A. Munn et al. to H.B. Clyde Lake, 12 Oct. 1931.
78. F. Barnes, "Bringing Another Empire Alive? The Empire Marketing Board and the Construction of Dominion Identity, 1926–33," *Journal of Imperial and Commonwealth History* 42, no. 1 (2014): 61–85; U. Kothari, "Trade, Consumption and Development Alliances: The Historical Legacy of the Empire Marketing Board Poster Campaign," *Third World Quarterly* 35, no. 1 (2014): 43–64; D. Meredith, "Imperial Images: The Empire Marketing Board, 1926–1932," *History Today* 37, no. 1 (1987): 30–36.
79. BT, *Annual Report*, 1927, 30; TRPAD, MG 73, Box 19, File 7, A.H. Murray to J.F. Meehan, 12 Sept. 1927.
80. Baker and Ryan, "The Newfoundland Fishery Research Commission," 165.
81. Ibid.; Rose, *Cod*, 338–39.
82. *DN*, "Recalls Demand in 1916 for Scientific Fisheries Research," 7 Apr. 1932, 6.
83. "The 'Real' Start," *Decks Awash* 10, no. 6 (1981): 5.
84. J.R. Smallwood, *The New Newfoundland: An Account of the Revolutionary Developments Which Are Transforming Britain's Oldest Colony from "The Cinderella of the Empire" into One of the Great Small Nations of the World* (New York: Macmillan, 1931), 155–57; TRPAD, GN8/2, Richard A. Squires Papers, file 31.ii, Passfield to Governor Sir John Middleton, 2 Dec. 1929.
85. *DN*, "Expert Addresses Rotary on Value of Cod Liver Oil," 9 Aug. 1929, 3.
86. DMF, *Annual Report*, 14; H. Thompson, *Reports of the Newfoundland Fishery Research Commission, No 1: A Survey of the Fisheries of Newfoundland and Recommendations for a Scheme of Research* (St. John's: Newfoundland Fishery Research Commission, 1930), 8; TRPAD, GN 8, Box 28, 8.252, Folder 1, "Memorandum of Proposals for Fishery Research in Newfoundland Agreed between the Prime Minister of Newfoundland and the Officers of the Empire Marketing Board," n.d.; ibid., GN 34/2, Box 147, File: Fishery:

Research Commission, 1931–1932, Arthur Mews to H.B.C. Lake, 2 Apr. 1931; ibid., GN 8.125, Folder 2, Passfield to Middleton, 2 Dec. 1929.

87. For details of the full agreement, see Smallwood, *The New Newfoundland*, 155–57.
88. TRPAD, GN 8.125, Folder 2, W.C .Job to R.A. Squires, 9 July 1930.
89. J.B. Tait, "Harold Thompson, 1890–1957," *Journal du Conseil International pour l'Exploration de la Mer* 23, no. 2 (1958): 151–54. For a copy of his CV, see TRPAD, GN 8, Box 28, 8.252, Folder 1, "Dr. Harold Thompson, CV," n.d.
90. Thompson, *Reports*, 8.
91. TRPAD, GN 34/2, Box 147, File: Fishery Research Commission, 1930–1931, "Progress Report by Dr. Harold Thompson," 23 Aug. 1930.
92. *DN*, "Dr. Thompson's Lecture on Marine Research," 7 Apr. 1932, 7.
93. TRPAD, GN 34/2, Box 147, File: Fishery Research Commission, 1930–1931, Harold Thompson to Mr. Noonan, 16 Aug. 1930.
94. For his full report, see H. Thompson, *A Survey of the Fisheries of Newfoundland and Recommendations for a Scheme of Research*, Newfoundland Economic Bulletin No. 1 (St. John's: Fishery Research Commission, 1930).
95. TRPAD, GN 34/2, Box 147, File: Fishery Research Commission, 1930–1931 (2), Harold Thompson to H.B.C. Lake, 17 Dec. 1930; ibid., GN 8, Box 28, 8.252, Folder 1, "Recommendations for a Scheme of Fishery Research in Newfoundland," n.d.
96. BT, *Annual Report*, 1931, 29; TRPAD, GN 34/2, Box 147, File: Fishery: Research Commission, 1931–1932, Arthur Mews to H.B.C. Lake, 2 Apr. 1931.
97. FRC, *Annual Report*, 1931, 8–10. See also TRPAD, GN 34/2, Box 146, File: Cape Agulhas S.S., Unsigned to Captain Gabriel Fudge, 14 Jan. 1931; ibid., Box 147, File: Fishery Research Commission, 1930–1931, Minutes of Fifth Meeting of Fishery Research Commission, 24 Feb. 1931; ibid., File: Fishery Research Commission, 1930–1931 (2), Report on Course for Fishermen, 1931 by H.R. Chipman, n.d.; H.B.C. Lake to Harold Thompson, 21 Feb. 1930; H.B.C. Lake to Professor Leim, 24 Jan. 1931; ibid., File: Fishery: Research Commission, 1931–1932, Bay Bulls lease agreement.
98. TRPAD, GN 34/2, Box 147, File: Fishery Research Commission, 1930–1931 (2), Harold Thompson to H.B.C. Lake, 27 Feb. 1931.
99. H. Thompson, "Fishery Research in Newfoundland," in J.R. Smallwood, ed., *The Book of Newfoundland, Vol. 2* (St. John's: Newfoundland Book

Publishers, 1937), 211; TRPAD, GN 8, Box 28, File 8.252, Folder 2, Résumé of the establishment, functions and operations of the biological laboratory of the fishery research commission Bay Bulls, Newfoundland by Harold Thompson, 23 Feb. 1933.

100. TRPAD, GN 8, Box 28, 8.252, Folder 1, Some points for first year's work at Bay Bulls Laboratory, n.d., no author; ibid., GN 34/2, Box 147, File: Fishery: Research Commission, 1931–1932, "Recommendations for a scheme of fishery research in Newfoundland," n.d.

101. Ibid., GN 8, Box 28, File 8.252, Folder 2, Résumé . . . , 23 Feb. 1933.

102. For research summaries, see FRC, *Annual Report*, 1931 and 1932. The full list of publications is compiled in the bibliography under "Fisheries Research Commission Publications."

103. BT, *Annual Report*, 1932; ibid., 1932, 23; FRC, *Annual Report*, 1931, 76–81; Macpherson, *Technical Investigations*; Macpherson, *The Dried Codfish Industry*. See also *DN*, "Codfish Curing and Classification," 25 Nov. 1932, 5, 9; TRPAD, GN 8, Box 28, 8.252, Folder 1, Agenda for Eleventh Meeting of the Fishery Research Commission, 5 Apr. 1932.

104. FRC, *Annual Report*, 1932, 97; ibid., 1933, 11; TRPAD, GN 8, Box 28, File 8.252, Folder 2, Minutes of twelfth meeting of Fishery Research Commission, 6 June 1933. For a report on the fisheries course conducted at the Bay Bulls laboratory from 18 May 1933 to 3 Aug. 1933, see ibid., Fisheries Course Report by Dr. Thompson, Director.

105. FRC, *Annual Report*, 14; NACFI, *North American Council on Fishery Investigations Proceedings 1931–1933*, No. 2 (Ottawa: J.O. Patenaude, 1935); NACFI, *North American Council on Fishery Investigations Proceedings 1934–1936*, No. 3 (Ottawa: J.O. Patenaude, ISO, 1939).

106. G. Whiteley, *Northern Seas, Hardy Sailors* (New York: W.W. Norton, 1982), 111. For an interesting interview with Whiteley, where he reflects on his life and work, see M. Macleod, ed., *Crossroads Country: Memories of Pre-Confederation Newfoundland, at the Intersection of American, British and Canadian Connections* (St. John's: Breakwater Books, 1999), 42–53.

107. TRPAD, GN 34/2, Box 147, File: Fishery Research Commission, 1930–1931, Geo. Whiteley Jr. to H.B.C. Lake, 17 June 1930; ibid., File: Fishery Research Commission, 1931–1932, H.B.C. Lake to D. James Davies, 9 Apr. 1931.

108. G. Whiteley, "Marine Research and the Scientific Method," *Newfoundland Quarterly* 31, no. 4 (1932): 29.

109. Ibid., 28.
110. Ibid. Cf. D. Demeritt, "Scientific Forest Conservation and the Statistical Picturing of Nature's Limits in the Progressive-Era United States," *Environment and Planning D: Society and Space* 19, no. 4 (2001): 431–59.
111. Whiteley, "Marine Research," 29.
112. Ibid.
113. Ibid., 30.
114. BT, *Annual Report*, 1932, 21.
115. TRPAD, GN 8, Box 28, 8.252, Folder 1, Harold Thompson to Sir Richard Squires, 24 Sept. 1931; ibid., Dr. Harold Thompson to Secretary of Empire Marketing Board, 24 Sept. 1931.
116. Ibid., Minutes of Ninth Meeting of Commission, 9 Jan. 1932.
117. Baker and Ryan, "The Newfoundland Fishery Research Commission," 169; Barnes, "Bringing Another Empire Alive?" 65; Kothari, "Trade, Consumption and Development Alliances," 56.
118. TRPAD, MG 73, Box 30, File 14, "Extract from Report of Dr. Thompson, Director, Fishery Research Bureau, Bay Bulls," 24 Sept. 1936.
119. Ibid.
120. Ibid.
121. W. Templeman, "Fisheries Research," in J.R. Smallwood, C.F. Horan, R.D.W. Pitt, and B.G. Riggs, eds., *Encyclopedia of Newfoundland and Labrador, Vol. 2* (St. John's: Newfoundland Book Publishers, 1984), 169.
122. FRC, *Annual* Report, 1936–37, 5; Rozwadowski, *The Sea Knows No Boundaries*, 309, n. 21; Tait, "Harold Thompson," 152–53; TRPAD, MG 73, Box 30, File 14, Claude Fraser to H.T. Renouf, 25 Sept. 1936.
123. "The Directors Past and Present," *Decks Awash* 10, no. 6 (1981): 10.
124. M. Macleod, "Prophet with Honour: Dr. William F. Hampton, 1908–1968, Newfoundland Scientist," *Newfoundland Quarterly* 81, no. 1 (1985): 29–36.
125. Newfoundland, *Report of the Commission of Enquiry*, 156.
126. Newfoundland, *Report of Fisheries Research Committee*, Economic Bulletin No. 4 (St. John's: Department of Natural Resources, 1937), 19.
127. TRPAD, MG 73, Box 30, File 14, H.T. Renouf to R.B. Ewbank, 7 June 1938.
128. FRC, *Annual Report*, 1936–37, 20; "The 'Real' Start," *Decks Awash* 10, no. 6 (1981): 7; TRPAD, MG 73, Box 30, File 14, A.T. Goodridge et al. to Renouf, 31 May 1938.
129. Templeman, "Fisheries Research," 170.

130. TRPAD, MG 73, Box 30, File 14, Renouf to Claude Fraser, 16 Oct. 1936; ibid., Renouf to Ewbank, 16 Feb. 1937; ibid., Renouf to Ewbank, 8 Mar. 1937; ibid., Goodridge et al. to Renouf, 31 May 1938; ibid., Renouf to Ewbank, 7 June 1938.
131. "Rising from the Ashes," *Decks Awash* 10, no. 6 (1981): 7
132. Whiteley, "Marine Research," 31.
133. Ibid.
134. *DN*, "Prof. Sleggs' Address to Rotary Club," 26 Oct. 1926, 7.
135. Whiteley, *Northern Seas*, 107–10.
136. Harvey, *Newfoundland As It Was*, 160.
137. TRPAD, GN 8, Box 28, File 8.252, Folder 2, Résumé . . . , 23 Feb. 1933.
138. *DN*, "Board of Trade Hears Lecture on Fisheries Research," 19 Sept. 1923, 4.

Chapter 5

1. Newfoundland, *Statement of Policy by the Commission of Government, Newfoundland: Press Communiqué of the Seventh Meeting of the Commission of Government Issued Saturday, January 26th, 1935* (St. John's: Harvey & Company, 1935).
2. Ibid., 1.
3. Ibid., 2.
4. Macpherson, *The Dried Codfish Industry*, 10.
5. *ET*, "Confederation or No Confederation," 13 Mar. 1888, 4.
6. Nielsen, *Report on the Cure.*
7. Ibid., 21.
8. Ibid., 24.
9. DF, *Annual Report*, 1894, 46.
10. Ibid.
11. Ibid, 51 (emphasis added).
12. *ET*, "Confederation or No Confederation," 13 Mar. 1888, 4.
13. DF, *Annual Report*, 1894, 18–19.
14. Ibid., 17.
15. Ibid., 46.
16. Ibid., 54.
17. Ibid., 1895, 49.
18. Ibid., 1896, Appendix, 12.

19. *ET*, "At the 'Ouse," 8 Feb. 1898, 4. See also J.K. Hiller, "A History of Newfoundland, 1874–1901," PhD dissertation (Department of History, University of Cambridge, 1971), 338–39.
20. *JHA*, 1897, 21.
21. J.K. Hiller, "The Origins of the Pulp and Paper Industry in Newfoundland," *Acadiensis* 11, no. 2 (1982): 42–68; J. Malpas and A.F. King, "Pioneers of Geological Exploration, Mapping and Mining in Newfoundland," in D.H. Steele, ed., *Early Science in Newfoundland and Labrador* (St. John's: Chapter of Sigma Xi, 1987), 8–26; Noel, *Politics*, 34; W. Reeves, "Alexander's Conundrum Reconsidered: The American Dimension in Newfoundland Resource Development, 1898–1910," *Newfoundland Studies* 5, no. 1 (1989): 1–37.
22. DMF, *Annual Report*, 1902, 9.
23. TRPAD, File GN 2.15.25, Suggestions for improving the cure of codfish — 8 Apr. 1903, 2. See also ibid., MG 73, Box 70, File 3, "Directions," n.d.
24. Ibid., GN 1/3/A, Box 30, Despatch 302, H.E. McCallum to E.C. Watson, 30 Nov. 1899.
25. *ET*, "The Premier Favours a Pension Scheme," 23 Mar. 1906, 3.
26. TRPAD, GN 1/3/A, Box 60, Despatch 36, "Report on the Foreign Trade and Commerce of Newfoundland, 1905–06," VI.
27. *ET*, "The Price of Fish," 8 Oct. 1908, 6. For a more granular analysis of the crisis and its effects, see M. Baker, "Challenging the 'Merchants' Domain': William Coaker and the Price of Fish, 1908–1919," *Newfoundland and Labrador Studies* 29, no. 2 (2014): 189–226; McDonald, *"To Each His Own"*, 14–33.
28. *PHA*, 1909, 22. See also *ET*, "The Fishery and the Fish Markets," 30 Nov. 1908, 5.
29. *PHA*, 1909, 26.
30. DMF, *Annual Report*, 1907, 8.
31. DMF, *Annual Report*, 1911, 49.
32. The literature on the FPU is extensive. Ian McDonald's *"To Each His Own"* is the classic study. For a more recent appraisal, see M. Baker, "William Ford Coaker, the Formative Years, 1871–1908," *Newfoundland and Labrador Studies* 27, no. 2 (2012): 223–66 and Baker, "Challenging," 189–226.
33. Coaker, *Twenty Years*, 3.
34. McDonald, *"To Each His Own"*, 155.
35. Coaker, *Twenty Years*, 22–26.

36. Ibid., 33.
37. Baker, "Challenging," 198; P. O'Flaherty, *Lost Country: The Rise and Fall of Newfoundland, 1843–1933* (St. John's: Long Beach Press, 2005), 242.
38. For his full manifesto, see *DN*, "Address of Sir Edward Morris, Leader of the People's Party," 5 Mar. 1908, 4.
39. *DN*, "Board of Trade: Saturday Night's Meeting," 15 Mar. 1909, 4.
40. *PHA*, 1909, 77.
41. The formation of the Newfoundland Board of Trade has received less attention than the FPU. For an in-depth study, see R.G. Hong's 1998 MA thesis, "'An Agency for the Common Weal.'" The "Knights of the leather chairs" comes from TRPAD, MG 73, Box 25, File 8, Marjorie Thomson to H.G.R. Mews, 13 Dec. 1933.
42. *ET*, "Board of Trade meeting," 7 June 1909, 6. See also Hong, "'An Agency,'" 36; H.T. Renouf, "The Newfoundland Board of Trade," in J.R. Smallwood, ed., *The Book of Newfoundland, Vol. 2* (St. John's: Newfoundland Book Publishers, 1937), 207–08.
43. BT, *Annual Report*, 1909, 7.
44. TRPAD, MG 73, Box 2, File 9, A.E. Hickman to G.C. Fearn, 15 Nov. 1910; ibid., File 1, John Munn to G.C. Fearn, 11 May 1910; ibid., Box 6, File 4, G.C. Fearn to President, Board of Trade, 26 Jan. 1915.
45. Coaker, *Twenty Years*, 4.
46. Coaker, *Twenty Years*, 2.
47. Baker, "Challenging," 198–99. McDonald, *"To Each His Own"*, 29–33.
48. TRPAD, GN 8.21, Folder 1, G.C. Fearn to E.P. Morris, 10 Nov. 1910. Cf. Baker, "Challenging," passim.
49. Baker, "Challenging," 221, n. 42; McDonald, *"To Each His Own"*, 36; *PHA*, 1920, 311.
50. Coaker, *Twenty Years*, 120.
51. McDonald, *"To Each His Own"*, 161–62; Noel, *Politics*, 113.
52. Coaker, *Twenty Years*, 37.
53. Ibid., 50.
54. Ibid., 65.
55. Ibid., 80; *PHA*, 1914, 162.
56. S. Cadigan, *Death on Two Fronts: National Tragedies and the Fate of Democracy in Newfoundland, 1914–1934* (London: Allen Lane, 2013), 30; McDonald, *"To Each His Own"*, 162.

57. Newfoundland, *Report of the Commission on Fishery Matters*, 1.
58. Ibid., 3.
59. Ibid.
60. Ibid., 4–6.
61. Cadigan, *Death on Two Fronts*, 33–58; O'Flaherty, *Lost Country*, 267–69.
62. *ET*, "The Fish Situation,"30 Sept. 1914, 4.
63. TRPAD, GN 8.58, P.F. Kirkman to L.V. Harcourt, 28 May 1915; ibid., MG 73, Box 6, File 7, W.S. Monroe to E.P. Morris, 17 Aug. 1915. See also DMF, *Annual Report*, 1914, 15–16; McDonald, *"To Each His Own"*, 47–48.
64. TRPAD, GN 8.58, "Memorandum on the Shortage of Fish and the Practicability of Obtaining a Supply from Newfoundland," n.d. See also Wright, *A Fishery for Modern Times*, 14.
65. DMF, *Annual Report*, 1918, 6.
66. *Proceedings of the Legislative Council of Newfoundland* (*PLC*), 1917, 206.
67. McDonald, *"To Each His Own"*, 87.
68. *ET*, "The Fish Situation,"30 Sept. 1914, 4.
69. DMF, *Annual Report*, 1918, 7.
70. TRPAD, MG 73, Box 10, File 5, "Memorandum on the Fisheries of Newfoundland," 18 Dec. 1918, 12. See also Cadigan, *Death on Two Fronts*, 217; McDonald, *"To Each His Own"*, 73.
71. McDonald, *"To Each His Own"*, 88.
72. Roughly translated as the "Consortium for the Importation and Distribution of Cod and Dried Fish," this body was referred to as simply "the Consorzio" in Newfoundland at the time. BT, *Annual Report*, 1919, 9; *St. John's Daily Star (SJDS)*, "Italian Market Reviewed by Exporters at the Grenfell Hall, September 3rd," 9 Sept. 1920, 7. For an exhaustive examination of the history of Consorzio and the Coaker Regulations, see McDonald, *"To Each His Own"*, 86–105. See also Baker, "Challenging," 213–17; W.F. Coaker, *Hon. W.F. Coaker's Speech on the Fish Regulations, House of Assembly, April 27th 1920* (St. John's: Union Publishing Co., 1920), 2; Innis, *The Cod Fishery*, 463–70; Noel, *Politics*, 142–48; I.D.H. McDonald, "The Reformer Coaker: A Brief Biographical Introduction," in J.R. Smallwood, G.J. Power, and J.R. Thoms, eds., *The Book of Newfoundland, Vol. 6* (St. John's: Newfoundland Book Publishers, 1974), 71–96; O'Flaherty, *Lost Country*, 294–309.
73. *ET*, "House of Assembly," 27 Apr. 1920, 7.
74. BT, *Annual Report*, 1919, 10.

75. TRPAD, MG 73, Box 10, File 7, Consorzio to Editor of Trade Review, 6 Oct. 1919.
76. *PHA*, 1920, 138.
77. For reproductions of the circulars issued to the trade by Coaker, detailing these regulations, see BT, *Annual Report*, 1919, 39–48.
78. Cadigan, *Death on Two Fronts*, 206–07.
79. *SJDS*, "Minister of Marine and Fisheries Points Out Necessity for the Fish Export Regulations," 14 Jan. 1920, 2; TRPAD, MG 73, Box 11, File 1, James P. Blackwood to E.A. Payn, 24 Aug. 1920.
80. *ET*, "Board of Trade Continues Discussion of Fish Regulations," 6 Feb. 1920, 8; *SJDS*, "Editorial Comment," 10 Feb. 1920, 4; TRPAD, MG 73, Box 69, File 13, "Minutes of Meeting of Fish Exporters," 4 Jan. 1921, Mr. Long, 9 Feb. 1920, 9/48–9/49; ibid., File 12, "Half Yearly Report of the Newfoundland Board of Trade," 1920.
81. Ibid., Box 11, File 11, "Reports RE — Fish Export Regulations," Mr. Barr, 3 Feb. 1920, 3/4; *SJDS*, "Board Trade Takes Up Export Regulations," 4 Feb. 1920, 10; *SJDS*, "Our Letter Box: Those Regulations," 7 Feb. 1920, 13.
82. *Statutes of Newfoundland*, 1920, 82–89.
83. *SJDS*, "Rules and Regulations Made under the Codfish Exportation Act," 11 Sept. 1920, 8–10.
84. *ET*, "Mr. Hawes Incapacitated," 10 Dec. 1920, 11; TRPAD, MG 73, Box 11, File 12, "1922 Protest."
85. Ibid., "The Italian Market: A Serious Situation," 15 Dec. 1920, 8.
86. Ibid., "A Test Case," 18 Dec. 1920, 8.
87. Ibid., "The Hampden of Newfoundland," 18 Dec. 1920, 5.
88. Ibid., "Regulations Modified, Says Dame Rumour," 29 Dec. 1920, 6.
89. Ibid., "Economic Conditions," 21 Jan. 1921, 4.
90. Coaker, *Twenty Years*, 285.
91. DMF, *Annual Report*, 1923, 20; G.M. Gerhardsen, *Salted Cod and Related Species*, FAO Fisheries Study No. 1 (Washington: FAO, 1949); S. Gorostiza, and M. Ortega Cerdà, "'The Unclaimed Latifundium': The Configuration of the Spanish Fishing Sector under Francoist Autarky, 1939–1951," *Journal of Historical Geography* 52 (2016): 26–35; P. Holm, "The Dynamics of Institutionalization: Transformation Processes in Norwegian Fisheries," *Administrative Science Quarterly* 40, no. 3 (1995): 398–422; Innis, *Cod Fisheries*, 467–72; A. Sverrisson, "Small Boats and Large Ships: Social Continuity and

Technical Change in the Icelandic Fisheries, 1800–1960," *Technology and Culture* 43, no. 2 (2002): 227–53.

92. King, *Marketing of Fishery Products*, 16.
93. TRPAD, MG 73, Box 23, File 11, W.H. Greenland to J.J. Bates, 10 Mar. 1931; ibid., Box 32, File 25, Board of Trade Fish Committee to Acting Secretary, Department of Natural Resources, 30 Nov. 1937.
94. BT, *Annual Report*, 1923, 12–13.
95. Neary, *Newfoundland in the North Atlantic World*, 13.
96. H.B. Mayo, "Newfoundland's Entry into the Dominion," *Canadian Journal of Economics and Political Science* 15, no. 4 (1949): 505–22. See also Neary, *Newfoundland in the North Atlantic World*, 34; Noel, *Politics*, 187–89; Wright, *A Fishery for Modern Times*, 14.
97. *Statutes*, 1931, 453–61.
98. BT, *Annual Report*, 1931, 50.
99. For the updated act, see *Statutes*, 1933, 293–302. See also Alexander, *Decay of Trade*, 28; R. Apostle, G. Barrett, P. Holm, S. Jentoft, L. Mazany, B. McCay, and K. Mikalsen, *Community, State, and Market on the North Atlantic Rim: Challenges to Modernity in the Fisheries* (Toronto: University of Toronto Press, 1998), 45.
100. Quoted in Alexander, *Decay of Trade*, 26.
101. TRPAD, GN 8, Box 28, 8.252, Folder 1, "Memorandum of Proposals for Fishery Research in Newfoundland . . ." (*c.* 1929); ibid., MG 73, Box 30, File 14, "Extract from Report of Dr. Thompson, Director, Fishery Research Bureau, Bay Bulls," 24 Sept. 1936.
102. Thompson, *Reports*, 10. See also TRPAD, GN 34/2, Box 147, File: Fishery: Research Commission, 1931–1932, "Recommendations for a Scheme of Fishery Research in Newfoundland," n.d.
103. Newfoundland, *Report of the Commission of Enquiry*, 112–13. See also TRPAD, MG 73, Box 32, File 25, Acting Secretary, Department of Natural Resources to Board of Trade, 21 Oct. 1937.
104. FRC, *Annual Report*, 1931, 76–79; FRC, *Annual Report*, 1933, 14–23; Macpherson, *Technical Investigations*.
105. For a detailed discussion, see Neary, *Newfoundland in the North Atlantic World*, 12–43; Noel, *Politics*, 186–203; J. Overton, "Economic Crisis and the End of Democracy: Politics in Newfoundland during the Great Depression," *Labour/Le Travail* 26 (1990): 85–124. For a more recent appraisal, see Cullen,

"Race, Debt and Empire," 1–14. For historical accounts, see A.M. Fraser, "Newfoundland, Economic and Political II: Government-by-Commission (1934–6): A Survey," *Canadian Journal of Economics and Political Science* 3, no. 1 (1937): 71–83; Mayo, "Newfoundand's Entry," 502–22; A.F.W. Plumptre, "Newfoundland, Economic and Political I: The Amulree Report (1933): A Review," *Canadian Journal of Economics and Political Science* 3, no. 1 (1937): 58–71.

106. Neary, *Newfoundland in the North Atlantic World*, 14; Noel, *Politics*, 194–96; Overton, "Economic Crisis," 105.
107. Quoted in Noel, *Politics*, 203.
108. Great Britain, *Newfoundland Royal Report*, 195.
109. Ibid., 197.
110. Overton, "Economic Crisis," passim.
111. "Commission of Government: Proclamation and Biographical Sketches," *Newfoundland Quarterly* 34, no. 4 (1934): 21–24.
112. Department of Natural Resources (DNR), *Annual Report*, 1934, 1–2.
113. *Statutes*, 1935, 137–45. See also Apostle et al., *Community*, 60.
114. For a summary of the Kent Commission's findings, see TRPAD, MG 73, Box 32, File 25, Acting Secretary, Department of Natural Resources, to Board of Trade, 21 Oct. 1937; ibid., 29 Oct. 1937; ibid., Acting Secretary, Department of Natural Resources, to Secretary, 6 Nov. 1937; ibid., Acting Secretary, Department of Natural Resources, to Board of Trade, 22 Nov. 1937.
115. The full list of publications is compiled in the bibliography under "Fisheries Research Commission Publications."
116. FRC, *Annual Report*, 1936–37, 36.
117. TRPAD, MG 73, Box 32, File 25, Advisory Council to the Salt Codfish Association to Secretary, Department of Natural Resources, 13 Nov. 1937.
118. Ibid., GN 8, Box 28, 8.252, Folder 1, Some points for first year's work at Bay Bulls Laboratory (*c.* 1932); ibid., Fishery Research Laboratory, Bay Bulls — A Summary of the functions of the Research Station with a brief Resumé of the work accomplished since its inception April 1931.
119. FRC, *Annual Report*, 1931, 83.
120. FRC, *Annual Report*, 1936–37, 38.
121. *ET*, "Suggestions for Improving Our Industry," 16 July 1925, 6.
122. TRPAD, GN 127, Box 1, "Evidence: Dr. Norman L. Macpherson," 26 May 1936. For a history of artificial drying, first attempted in the 1870s, see ibid.,

PANL GN 34/2, Box 49, File 40/1, "Artificial Drying of Fish, by Bertrand Menard," 17 Nov. 1950.

123. FRC, *Annual Report*, 1933, 16; Macpherson, *Dried Codfish Industry*, 44.
124. Macpherson, *Dried Codfish Industry*, 44.
125. TRPAD, GN 8, Box 28, 8.252, Folder 1, Harold Thompson to F.C. Alderdice, 6 Dec. 1932.
126. Ibid., GN 34/2, Box 49, File 40/6, press clipping, 22 Nov. 1952.
127. Alexander, *Decay of Trade*, 23; Commission of Government (CG), *Annual Report*, 1935, 15; Newfoundland, *Report of the Commission of Enquiry*, 62. For Hope Simpson's take, see J.H.S. to Betty, 25 Sept. 1935, in Neary, *White Tie*, 221–22. See also TRPAD, GN 127, Box 1, "Evidence: George Hawes," 6 Apr. 1936; ibid., MG 73, Box 34, File 3, Salt Codfish Association Executive to Commissioner for Natural Resources, 1 Apr. 1938.
128. Ibid., GN 127, Box 1, "Evidence: George Hawes," 6 Apr. 1936.
129. Alexander, *Decay of Trade*, 29–30; Apostle et al., *Community*, 36–44; Holm, "Dynamics of Institutionalization," 405–09.
130. J.H.S. to Ian and Sheila, 7 Apr. 1936, in Neary, *White Tie*, 283–84.
131. J.H.S. to Maisie, 20 Apr. 1936, in Neary, *White Tie*, 288–89.
132. CG, *Annual Report*, 1936, 54–55; R. Gushue, *The Fisheries of Newfoundland, Retrospect and Prospect, an Address Delivered at a Meeting of the Rotary Club of St. John's, Nfld., September 12, 1946* (n.p., 1946); R. Gushue, "Newfoundland's Salt Codfish Industry Adopts the Pool Plan of Marketing," *Atlantic Guardian* 4, no. 1 (1947): 10–13.
133. Gushue, *Fisheries of Newfoundland*, 3.
134. Alexander's *Decay of Trade* is the definitive account of NAFEL.
135. Gushue, *Fisheries of Newfoundland*, 2.
136. Newfoundland, *Statement*, 1.
137. Hampton, *Approved Methods*, 14–16; TRPAD, GN 8, Box 28, 8.252, Folder 1, Agenda for Eleventh Meeting, 5 Apr. 1932.
138. Hampton, *Approved Methods*, 21.
139. Alexander, *Decay of Trade*.

Chapter 6

1. J. Hatton and M. Harvey, *Newfoundland: Its History, Its Present Condition, and Its Prospects in the Future* (Boston: Doyle & Whittle, 1883), 245.

2. Ibid.
3. Ghaly et al., "Fish Spoilage," 859–77; Kurlansky, *Cod*, 34.
4. Archaeologist-cum-social-anthropologist Peter Pope explains that cod oil was known as *train oil* "because it was used to lubricate heavy mechanisms, or 'trains,' in early modern parlance." Pope, *Fish into Wine*, 28–29.
5. G. Cell, *English Enterprise in Newfoundland 1577–1660* (Toronto: University of Toronto Press, 1969), 150.
6. Marx, *Grundrisse*, 409.
7. S. Ryan, *The Ice Hunters: A History of Newfoundland Sealing to 1914* (St. John's: Breakwater Books, 1994), 65–69.
8. Munn, *Cod Liver Oil Industry*, 5.
9. G. Wolf, "A Historical Note on the Mode of Administration of Vitamin A for the Cure of Night Blindness," *American Journal of Clinical Nutrition* 31, no. 2 (1978): 290–92.
10. R.A. Guy, "The History of Cod Liver Oil as a Remedy," *American Journal of Diseases of Children* 26, no. 2 (1923): 112.
11. Ibid., 115. See also J.C. Drummond and T.P. Hilditch, *The Relative Values of Cod Liver Oils from Various Sources (EMB 35)* (London: His Majesty's Stationery Office, 1930), 7; N.L. Macpherson, *Newfoundland Cod Liver Oil*, Service Bulletin No. 3 (St. John's: Department of Natural Resources, 1937), 7. For a nineteenth-century perspective, see J.H. Bennett, *Treatise on the Oleum Jecoris Aselli, or, Cod Liver Oil, as Therapeutic Agent in Certain Forms of Gout, Rheumatism, and Scrofula: with Cases* (London: S. Highley, 1841), 13–14.
12. Guy, "History of Cod Liver Oil," 112–15.
13. As biochemist C.E. Bills correctly pointed out in 1927, this process is autolytic rather than putrefactive. It is more accurately described as a process of fermentation, similar to the production of fish sauce. See C.E. Bills, "The Principal Chemical Researches on Cod Liver Oil," *Chemical Reviews* 3, no. 4 (1927): 425–42. Recently, there is a renewed interested in lactic acid-fermented cod liver oil in the health foods and naturopathic community, as this is more potent than refined oils and is more easily absorbed by the body.
14. Macpherson, *Newfoundland Cod Liver Oil*, 6–7; S.S. Zilva and J.C. Drummond, "The Cod Liver Oil Industry in Newfoundland," *Journal of the Society of Chemical Industry Transactions* 42, no. 18 (1923): 185T–88T.
15. DRC, *Royal Commission*, 50.

16. TRPAD, MG 73, Box 70, File 5, "Cod Liver Oil," n.d.
17. F.P. Møller, *Cod Liver Oil and Chemistry* (London: Peter Møller, 1895), lvi.
18. Ibid. See also *ET*, "Improved Manufacture," 5 Dec. 1898, 4.
19. Møller, *Cod Liver Oil*, lv.
20. Bills, "Principal Chemical Researches," 425–26; Cutting, *Fish Saving*, 152; B. Davies, "Atlantic Guardian Visits Munn's," *Atlantic Guardian* 3, no. 1 (1947): 48–57; Zilva and Drummond, "Cod Liver Oil Industry."
21. Munn, *Cod Liver Oil Industry*, 9.
22. D.J. Davies, *Newfoundland Cod Liver Oil* (St. John's: Manning & Rabbitts, 1930), 6. For more on Fox's method, see Munn, *Cod Liver Oil Industry*, 9; A. Nielsen, *Directions for the Manufacture of Cod-Liver Oil* (St. John's: Bowden & Co., Printers, 1896), 6–7.
23. A healthy liver — according to the criteria of export cod liver producers, at least — was cream-coloured and tender enough that a finger can be pushed through it without any effort. Lean livers were darker and tougher. Diseased livers were spotted or green.
24. H.F. Shortis, "Paper 144: History of the Cod Liver Oil Industry in Newfoundland," in *Shortis Papers*, Vol. 4, Part 1 (n.p., 1906).
25. Davies, *Newfoundland Cod Liver Oil*, 5.
26. Møller, *Cod Liver Oil*, lvi.
27. Stearine had several technical uses, most importantly as a non-polar base for the manufacture of soap. Later studies proved that stearine had significant medicinal value, even curing experimental rickets in dogs, which raised questions over the practice of removing it. See J.C. Drummond and S.S. Zilva, "The Preparation of Cod Liver Oil and the Effect of the Processes on the Vitamin Value of the Oils," *Journal of the Society of Chemical Industry* 41, no. 15 (1922).
28. A. Nielsen, *Directions for the Manufacture of Cod-Liver Oil, Part II: The Freezing Process* (St. John's: Bowden & Co., Printers, 1896).
29. Davies, *Newfoundland Cod Liver Oil*, 7.
30. Bills, "Principal Chemical Researches," 427.
31. Nielsen, *Directions, Part II*, 3.
32. *ET*, "Newfoundland Cod Liver Oil," 28 Dec. 1893, 4.
33. For very detailed descriptions of the process for producing non-freezing cod liver oil, see Nielsen, *Directions, Part II*; Munn, *Cod Liver Oil Industry*, 10–11.

34. Nielsen, *Directions, Part II*, 9.
35. Davies, *Newfoundland Cod Liver Oil*, 7.
36. Macpherson, *Newfoundland Cod Liver Oil*, 9.
37. Cutting, *Fish Saving*, 153; Davies, "Atlantic Guardian Visits Munn's," 49; Munn, *Cod Liver Oil Industry*, 11.
38. Macpherson, *Newfoundland Cod Liver Oil*, 7; TRPAD, MG 73, Box 12, File 3, H.R. Brookes (Job Bros.) to E.A. Payn, 20 Oct. 1921.
39. Munn, *Cod Liver Oil Industry*, 11.
40. TRPAD, MG 73, Box 6, File 6, W.A. Munn to W.S. Monroe, 22 Nov. 1915.
41. Imperial Economic Committee (IEC), *Report of the Imperial Economic Committee on Marketing and Preparing for Market of Foodstuffs Produced within the Empire: Fifth Report — Fish*, Cmd. 2934 (London: His Majesty's Stationery Office, 1927), 56. See also TRPAD, MG 73, Box 9, File 7, W.A. Munn to W.B. Grieve, 2 Aug. 1917; ibid., H.R. Brookes to W.B. Grieve, 3 Aug. 1917; ibid., GN 34/2, Box 146, File: Cod Liver Oil, W.A. Munn to H.B.C. Lake, 12 Nov. 1931.
42. D. Wendt, "The Man with a Fish on His Back: Science, Romance, and Repugnance in the Selling of Cod-Liver Oil," *Chemical Heritage Magazine* 28, no. 1 (2010): 33.
43. DRC, *Royal Commission*, 51; FRC, *Annual Report*, 1931, 73; TRPAD, MG 73, Box 13, File 10, W.A. Munn to E.A. Payn, 24 Mar. 1922.
44. J. Deas, "Vitamin A and Its Variations in Cod Liver Oil," *Canadian Medical Association Journal* 14, no. 10 (1924): 960; *ET*, "Rotary Luncheon: The Curative Effects of Cod Liver Oil," 23 Aug. 1924, 4; TRPAD, MG 73, Box 12, File 3, W.A. Munn to E.A. Payn, 12 Oct. 1921; ibid., H.R. Brookes to E.A. Payn, 20 Oct. 1921; ibid., Box 13, File 10, J.C. Drummond to Edgar Bowring, 5 Dec. 1921; ibid., W.A. Munn to E.A. Payn, 24 Mar. 1922.
45. Bills, "Principal Chemical Researches," 426.
46. Davies, *Newfoundland Cod Liver Oil*, 11; Munn, *Cod Liver Oil Industry*, 7.
47. Drummond and Zilva, "Preparation of Cod Liver Oil," 280 T; Macpherson, *Newfoundland Cod Liver Oil*, 22.
48. Møller, *Cod Liver Oil*, liii. See also TRPAD, MG 73, Box 9, File 7, W.A. Munn to W.B. Grieve, 2 Aug. 1917; ibid., GN 34/2, Box 147, File: L Miscellaneous, 1930–31, "Newfoundland Medicinal Cod Liver Oil," n.d. (*c.* 1930–31).
49. TRPAD, GN 34/2, Box 148, File: P Miscellaneous, 1927–31, Allen & Hanburys Ltd. to J.C. Drummond, 20 Dec. 1927.

50. DMF, *Annual Report*, 1912, 56.
51. TRPAD, MG 73, Box 9, File 7, H.R. Brookes to W.B. Grieve, 3 Aug. 1917; ibid., W.A. Munn to W.B. Grieve, 2 Aug. 1917; ibid., Box 7, File 8, R.B. Job to E.P. Morris, 16 Sept. 1916.
52. D. Alexander, "Newfoundland's Traditional Economy and Development to 1934," in J. Hiller and P. Neary, eds., *Newfoundland in the Nineteenth and Twentieth Centuries: Essays in Interpretation* (Toronto: University of Toronto Press, 1980), 20.
53. DMF, *Annual Report*, 1910, 38; TRPAD, GN 2.5.32, File 32.M, W.A. Munn to E.P. Morris, 21 Apr. 1911.
54. DMF, *Annual Report*, 1910, 39.
55. Ibid., 37–38. See also TRPAD, GN 2.5.32, File 32.M, Alan Goodridge to E.P. Morris, 29 Apr. 1911; ibid., R. Watson to A.W. Piccott, 2 May 1911.
56. *ET*, "New Job: Norwegian Cod Oil Man Imported by Government," 14 June 1911, 4. For full details of Simonsen's contract, see TRPAD, MG 73, Box 3, File 9, M.B. Simonsen to G.C. Fearn, 29 Aug. 1911; ibid., File 14, unaddressed mimeographed letter, 4 Sept. 1911.
57. *ET*, "New Job," 4; TRPAD, MG 73, Box 3, File 3, Alan Goodridge to G.C. Fearn, 21 June 1911.
58. TRPAD, MG 73, Box 3, File 14, "Report No.1" by M.B. Simondsen [*sic*].
59. Ibid. See also DMF, *Annual Report*, 1911, Appendix, XXXIII–XXXIV; TRPAD, MG 73, Box 9, File 5 (1918), "Rules for Making Cod Liver Oil."
60. DMF, *Annual Report*, 1911, 34; ibid., 1913, 60; TRPAD, MG 73, Box 3, File 6, W.A. Munn to G.C. Fearn, n.d. (*c.* 1911); ibid., GN 2.5.32, File 32.M, A. Goodridge to R. Watson, 27 Sept. 1911; ibid., G.C. Fearn to E.P. Morris, 4 Sept. 1911.
61. Quoted in Hong, "'An Agency,'" 96–97.
62. DMF, *Annual Report*, 1915, 9.
63. "Cod Oil," *Canadian Fisherman* 2, no. 12 (1915): 404–05; TRPAD, MG 73, Box 9, File 2 (1918), L.O. Crane to E.A. Payn, 3 Oct. 1918.
64. J.C. Drummond, *Lane Medical Lectures: Biochemical Studies of Nutritional Problems* (Stanford, CA: Stanford University Press, 1934), 7–8.
65. Newfoundland Customs Returns (NCR), 1914–15, 77; NCR, 1915–16, 71; NCR, 1916–17, 75; NCR, 1917–18, 72. See also TRPAD, MG 73, Box 9, File 6, R.A. Squires to E.A. Payn, 5 Oct. 1917.
66. Quote from DMF, *Annual Report*, 1915, 10. See also TRPAD, MG 73, Box 6, File 6, W.A. Munn to W.S. Monroe, 22 Nov. 1915.

67. TRPAD, MG 73, Box 7, File 8, E.A. Payn to E.P. Morris, 28 Apr. 1916; ibid., Box 8, File 1, James S. Benedict to E.A. Payn, 23 Nov. 1917.
68. DMF, *Annual Report*, 1915, 10.
69. *Statutes*, 1916, 193. See also Newfoundland, *Rules and Regulations for the Manufacturing and Refining of Cod Liver Oil* (St. John's: Department of Marine and Fisheries, 1919).
70. TRPAD, MG 73, Box 9, File 5 (1918), "Rules for Making Cod Liver Oil." This bill was modelled on the licensing and inspection law for lobster canning developed by Nielsen in 1889. See K. Korneski, "Development and Degradation: The Emergence and Collapse of the Lobster Fishery on Newfoundland's West Coast, 1856–1924," *Acadiensis* 41, no. 1 (2012): 21–48.
71. DMF, *Annual Report*, 1916, Appendix, 25; *ET*, "Notice," 28 Apr. 1917, 6.
72. Macpherson, *Newfoundland Cod Liver Oil*, 11.
73. For the views of large-scale cod liver oil refiners W.A. Munn and H.R. Brookes on the short-term effects of the 1916 legislation, see TRPAD, MG 73, Box 9, File 7, Munn to W.B. Grieve, 2 Aug. 1917; ibid., Brookes to Grieve, 3 Aug. 1917.
74. DMF, *Annual Report*, 1917, 11. For more on Dunstan's report, see TRPAD, MG 73, Box 9, File 7, W. Dunstan to J.G. Stone, 26 June 1917; ibid., H.R. Brookes to W.B. Grieve, 3 Aug. 1917; ibid., W.A. Munn to W.B. Grieve, 2 Aug. 1917; ibid., File 7 (1918), J.G. Stone to E.A. Payn, 20 July 1918; ibid., Box 12, File 3, D. James Davies to E.A. Payn, 13 Oct. 1921.
75. Ibid., Box 9, File 7, W.A. Munn to W.B. Grieve, 2 Aug. 1917.
76. Ibid., Box 12, File 3, Walter Fletcher to Victor Gordon, 19 Aug. 1921.
77. K.J. Carpenter, "A Short History of Nutritional Science: Part 1 (1785–1885)," *Journal of Nutrition* 133, no. 3 (2003): 643.
78. K.C. Carter, "The Germ Theory, Beriberi, and the Deficiency Theory of Disease," *Medical History* 21, no. 2 (1977): 121.
79. Guy, "History of Cod Liver Oil," 114.
80. Carter, "Germ Theory," 126; A. Maltz, "Casimer Funk, Nonconformist Nomenclature, and Networks Surrounding the Discovery of Vitamins," *Journal of Nutrition* 143, no. 7 (2013): 1014.
81. H.C. Sherman and S.L Smith, *The Vitamins* (New York: Chemical Catalog Company, 1922), 7. The theory that humans (and animals) required a combination of proteins, fats, and carbohydrates for survival was rooted in the work of German chemist Justus von Liebig — the same person who

inspired Marx's thinking around the "metabolic rift" between town and countryside. Fun facts: Liebig's theory that the essential nutrients in meat were contained in the muscle fluids, not flesh, led to the proliferation of a new cooking method — whereby meat was seared to "seal in the juices" before being roasted at a lower temperature — and led to his invention of techniques for the industrial production of the beef bouillon cube in 1847, now owned by the OXO brand. See McGee, *On Food*, 161, 601–02; H.F. DeLuca, "History of the Discovery of Vitamin D and Its Active Metabolites," *BoneKey Reports* 3, no. 479 (2014): 1. On the metabolic rift, see J.B. Foster, *Marx's Ecology* (New York: Monthly Review Press, 2000); J.B. Foster and F. Magdoff, "Liebig, Marx, and the Depletion of Soil Fertility," *Monthly Review* 50, no. 3 (1998): 32–45; J.W. Moore, "Transcending the Metabolic Rift: A Theory of Crises in the Capitalist World-Ecology," *Journal of Peasant Studies* 38, no. 1 (2011): 1–46.

82. W. Boyd, "Making Meat: Science, Technology and American Poultry Production," *Technology and Culture* 42, no. 4 (2001): 631–64; K.J. Carpenter, "The Discovery of Thiamin," *Annals of Nutrition & Metabolism* 61, no. 3 (2012): 219–23; K.J. Carpenter and B. Sutherland, "Eijkman's Contribution to the Discovery of Vitamins," *Journal of Nutrition* 125, no. 2 (1995): 155–63; DeLuca, "History of the Discovery of Vitamin D," 1–8.
83. Carter, "Germ Theory"; A.J. Ihde and S.L. Becker, "Conflict of Concepts in Early Vitamin Studies," *Journal of the History of Biology* 4, no. 1 (1971): 1–33.
84. Quoted in Sherman and Smith, *The Vitamins*, 18.
85. C. Funk, "The Etiology of the Deficiency Disease," *Journal of State Medicine* 20 (1912): 366.
86. Maltz, "Casimer Funk," 1018.
87. Sherman and Smith, *The Vitamins*, 11.
88. F.G. Hopkins, "Feeding Experiments Illustrating the Importance of Accessory Factors in Normal Dietaries," *Journal of Physiology* 44, nos. 5–6 (1912): 425–60.
89. E.V. McCollum and M. Davis, "The Essential Factors in the Diet during Growth," *Journal of Biological Chemistry* 23, no. 1 (1915): 231–46.
90. J.C. Drummond, "The Nomenclature of the So-called Accessory Food Factors (Vitamins)," *Biochemical Journal* 14, no. 5 (1920): 660.
91. McCollum and Davis, "Essential Factors." See also L. Rosenfeld, "Vitamine-Vitamin: The Early Years of Discovery," *Clinical Chemistry* 43, no. 4

(1997): 680–85; R.D. Semba, "On the 'Discovery' of Vitamin A," *Annals of Nutrition & Metabolism* 61, no. 3 (2012): 192–98.

92. T.B. Osborne and L.B. Mendel, "The Relation of Growth to the Chemical Constituents of the Diet," *Journal of Biological Chemistry* 15, no. 2 (1913): 311–26; Osborne and Mendel, "The Influence of Butter-fat on Growth," *Journal of Biological Chemistry* 16, no. 4 (1914): 423–47; Osborne and Mendel, "The Influence of Cod Liver Oil and Some Other Fats on Growth," *Journal of Biological Chemistry* 17, no. 3 (1914): 401–08; E.V. McCollum and M. Davis, "The Necessity of Certain Lipids in the Diet during Growth," *Journal of Biological Chemistry* 15, no. 1 (1913): 167–75; McCollum and Davis, "Essential Factors."
93. E. Mellanby, "An Experimental Investigation on Rickets," *The Lancet* 193, no. 4985 (1919): 407–12. See also K.J. Carpenter, "A Short History of Nutritional Science: Part 3 (1912–1944)," *Journal of Nutrition* 133, no. 10 (2003): 3023–32.
94. *ET*, "Vitamines and Newfoundland Cod Oil," 1 Aug. 1922, 6.
95. Ibid., "Wonders of Cod Liver Oil," 30 Aug. 1924, 10.
96. Ibid.
97. H.C. Sherman and H.E. Munsell, "The Quantitative Determination of Vitamin A," *Journal of the American Chemical Society* 47, no. 6 (1925): 1639–46; S.S. Zilva and M. Miura, "The Quantitative Estimation of the Fat-soluble Factor," *Biochemical Journal* 15, no. 5 (1921): 654–59.
98. S.S. Zilva and M. Miura, "A Note on the Relative Activity of the Fat-soluble Accessory Factor in Cod-Liver Oil and Butter," *The Lancet* 197, no. 5085 (1921): 323.
99. Ibid. See also S.S. Zilva, "The Action of Ozone on the Fat-soluble Factor in Fats: Preliminary Note," *Biochemical Journal* 14, no. 6 (1920): 740–41.
100. *ET*, "To Study Cod Liver Oil," 1 Aug. 1922, 6; TRPAD, MG 73, Box 12, File 3, Walter Fletcher to Victor Gordon, 19 Aug. 1921.
101. Medical Research Council (MRC), *Report of the Medical Research Council for the year 1921–22*, (London: His Majesty's Stationery Office, 1922), 59.
102. Drummond and Zilva, "Preparation of Cod Liver Oil," 283T.
103. Zilva and Drummond, "Cod Liver Oil Industry in Newfoundland;" Zilva, Drummond, and M. Graham, "Relation of Vitamin A."
104. TRPAD, MG 73, Box 14, File 5, H.R. Brookes, C.C. Pratt, and W.A. Munn to A.E. Hickman, 29 Mar. 1922.

105. *ET*, "Dr. Zilva Addresses Board of Trade," 31 July 1922, 6; ibid., "Lecture by Dr. Zilva," 26 Aug. 1922, 6.
106. Zilva, Drummond, and Graham, "Relation of Vitamin A," 178.
107. TRPAD, MG 73, Box 13, File 10, W.A. Munn to E.A. Payn, 24 Mar. 1922.
108. DMF, *Annual Report*, 1922, 57; TRPAD, GN 8.200, "Note on the Export Trade of Newfoundland with the United Kingdom," n.d. (*c.* 1923).
109. *ET*, "Newfoundland Cod Liver Oil," 18 May 1923, 7.
110. Alexander, *Decay of Trade*, 29–31.
111. Munn, *Cod Liver Oil Industry*, 17; *ET*, "Rotary Luncheon: The Curative Effects of Cod Liver Oil," 23 Aug. 1924, 4.
112. C.E. Bills, "Early Experiences with Fish Oils — A Retrospect," *Nutrition Reviews* 13, no. 3 (1955): 65; *ET*, "Cod Liver Oil Exports," 3 July 1924, 6; ibid., "Scientific Demonstration of Curative Power of Cod Liver Oil," 21 Aug. 1924, 6.
113. *ET*, "Rotary Luncheon: The Curative Effects of Cod Liver Oil," 23 Aug. 1924, 4.
114. Ibid.
115. M.E. Condon, *The Fisheries and Resources of Newfoundland: 'The Mine of the Sea' (National, International and Co-operative)* (St. John's: n.p., 1925), 45; Munn, *Cod Liver Oil Industry*, 18.
116. DMF, *Annual Report*, 1924, 20; ibid., 1926, 11; *ET*, "Cod Liver Oil Industry," 10 July 1925, 7; TRPAD, GN 34/2, Box 148, File: P Miscellaneous, 1927–31, Arthur D. Holmes to J.C. Drummond, 28 Dec. 1927; ibid., F.W. Nitardy to J.C. Drummond, 4 Jan. 1927.
117. DMF, *Annual Report*, 1927, 13.
118. W.J. Browne, J.B. Baird, D.J. Davies, J. Grieve, J.W. Morris, C.L. Parkins, R.J. Stevenson, J.S. Woods, C.F. Horwood, and W. Watson, *The By-Products of the Fisheries of Nfld: A Paper Prepared by the Group on "Our Economic and Commercial Problems" for Presentation to the University Graduates' Association* (St. John's: Robinson & Co., 1928); *ET*, "Cod Liver Oil Industry," 10 July 1925, 7; ibid., "The Fish Meal, Fish Oil, and Fish Guano Industries of Canada," 14 Jan. 1926, 10; ibid., "Commercialize the Waste Products," 16 Jan. 1926, 4. For cod liver oil's role in poultry farming, see L.C. Norris, "The Significant Advances of the Past Fifty Years in Poultry Nutrition," *Poultry Science* 37, no. 2 (1958): 259; Boyd, "Making Meat," 638–39.
119. NCR, 1926–27, 94; ibid., 1928–29, 102.

120. DMF, *Annual Report*, 1927, 15.
121. TRPAD, MG 73, Box 17, File 6, P.T. McGrath to W.S. Monroe, 16 Apr. 1925.
122. Ibid., Box 16, File 3, George J. Saunders to F.H. Steer, 19 June 1924.
123. IEC, *Fifth Report — Fish*, 57.
124. TRPAD, MG 73, Box 17, File 6, P.T. McGrath to W.S. Monroe, 16 Apr. 1925.
125. *ET*, "Sir H. Mackinder's Address," 10 Sept. 1927, 4; ibid., "Chairman of the Imperial Economic Committee Addressed the Board of Trade," 10 Sept. 1927, 7; TRPAD, MG 73, Box 19, File 7, A.H. Murray to J.F. Meehan, 12 Sept. 1927; ibid., GN 8, Box 28, 8.252, Folder 1, Harold Thompson to Sir Richard Squires, 13 Oct. 1931.
126. Ibid., MG 73, Box 17, File 6, W.A. Munn and John Clouston to Tasker Cook, 21 May 1925; ibid., GN 34/2, Box 146, File: Cod Liver Oil, "Minutes of Meeting of Cod Liver Oil Exporters and Representatives of the Department of Marine and Fisheries," 8 Oct. 1931; ibid., W.A. Munn et al. to H.B.C. Lake, 12 Oct. 1931.
127. IEC, *Fifth Report — Fish*, 59.
128. Ibid., 60.
129. Drummond and Hilditch, *Relative Values*, 3. For more information on T.P. Hilditch's career, see F.D. Gunstone, "T.P. Hilditch, CBE, DSc, FRIC, FRS," *Journal of the American Oil Chemists' Society* 42, no. 9 (1965): a474–a530.
130. Drummond and Hilditch, *Relative Values*, 17–19; DMF, *Annual Report*, 1929, 12; *DN*, "Expert Addresses Rotary on Value of Cod Liver Oil," 9 Aug. 1929, 3.
131. Drummond and Hilditch, *Relative Values*, 21.
132. Ibid.
133. Ibid., 26–29, 49–51.
134. Ibid., 63.
135. Ibid., 124. This conclusion corroborated the research findings of private laboratories of companies. For the opinions of these different corporations, see the following letters found in TRPAD, GN 34/2, Box 148, File: P Miscellaneous, 1927–31: F.W. Nitardy to J.C. Drummond, 4 Jan. 1927; P.F. Wild to Drummond, 20 Dec. 1927; Boots Pure Drug Co. Ltd. to Drummond, 20 Dec. 1927; Allen & Hanburys Ltd. to Drummond, 20 Dec. 1927; Arthur D. Holmes to Drummond, 28 Dec. 1927; E.M. Johnson Jr. and C. E. Bills to Drummond, 31 Dec. 1927; Parke, Davis & Co. to Drummond, 23 Jan. 1928.
136. In addition to the Great Depression, Munn attributed the fall in exports to Norway's "considerable carry over from previous years," which made them

start cutting prices. TRPAD, GN 34/2, Box 148, File: M Miscellaneous, 1930–31, W.A. Munn to W.P. Rogerson, 11 Mar. 1931.

137. Ibid., Box 147, File: High Commissioners Office, 1930–31, D. James Davies to H.B.C. Lake, 5 Jan. 1931. See also ibid., Box 148, File: M Miscellaneous, 1930–31, W.A. Munn to W.P. Rogerson, 11 Mar. 1931

138. Ibid., Box 147, File: High Commissioners Office, 1930–31, "Newfoundland Cod Liver Oil," n.d.

139. Drummond and Hilditch, *Relative Values*, 63; "Secrets of Cod Liver Oil," *Newfoundland Quarterly* 30, no. 4 (1931): 36.

140. TRPAD, GN 34/2, Box 147, File: High Commissioners Office, 1930–31, "Newfoundland Cod Liver Oil," n.d.; ibid., D. James Davies to H.B.C. Lake, 17 Mar. 1931; ibid., Davies to Lake, 4 June 1931.

141. DRC, *Royal Commission*, 51; TRPAD, GN 34/2, Box 147, File: High Commissioners Office, 1930–31, "Newfoundland Cod Liver Oil," n.d.

142. Ibid., GN 9.244, Folder 4, "Ottawa Conference" [Imperial Economic Conference, Ottawa], n.d.; ibid., GN 34/2, Box 146, File: Cod Liver Oil, William C. Job to H.B.C Lake, 20 Nov. 1931; ibid., Harold Thompson to Lake, 17 Dec. 1931; ibid., W.A. Munn to unaddressed, 21 Jan. 1932; ibid., Box 147, File: High Commissioners Office, 1931–32, D. James Davies to Lake, 21 Oct. 1932; ibid., Davies to Lake, 26 Feb. 1932.

143. Ibid., File: High Commissioners Office, 1930-31, "Newfoundland Cod Liver Oil," n.d. (emphasis added).

144. Ibid., Box 148, File: M Miscellaneous, 1930–31, W.A. Munn to H.B.C. Lake, 17 Jan. 1931.

145. Ibid., Box 146, File: Cod Liver Oil, W.A. Munn to H.B.C. Lake, 12 Nov. 1931. See also ibid., Box 147, File: High Commissioners Office, 1931–32, "Cod Liver Oil," n.d.; ibid., MG 73, Box 24, File 9, Avalon Goodridge to H.G.R. Mews, 9 June 1932.

146. Ibid., GN 34/2, Box 146, File: Cod Liver Oil, W.A. Munn to H.B.C. Lake, 12 Nov. 1931.

147. Ibid. For an examination of the historical legacy of this marketing campaign, see U. Kothari, "Trade, Consumption and Development Alliances: The Historical Legacy of the Empire Marketing Board Poster Campaign," *Third World Quarterly* 35, no. 1 (2014): 43–64.

148. TRPAD, GN 34/2, Box 148, File: M Miscellaneous, 1930–31, W.A. Munn to H.B.C. Lake, 17 Jan. 1931. Scottish doctor, politician, and chairman of the

EMB's Research Committee, Walter Elliot, highlighted the delicate compromises the EMB had to negotiate in the wording of these posters: "A confident assentation 'New Zealand Butter is the best' would have drawn instant protest from Canada and Australia. . . . We had to find some line along which a great group of producers would cooperate, which would lead to no recriminations." W. Elliot, "The Work of the Empire Marketing Board," *Journal of the Royal Society of Arts* 79, no. 4191 (1931): 738–39.

149. TRPAD, GN 34/2, Box 147, File: High Commissioners Office, 1931–32, D. James Davies to H.B.C. Lake, 26 Feb. 1932.
150. Great Britain, *Newfoundland Royal Report*, 120; TRPAD, GN 34/2, Box 147, File: High Commissioners Office, 1931–32, D. James Davies to H.B.C. Lake, 21 Oct. 1932.
151. Norwegian cod liver oil exports to Great Britain fell from 520,000 gallons in 1930 to 281,000 gallons in 1934. Newfoundland exports to Great Britain grew from 10,684 gallons to 91,517 gallons. Domestic production, however, received the biggest boon: growing from 512,000 gallons in 1930 to 2,575,600 gallons in 1934. See FRC, *Annual Report*, 8–9; Macpherson, *Newfoundland Cod Liver Oil*, 14.
152. TRPAD, GN 34/2, Box 146, File: Cod Liver Oil, "Minutes of Meeting of Cod Liver Oil Exporters and Representatives of the Department of Marine and Fisheries," 8 Oct. 1931. For details of these experiments, see FRC, *Annual Report*, 1933: 9; ibid., 1934, 10; ibid., 1935, 21; ibid., 1936–37, 48–49.
153. TRPAD, GN 8, Box 28, 8.252, Folder 1, Fishery Research Laboratory, Bay Bulls — A Summary of the functions of the Research Station with a brief Resumé of the work accomplished since its inception April 1931; ibid., Harold Thompson to Sir Richard Squires, 13 Oct. 1931.
154. FRC, *Annual Report*, 1931, 72–73; N.L. Macpherson, "Vitamin A Concentration of Cod Liver Oil Correlated with Age of Cod," *Nature* 132, no. 3322 (1933): 26.
155. Macpherson, "Vitamin A Concentration." See also FRC, *Annual Report*, 1932, 32–37; ibid., 1933, 31–36.
156. Drummond and Hilditch, *Relative Values*, 124.
157. Macpherson, "Vitamin A Concentration," 27.
158. TRPAD, GN 127, Box 1, "Evidence: Dr. Norman L. Macpherson," 26 May 1936.
159. C.E. Bills, "Antiricketic Substances VI. The Distribution of Vitamin D, with Some Notes on Its Possible Origin," *Journal of Biological Chemistry* 72, no.

2 (1927): 751–58; Macpherson, *Newfoundland Cod Liver Oil*, 39–40; TRPAD, MG 73, Box 23, File 1, D.S. Bell to H.G.R. Mews, 1 June 1931; ibid., Box 34, File 6, "Report on Cod Liver Oil Studies in Canada and the U.S.A., 10 March to 16 April, 1938" by W.F. Hampton.

160. Bills, "Early Experiences," 67.
161. TRPAD, MG 73, Box 26, File 7, H.G.R. Mews to John Hope Simpson, 2 June 1934.
162. Macpherson, *Newfoundland Cod Liver Oil*, 11.
163. TRPAD, GN 34/2, Box 146, File: C Miscellaneous, H.B.C. Lake to Acting Commercial Counsellor, British Embassy, Washington, DC, 9 Jan. 1930. Newfoundland producers stated in an advertisement in the London Directory that Newfoundland cod liver oil "is made from the LIVERS OF COD only, taken immediately from perfectly fed fish during the Summer season." TRPAD, GN 34/2, Box 147, File: L Miscellaneous, 1930–31, "Newfoundland Medicinal Cod Liver Oil," n.d.
164. Munn, *Cod Liver Oil Industry*, 18.
165. Macpherson, *Newfoundland Cod Liver Oil*, 42.
166. TRPAD, MG 73, Box 34, File 6, "Report on Cod Liver Oil Studies in Canada and the U.S.A., 10 March to 16 April, 1938" by W.F. Hampton.
167. R.D. Apple, *Vitaminia: Vitamins in American Culture* (New Brunswick, NJ: Rutgers University Press, 1996), 5–6.
168. Carpenter, "Short History, Part III," 3025–26; J. Waddell and E.L. Rohdenburg, "The Provitamin D of Cholesterol. 1. The Antirachitic Efficacy of Irradiated Cholesterol," *Journal of Biological Chemistry* 105, no. 4 (1934): 711–39.
169. Wendt, "Man with a Fish on His Back," 36.
170. Hatton and Harvey, *Newfoundland*, 245.
171. Marx, *Grundrisse*, 409.

Chapter 7

1. Unless otherwise noted, the quotations come from J.H.S. to Ian, 8 Mar. 1936, in Neary, *White Tie*, 275–77.
2. J.H.S. to Greta, 28 May 1936, in Neary, *White Tie*, 296.
3. Rhoda Dawson, interview by Hiram Silk. 2 Oct. 1987. Available at: http://collections.mun.ca
4. MUNA, COLL-198, File 4.02.032, "Essay on Newfoundland."

5. Ibid.
6. For early plans and drafts of her thesis, see: MUNA, COLL-198, File 4.0, "Memoirs of Newfoundland and Labrador by Rhoda Dawson." For a taste of her perceptive analysis, see R. Dawson, "The Folk Art of the Labrador," *Among the Deep-Sea Fishers* 36, no. 2 (1938): 39–49.
7. R. Dawson, "The Wharves of St. John's, Newfoundland," *Canadian Parliamentary Review* 15, no. 2 (1992): 2–5; P. Laverty, *Silk Stocking Mats: Hooked Mats of the Grenfell Mission* (Montreal and Kingston: McGill-Queen's University Press, 2005), 34–36; P. Neary, "'Wry Comment': Rhoda Dawson's Cartoon of Newfoundland Society, 1936," *Newfoundland Studies* 8, no. 1 (1992): 1–14; G. Rudge, "Rhoda Dawson, A Missionary Zeal for Rag Rugs and Ruskin," *The Guardian*, 31 Mar. 1992.
8. Neary, "'Wry Comment,'" 13.
9. Ibid.
10. Ibid., 1.
11. Bukharin, *Science at the Crossroads*, 174.
12. J.H.S. to Greta, 7 May 1936, in Neary, *White Tie*, 292.
13. Noel, *Politics*, 149.
14. Quita Hope Simpson to Edgar and Eleanor, 8 Apr. 1934, in Neary, *White Tie*, 66.
15. J.H.S. to Betty, 19 July 1935, in Neary, *White Tie*, 189.
16. Murray, *Commercial Crisis in Newfoundland*, 4. For a detailed analysis, see Banoub, "Black Monday, 1894."
17. MUNA, COLL-198, File 4.02.031, "Essay on Newfoundland," 22 (emphasis added).
18. Radical Science Journal Collective, "Science, Technology, Medicine and the Socialist Movement," *Radical Science Journal* 11 (1981): 3–70; G. Werskey, *The Visible College: A Collective Biography of British Scientists and Socialists of the 1930s* (London: Allen Lane, 1978); G. Werskey, "The Marxist Critique of Capitalist Science: A History in Three Movements?" *Science as Culture* 16, no. 4 (2007): 397–461; R. Young, "Science Is a Labour Process," *Science for People* 43/44 (1979): 31–37; R. Young, "Marxism and the History of Science," in R.C. Olby, ed., *Companion to the History of Modern Science* (London: Routledge, 1990), 77–86.
19. P. Mirowski and E.M. Sent, "The Commercialization of Science and the Response of STS," in E. Hackett, O. Amsterdamska, and M. Lynch, eds.,

Handbook of Science, Technology and Society Studies (Cambridge, MA: MIT Press, 2007), 638. See also M. Arboleda, "Revitalizing Science and Technology Studies: A Marxian Critique of More-Than-Human Geographies," *Environment and Planning D: Society and Space* 35, no. 2 (2017): 360–78.

20. A. Ashforth, *The Politics of Official Discourse in Twentieth-Century South Africa* (Oxford: Clarendon Press, 1990), 5.
21. T. Mitchell, *Rule of Experts: Egypt, Techno-Politics, Modernity* (Berkeley: University of California Press, 2002), 115–16.
22. J.H.S. to Greta, 28 May 1936, in Neary, *White Tie*, 296.
23. Marx, "Postface to the Second Edition," in *Capital, Vol. 1*, 103.
24. A. Gramsci, *Selections from the Prison Notebooks* (New York: International Publishers, 1971), 423. See also K. Crehan, *Gramsci's Common Sense: Inequality and Its Narratives* (Durham, NC: Duke University Press, 2016).
25. Gramsci, *Prison Notebooks*, 422.
26. Marx to Kuglemann, 17 Mar. 1868 in K. Marx and F. Engels, *Collected Works, Vol. 42, Letters, 1864–68* (New York: International Publishers, 1987), 551–53.
27. Marx, *Grundrisse*, 704.
28. Ibid.
29. Ibid., 409 (emphasis added).
30. Ibid., 706.
31. Mandel, *Late Capitalism*, 268.
32. R. Clark, "Romancing the Harlequins: A Note on Class Struggle in the Newfoundland Village," in R. Clark, ed., *Contrary Winds: Essays on Newfoundland Society in Crisis* (St. John's: Breakwater Books, 1986), 19.
33. U. Sinclair, *The Brass Check: A Study of American Journalism* (Pasadena, CA: Published by the author, 1919), 77–78 (emphasis added). See also R.W. McChesney and B. Scott, "Upton Sinclair and the Contradictions of Capitalist Journalism," *Monthly Review* 54, no. 1 (2002): n.p.
34. S. Terkel, *Working: People Talk about What They Do All Day and How They Feel about What They Do* (New York: New Press, 2004 [1972]), xi–xii.
35. Marx, *Capital, Vol. 1*, 301–02 (emphasis added).

BIBLIOGRAPHY

Abbreviations

BT	Board of Trade
CG	Commission of Government
CNS	Centre for Newfoundland Studies
CO	Cod oil (for technical uses)
CLO	Cod liver oil (for medicinal uses)
DF	Department of Fisheries
DMF	Department of Marine and Fisheries
DN	*Daily News*
DNE	*Dictionary of Newfoundland English*
DNR	Department of Natural Resources
DRC	Dominions Royal Commission
EH	*Evening Herald*
EM	*Evening Mercury*
EMB	Empire Marketing Board
ET	*Evening Telegram*
FAO	Food and Agriculture Organization
FC	Fisheries Commission
FPU	Fishermen's Protective Union
FRC	Fishery Research Commission
ICES	European International Council for the Exploration of the Sea
IEC	Imperial Economic Committee

JHA	*Journal of House of Assembly of Newfoundland*
MHA	Member of the House of Assembly
MRC	Medical Research Council
MUC	Memorial University College
MUN	Memorial University (of Newfoundland)
MUNA	Memorial University Archives
NACFI	North American Council on Fishery Investigations
NAFEL	Newfoundland Associated Fish Exporters Limited
NFB	Newfoundland Fisheries Board
NCR	Newfoundland Census Returns
qtl(s)	Quintal(s): A measure of saltfish ready for the market (112 lbs or 50.8 kg)
PCLCE	*Proceedings of the Convention of Licensed Codfish Exporters*
PHA	*Proceedings of the House of Assembly of Newfoundland*
PLC	*Proceedings of the Legislative Council of Newfoundland (PLC)*
SJDS	*St. John's Daily Star*
TR	*The Trade Review*
TRPAD	The Rooms Provincial Archives Division
USFC	United States Fish Commission
WS	*Western Star*

Newspapers

Boston Evening Transcript, Boston
Daily Colonist, St. John's (1886–1892)
Daily News, St. John's (1894–1937)
Evening Herald, St. John's (1890–1920)
Evening Mercury, St. John's (1882–1890)
Evening Telegram, St. John's (1887–1937)
St. John's Daily Star, St. John's (1915–1921)
The Trade Review, St. John's (1892–1895)
Western Star, Corner Brook (1900–1937)

Annual Reports and Series

Board of Trade (BT), 1909–1938.
Centre for Newfoundland Studies, MUN.

Commission of Government (CG), 1935–1938.
Department of Fisheries (DF), 1893–1897.
Department of Marine and Fisheries (DMF), 1898–1934.
Department of Natural Resources (DNR), 1934–1949.
Fisheries Commission (FC), 1888–1892.
Fishery Research Commission (FRC), 1931–1937.
Journal of House of Assembly of Newfoundland (*JHA*), 1887–1937.
Newfoundland Census Returns (NCR), 1891, 1901, 1911, 1921.
Proceedings of the House of Assembly of Newfoundland (*PHA*), 1887–1937.
Proceedings of the Legislative Council of Newfoundland (*PLC*), 1887–1937.
Statutes of Newfoundland, 1887–1937.

Archival Sources

MUNA, COLL-137, Geography Collection of Historical Photos.
MUNA, COLL-198, Rhoda Dawson papers.
MUNA, COLL-237, Robert Bond papers.
MUNA COLL-307, Michael Harrington papers.
MUNA, MF-055, George William Jeffers collection.
MUNA, President's Office, Box PO-9, file "Biology, JLP."
TRPAD, GN 1/3/A, Boxes 23-74, Governor's Office, Miscellaneous Letters.
TRPAD, GN 2, Colonial Secretary's Office, Series 2.5: Special Files.
TRPAD, GN 2, Colonial Secretary's Office, Series 2.15: Opinions, memoranda, correspondence.
TRPAD, GN 8, Prime Ministers' Papers, Edward Patrick Morris sous fonds.
TRPAD, GN 8, Prime Ministers' Papers, Richard Anderson Squires sous fonds.
TRPAD, GN 8, Prime Ministers' Papers, William Robertson Warren sous fonds.
TRPAD, GN 8, Prime Ministers' Papers, Frederick C. Alderdice sous fonds.
TRPAD, GN 20, Department of Marine and Fisheries fonds, Series: Marine and Fisheries (1930–1932) subject files.
TRPAD, GN 34/2, Department of Marine and Fisheries fonds, Boxes 146–49.
TRPAD, GN 38, Commission of Government, Natural Resources, General Administration.
TRPAD, GN 127, Royal Commission of Enquiry Investigating the Sea Fisheries of Newfoundland & Labrador, other than the Seal Fishery.
TRPAD, MG 73, Board of Trade Correspondence, Boxes 1–34, 69–71.

Fisheries Research Commission (FRC) Publications (in sequential order, 1930–1949)

Research Bulletins

Lindsay, S.T., and H. Thompson. *Biology of the Salmon (Salmo salar L.) Taken in Newfoundland Waters in 1931*. Research Bulletin No. 1. St. John's: Fishery Research Commission, 1932.

Sleggs, G.F. *Observations upon the Economic Biology of the Caplin (Mallotus villosus O.F. Müller)*. Research Bulletin No. 2. St. John's: Fishery Research Commission, 1933.

Frost, N. *I. Amphipoda from Newfoundland Water: II. Decapod Larvae from Newfoundland Waters*. Research Bulletin No. 3. St. John's: Fishery Research Commission, 1936.

Frowt, N. *Some Fishes of Newfoundland Waters*. Research Bulletin No. 4. St. John's: Fishery Research Commission, 1938.

Frost, N., and A.M. Wilson. *The Genus Ceratium and Its Use as an Indicator of Hydrographic Conditions in Newfoundland Waters: With an Appendix on Hydrographic Conditions*. Research Bulletin No. 5. St. John's: Fishery Research Commission, 1938.

Thompson, H. *The Occurrence and Biological Features of Haddock in the Newfoundland Area*. Research Bulletin No. 6. St. John's: Fishery Research Commission, 1939.

Templeman, W. *Investigations into the Life History of the Lobster (Homarus americanus) on the West Coast of Newfoundland, 1938*. Research Bulletin No. 7. St. John's: Fishery Research Commission, 1939.

Templeman, W. *Lobster Tagging on the West Coast of Newfoundland, 1938*. Research Bulletin No. 8. St. John's: Fishery Research Commission, 1940.

Frost, N. *A Preliminary Study of Newfoundland Trout*. Research Bulletin No. 9. St. John's: Fishery Research Commission, 1940.

Templeman, W. *The Washing of Berried Lobsters and the Enforcement of Berried Lobster Laws*. Research Bulletin No. 10. St. John's: Fishery Research Commission, 1940.

Templeman, W. *The Newfoundland Lobster Fishery: An Account of Statistics, Methods and Important Laws*. Research Bulletin No. 11. St. John's: Fishery Research Commission, 1941.

Blair, A.A. *Salmon Investigations: 1. Obstructions in Newfoundland and Labrador Rivers.* Research Bulletin No. 12. St. John's: Fishery Research Commission, 1943.

Blair, A.A. *Salmon Investigations: 2. Atlantic Salmon of the East Coast of Newfoundland and Labrador, 1939.* Research Bulletin No. 13. St. John's: Fishery Research Commission, 1943.

Thompson, H. *A Biological and Economic Study of Cod (Gadus callarias, L.) in the Newfoundland Area, including Labrador.* Research Bulletin No. 14. St. John's: Fishery Research Commission, 1943.

Templeman, W. *The Life History of the Spiny Dogfish (Squalus acanthias) and the Vitamin A. Values of Dogfish Liver Oil.* Research Bulletin No. 15. St. John's: Fishery Research Commission, 1944.

Templeman, W., and S.N. Tibbo. *Lobster Investigations in Newfoundland, 1938 to 1941.* Research Bulletin No. 16. St. John's: Fishery Research Commission, 1945.

Templeman, W. *The Life History of the Caplin (Mallotus villosus O.F. Müller) in Newfoundland Waters.* Research Bulletin No. 17. St. John's: Fishery Research Commission, 1948.

Templeman, W. *Abnormalities in Lobsters: A Possible Substitute for the Plugging and Banding of Lobster Claws; Body Form and Stage Identification in the Early Stage of the American Lobster; Growth per Moult in the American Lobster.* Research Bulletin No. 18. St. John's: Fishery Research Commission, 1948.

Service Bulletins

Macpherson, N.L. *The Dried Codfish Industry.* Service Bulletin No. 1. St. John's: Department of Natural Resources, 1935.

Thompson, H. *Memorandum on the Lobster Industry in Newfoundland.* Service Bulletin No. 2. St. John's: Department of Natural Resources, 1934.

Macpherson, N.L. *Newfoundland Cod Liver Oil.* Service Bulletin No. 3. St. John's: Department of Natural Resources, 1937.

Hampton, W.F. *Pink Fish: Its Cause and Prevention.* Service Bulletin No. 4. St. John's: Department of Natural Resources, 1938.

Hampton, W.F. *The Dogfish and How It Can Be Used.* Service Bulletin No. 5. St. John's: Department of Natural Resources, 1938.

Frost, N. *Trout and Their Conservation.* Service Bulletin No. 6. St. John's: Department of Natural Resources, 1938.

Wilson, A.M. *Production and Composition of Commercial Salt.* Service Bulletin No. 7. St. John's: Department of Natural Resources, 1938.

Frost, N. *Newfoundland Fishes: A Popular Account of Their Life Histories.* Service Bulletin No. 8. St. John's: Department of Natural Resources, 1938.

Hampton, W.F. *Approved Methods of Handling Codfish for Salting and Drying.* Service Bulletin No. 9. St. John's: Department of Natural Resources, 1938.

Murphy, J.F. *Production of Fish Meal with Simple Home-made Equipment.* Service Bulletin No. 10. St. John's: Department of Natural Resources, 1939.

Wilson, A.M. *Fish Meal and Its Uses.* Service Bulletin No. 11. St. John's: Department of Natural Resources, 1939.

Hampton, W.F. *Elementary Principles of Food Preservation.* Service Bulletin No. 12. St. John's: Department of Natural Resources, 1939.

Hampton, W.F. *A Guide to Canning Practice.* Service Bulletin No. 13. St. John's: Department of Natural Resources, 1940.

Frost, N. *Newfoundland Flat-fishes: A Popular Account of Their Life Histories.* Service Bulletin No. 14. St. John's: Department of Natural Resources, 1940.

Templeman, W. *The Life History of the Lobster.* Service Bulletin No. 15. St. John's: Department of Natural Resources, 1940.

Economic Bulletins

Thompson, H. *A Survey of the Fisheries of Newfoundland and Recommendations for a Scheme of Research.* Economic Bulletin No. 1. St. John's: Fishery Research Commission, 1930.

King, H. *The Marketing of Fishery Products in Newfoundland.* Economic Bulletin No. 2. St. John's: Fishery Research Commission, 1937.

Newfoundland. *Report of the Commission of Enquiry Investigating the Seafisheries of Newfoundland and Labrador Other Than the Sealfishery.* Economic Bulletin No. 3. St. John's: Department of Natural Resources, 1937.

Newfoundland. *Report of Fisheries Research Committee.* Economic Bulletin No. 4. St. John's: Department of Natural Resources, 1937.

Maurice, J. *United States of America Fishery Market Survey.* Economic Bulletin No. 5. St. John's: Fishery Research Commission, 1937.

Foote, W.H. *Methods of Production & Curing of Norwegian Fish.* Economic Bulletin No. 6. St. John's: Department of Natural Resources, 1938.

Maurice, J. *Cuba Fishery Market Survey, November 1937.* Economic Bulletin No. 7. St. John's: Department of Natural Resources, 1937.

Newfoundland Fisheries Board. *Report of the Newfoundland Fisheries Board and General Review of the Fisheries for the Years 1939 and 1940, with Statistical Survey.* Economic Bulletin No. 8. St. John's: Department of Natural Resources, 1940.

Newfoundland Fisheries Board. *Report of the Newfoundland Fisheries Board and General Review of the Fisheries for the Year 1941, with Statistical Survey.* Economic Bulletin No. 9. St. John's: Robinson & Co., Ltd., 1942.

Newfoundland Fisheries Board. *Report of the Newfoundland Fisheries Board and General Review of the Fisheries for the Year 1942, with Statistical Survey.* Economic Bulletin No. 10. St. John's: Office of the King's Printer, 1943.

Newfoundland Fisheries Board. *Report of the Newfoundland Fisheries Board and General Review of the Fisheries for the Year 1943, with Statistical Survey.* Economic Bulletin No. 11. St. John's: Bowden & Co., Ltd., 1944.

Newfoundland Fisheries Board. *Report of the Newfoundland Fisheries Board and General Review of the Fisheries for the Year 1944, with Statistical Survey.* Economic Bulletin No. 12. St. John's: Department of Natural Resources, 1945.

Newfoundland Fisheries Board. *Report of the Newfoundland Fisheries Board and General Review of the Fisheries for the Year 1945, with Statistical Survey.* Economic Bulletin No. 13. St. John's: Department of Natural Resources, 1946.

Newfoundland Fisheries Board. *Report of the Newfoundland Fisheries Board and General Review of the Fisheries for the Year 1946, with Statistical Survey.* Economic Bulletin No. 14. St. John's: Office of the King's Printer, 1948.

Newfoundland Fisheries Board. *Report of the Newfoundland Fisheries Board and General Review of the Fisheries for the Year 1947, with Statistical Survey.* Economic Bulletin No. 15. St. John's: Robinson & Co., Ltd., 1948.

Newfoundland Fisheries Board. *Report of the Newfoundland Fisheries Board and General Review of the Fisheries for the Year 1948, with Statistical Survey.* Economic Bulletin No. 16. Ottawa: Edmond Cloutier, 1949.

Published and Printed Sources

Alexander, D. *The Decay of Trade: An Economic History of the Newfoundland Saltfish Trade 1935–1965.* St. John's: ISER Books, 1977.

———. "Newfoundland's Traditional Economy and Development to 1934." In *Newfoundland in the Nineteenth and Twentieth Centuries: Essays in Interpretation*, edited by J. Hiller and P. Neary. Toronto: University of Toronto Press, 1980.

Ali, T., and E. Mandel. "The Luck of a Crazy Youth (Interview with Ernest Mandel)." *New Left Review* 213 (1995): 101–06.

Allard, D.C. "Spencer Fullerton Baird and the Foundations of American Marine Science." *Marine Fisheries Review* 50, no. 4 (1988): 124–29.

Anspach, L.A. *A History of Newfoundland.* London: Sherwood, Gilbert and Piper, 1819.

Apostle, R., G. Barrett, P. Holm, S. Jentoft, L. Mazany, B. McCay, and K. Mikalsen. *Community, State, and Market on the North Atlantic Rim: Challenges to Modernity in the Fisheries.* Toronto: University of Toronto Press, 1998.

Apple, R.D. *Vitamania: Vitamins in American Culture.* New Brunswick, NJ: Rutgers University Press, 1996.

Arboleda, M. "Revitalizing Science and Technology Studies: A Marxian Critique of More-Than-Human Geographies." *Environment and Planning D: Society and Space* 35, no. 2 (2017): 360–78.

———. *Planetary Mine: Territories of Extraction under Late Capitalism.* London: Verso, 2020.

——— and D. Banoub. "Market Monstrosity in Industrial Fishing: Capital as Subject and the Urbanization of Nature." *Social & Cultural Geography* 19, no. 1 (2018): 120–38.

Ashforth, A. *The Politics of Official Discourse in Twentieth-Century South Africa.* Oxford: Clarendon Press, 1990.

Banoub, D. "Black Monday, 1894: Saltfish, Credit, and the Ecology of Politics in Newfoundland." *Atlantic Studies* 17, no. 2 (2020): 227–43.

Baker, M. "William Ford Coaker, the Formative Years, 1871–1908." *Newfoundland and Labrador Studies* 27, no. 2 (2012): 223–66.

———. "Challenging the 'Merchants' Domain': William Coaker and the Price of Fish, 1908–1919." *Newfoundland and Labrador Studies* 29, no. 2 (2014): 189–226.

———, A.B. Dickinson, and C.W. Sanger. "Adolph Nielsen: Norwegian Influence on Newfoundland Fisheries in the Late 19th-Early 20th Century." *Newfoundland Quarterly* 27, no. 2 (1992): 25–35.

——— and S. Ryan. "The Newfoundland Fishery Research Commission, 1930–1934." In *How Deep Is the Ocean? Historical Essays on Canada's Atlantic Fishery*, edited by J.E. Candow and C. Corbin. Sydney, NS: University College of Cape Breton Press, 1997.

Barnes, F. "Bringing Another Empire Alive? The Empire Marketing Board and the Construction of Dominion Identity, 1926–33." *Journal of Imperial and Commonwealth History* 42, no. 1 (2014): 61–85.

Bavington, D. *Managed Annihilation: An Unnatural History of the Newfoundland Cod Collapse.* Vancouver: University of British Columbia Press, 2010.

Beatty, S.A., and G. Fougère. *The Processing of Dried Salted Fish.* Bulletin No. 112. Ottawa: Fisheries Research Board of Canada, 1957.

Bellofiore, R., G. Starosta, and P.D. Thomas. *In Marx's Laboratory: Critical Interpretations of the Grundrisse.* Leiden: Brill, 2013.

——— and T. Redolfi Riva. "The Neue Marx-Lektüre. Putting the Critique of Political Economy Back into the Critique of Society." *Radical Philosophy* 189 (2015): 24–36.

Bennett, J.H. *Treatise on the Oleum Jecoris Aselli, or, Cod Liver Oil, as Therapeutic Agent in Certain Forms of Gout, Rheumatism, and Scrofula: With Cases.* London: S. Highley, 1841.

Bills, C.E. "The Principal Chemical Researches on Cod Liver Oil." *Chemical Reviews* 3, no. 4 (1927): 425–42.

———. "Antiricketic Substances VI. The Distribution of Vitamin D, with Some Notes on Its Possible Origin." *Journal of Biological Chemistry* 72, no. 2 (1927): 751–58.

———. "Early Experiences with Fish Oils — A Retrospect." *Nutrition Reviews* 13, no. 3 (1955): 65–67.

Blackburn, R. "The Unexpected Dialectic of Structural Reforms." in *The Legacy of Ernest Mandel*, edited by G. Achard, 16–23. London: Verso, 1999.

Bloch, E. "Changing the World: Marx's *Theses on Feuerbach.*" In *On Karl Marx*, 54–105. London: Verso Books, 2018.

Bolster, W.J. *The Mortal Sea.* Cambridge, MA: Harvard University Press, 2012.

Bonefeld, W. "Abstract Labour: Against Its Nature and on Its Time." *Capital & Class* 34, no. 2 (2010): 257–76.

———. *Critical Theory and the Critique of Political Economy: On Subversion and Negative Reason.* London: Bloomsbury, 2014.

———, R. Gunn, and K. Psychopedis, eds. *Open Marxism: Dialectics and History.* London: Pluto Press, 1991.

Boyd, W. "Making Meat: Science, Technology and American Poultry Production." *Technology and Culture* 42, no. 4 (2001): 631–64.

Browne, W.J., J.B. Baird, D.J. Davies, J. Grieve, J.W. Morris, C.L. Parkins, R.J. Stevenson, J.S. Woods, C.F. Horwood, and W. Watson. *The By-Products of the Fisheries of Nfld: A Paper Prepared by the Group on "Our Economic and Commercial Problems" for Presentation to the University Graduates' Association.* St. John's: Robinson & Co., 1928.

Bukharin, N., et al. *Science at the Crossroads*, 2nd ed. London: Frank Cass & Co., 1971 [1931].

Cadigan, S. *Hope and Deception in Conception Bay: Merchant–Settler Relations in Newfoundland, 1785–1855.* Toronto: University of Toronto Press, 1995.

———. *Newfoundland and Labrador: A History.* Toronto: University of Toronto Press, 2009.

———. "Science, Industry, and Fishers in Fisheries Management: The Experience of Newfoundland and Labrador, 1890s–1990s." *Studia Atlantica* 13 (2009): 75–92.

———. *Death on Two Fronts: National Tragedies and the Fate of Democracy in Newfoundland, 1914–1934.* London: Allen Lane, 2013.

Callaci, E. "On Acknowledgments." *American Historical Review* 125, no. 1 (2020): 126–31.

Carpenter, K.J. "A Short History of Nutritional Science: Part 1 (1785–1885)." *Journal of Nutrition* 133, no. 3 (2003): 638–45.

———. "A Short History of Nutritional Science: Part 3 (1912–1944)." *Journal of Nutrition* 133, no. 10 (2003): 3023–32.

———. "The Discovery of Thiamin." *Annals of Nutrition & Metabolism* 61, no. 3 (2012): 219–23.

——— and B. Sutherland. "Eijkman's Contribution to the Discovery of Vitamins." *Journal of Nutrition* 125, no. 2 (1995): 155–63.

Carrera, J.I. *El Capital: Razón Histórica, Sujeto Revolucionario y Conciencia.* Buenos Aires: Imago Mundi, 2013 [2003].

———. "Method: From the Grundrisse to Capital." In *In Marx's Laboratory: Critical Interpretations of the Grundrisse*, edited by R. Bellofiore, G. Starosta, and P.D. Thomas, 43–69. Leiden: Brill, 2013.

———. "Dialectics on Its Feet, or the Form of the Consciousness of the Working Class as Historical Subject." In *Marx's Capital and Hegel's Logic*, edited by Fred Moseley and Tony Smith, 64–88. Leiden: Brill, 2014.

Carson, R. *The Sea Around Us.* Oxford: Oxford University Press, 2003 [1950].

Carter, K.C. "The Germ Theory, Beriberi, and the Deficiency Theory of Disease." *Medical History* 21, no. 2 (1977): 119–36.

Cell, G. *English Enterprise in Newfoundland 1577–1660.* Toronto: University of Toronto Press, 1969.

Chappell, E. *Voyage of His Majesty's Ship Rosamond to Newfoundland and the Southern Coast of Labrador.* London: J. Mawman, 1818.

Chekov, A. "O Women, Women!" *Conjunctions* 31 (1998): 31–33.

Clark, R. "Romancing the Harlequins: A Note on Class Struggle in the Newfoundland Village." In *Contrary Winds: Essays on Newfoundland Society in Crisis*, edited by R. Clark. St. John's: Breakwater Books, 1986.

Clarke, F.N. *The Newfoundland Bait Service: Historical Notes on the Catching and Preservation of the Bait Fishes.* n.p., 1969.

Cleaver, H. "The Zapatistas and the Electronic Fabric of Struggle." In *Zapatista! Reinventing Revolution in Mexico*, edited by John Holloway and Eloísa Peláez, 81–103. London: Pluto Press, 1998.

Coaker, W.F. *Hon. W.F. Coaker's Speech on the Fish Regulations, House of Assembly, April 27th 1920.* St. John's: Union Publishing Co. 1920.

———. *Twenty Years of the Fishermen's Protective Union of Newfoundland.* St. John's: Advocate Publishing Co., 1930.

Condon, M.E. *The Fisheries and Resources of Newfoundland: 'The Mine of the Sea' (National, International and Co-operative).* St. John's: n.p., 1925.

Cronon, W. *Nature's Metropolis: Chicago and the Great West.* New York: W.W. Norton, 1991.

Coulthard, G. *Red Skin, White Masks: Rejecting the Colonial Politics of Recognition.* Minneapolis: University of Minnesota Press, 2014.

Crehan, K. *Gramsci's Common Sense: Inequality and Its Narratives.* Durham, NC: Duke University Press, 2016.

Crosby, A. *The Measure of Reality: Quantification and Western Society, 1250–1600.* Cambridge: Cambridge University Press, 1997.

Cullen, D. "Race, Debt and Empire: Racialising the Newfoundland Financial Crisis of 1933." *Transactions of the Institute of British Geographers* 43, no. 4 (2018): 1–14.

Cushing, D.H. *The Provident Sea.* Cambridge: Cambridge University Press, 1988.

Cutting, C.L. *Fish Saving: A History of Fish Processing from Ancient to Modern Times.* New York: Philosophical Library, 1956.

Dannevig, G.M. "Apparatus and Methods Employed at the Marine Fish Hatchery at Flödevig, Norway." *Bulletin of the Bureau of Fisheries* 28, no. 2 (1910): 799–810.

———. "The Utility of Sea-Fish Hatching." *Bulletin of the Bureau of Fisheries* 28, no. 2 (1910): 811–16.

Daston, L. "Objectivity and the Escape from Perspective." *Social Studies of Science* 22, no. 4 (1992): 597–618.

Davies, B. "Atlantic Guardian Visits Munn's." *Atlantic Guardian* 3, no. 1 (1947): 48–57.

Davies, D.J. *Newfoundland Cod Liver Oil.* St. John's: Manning & Rabbitts, 1930.

——— and A. Oldford. *Report of the Tour of Inspection Which Was Made to the Newfoundland Foreign Fish Markets.* St. John's: Marine and Fisheries Department, 1933.

Dawson, R. "The Folk Art of the Labrador." *Among the Deep-Sea Fishers* 36, no. 2 (1938): 39–49.

———. "The Wharves of St. John's, Newfoundland." *Canadian Parliamentary Review* 15, no. 2 (1992): 2–5.

Dear, P. "From Truth to Disinterestedness in the Seventeenth Century." *Social Studies of Science* 22, no. 4 (1992): 619–31.

Deas, J. "Vitamin A and Its Variations in Cod Liver Oil." *Canadian Medical Association Journal* 14, no. 10 (1924): 959–61.

DeLuca, H.F. "History of the Discovery of Vitamin D and Its Active Metabolites." *BoneKey Reports* 3, no. 479 (2014): 1–8.

Demeritt, D. "Scientific Forest Conservation and the Statistical Picturing of Nature's Limits in the Progressive-Era United States." *Environment and Planning D: Society and Space* 19, no. 4 (2001): 431–59.

Dominions Royal Commission (DRC). *Royal Commission on the Natural Resources, Trade, and Legislation of Certain Portions of His Majesty's Dominions. Minutes of Evidence Taken in Newfoundland in 1914.* London: Eyre and Spottiswoode, 1915.

Drummond, I.M. *British Economic Policy and the Empire, 1919–1939.* London: George Allen and Unwin, 1972.

Drummond, J.C. "The Nomenclature of the So-called Accessory Food Factors (Vitamins)." *Biochemical Journal* 14, no. 5 (1920): 660.

———. *Lane Medical Lectures: Biochemical Studies of Nutritional Problems.* Stanford, CA: Stanford University Press, 1934.

——— and T.P. Hilditch. *The Relative Values of Cod Liver Oils from Various Sources (EMB 35).* London: His Majesty's Stationery Office, 1930.

——— and S.S. Zilva. "The Preparation of Cod Liver Oil and the Effect of the Processes on the Vitamin Value of the Oils." *Journal of the Society of Chemical Industry* 41, no. 15 (1922): 280T–84T.

Duff, W. *The Fisheries of Newfoundland: Lecture Delivered in St. John's by Mr. Walter Duff of the Fishery Board for Scotland.* St. John's: n.p., 1914. Available at CNS, MUN.

Dussel, E. *Towards an Unknown Marx: A Commentary on the Manuscripts of 1861–63.* Translated by Y. Angulo. London: Routledge, 2001 [1988].

Elden, S. "Missing the Point: Globalization, Deterritorialization and the Space of the World." *Transactions of the Institute of British Geographers* 30, no. 1 (2005): 8–19.

Elliot, W. "The Work of the Empire Marketing Board." *Journal of the Royal Society of Arts* 79, no. 4191 (1931): 736–48.

EPR Kirby and Company, Management Consultants Group. *Historic and Cultural Significance of Dildo Island.* n.p., 1995. Available at: CNS, MUN.

Fanon, F. *Black Skin, White Masks.* Translated by C.L. Markman. London: Pluto Press, 1986.

Faris, J. *Cat Harbour: A Newfoundland Fishing Settlement.* Newfoundland Social and Economic Studies No. 3. St. John's: ISER Books, 1973.

Federici, S. "Marx and Feminism." *tripleC: Communication, Capitalism & Critique.* 16, no. 2 (2018): 468–75.

Ferguson, M.E. "Making Fish: Salt-Cod Processing on the East Coast of Newfoundland — A Study in Historic Occupational Folklife." MA thesis, Department of Folklore, Memorial University of Newfoundland, 1996.

Firestone, M. *Brothers and Rivals: Patrilocality in Savage Cove.* Newfoundland Social and Economic Studies No. 5. St. John's: ISER Books, 1967.

Finley, C. *All the Fish in the Sea: Maximum Sustainable Yield and the Failure of Fisheries Management.* Chicago: University of Chicago Press, 2011.

Foster, J.B. *Marx's Ecology.* New York: Monthly Review Press, 2000.

——— and F. Magdoff. "Liebig, Marx, and the Depletion of Soil Fertility." *Monthly Review* 50, no. 3 (1998): 32–45.

Fraser, A.M. "Newfoundland, Economic and Political II: Government-by-Commission (1934–6): A Survey." *Canadian Journal of Economics and Political Science* 3, no. 1 (1937): 71–83.

Funk, C. "The Etiology of the Deficiency Disease." *Journal of State Medicine* 20 (1912): 341–69.

García Linera, A. *Hacia el gran ayllu universal: Pensar el mundo desde Los Andes* (Santiago: Editorial Arcis, 2014.

Garstang, W. "The Impoverishment of the Sea: A Critical Summary of the Experimental and Statistical Evidence Bearing upon the Alleged Depletion of the Trawling Grounds." *Journal of the Marine Biological Association of the United Kingdom* 6, no. 1 (1900): 1–69.

Gerhardsen, G.M. *Salted Cod and Related Species*. FAO Fisheries Study No. 1. Washington: FAO, 1949.

Ghaly, A.E., D. Dave, S. Budge, and M.S. Brooks. "Fish Spoilage Mechanisms and Preservation Techniques." *American Journal of Applied Sciences* 7, no. 7 (2010): 859–77.

Gonzalez, M. *In the Red Corner: The Marxism of José Carlos Mariátegui*. Chicago: Haymarket Books, 2019.

Gorostiza, S., and M. Ortega Cerdà. "'The Unclaimed Latifundium': The Configuration of the Spanish Fishing Sector under Francoist Autarky, 1939–1951." *Journal of Historical Geography* 52 (2016): 26–35.

Graham, M. *Report to the Director of Fishery Investigations Comprising Observations on the Natural History of the Newfoundland Shore Cod.* Lowestoft: Fisheries Laboratory, 1922.

Gramsci, A. *Selections from the Prison Notebooks*. New York: International Publishers, 1971.

Great Britain. *Newfoundland Royal Report: Presented by the Secretary of State for Dominion Affairs to Parliament by Command of His Majesty, November, 1933*. Cmd. 4480. London: His Majesty's Stationery Office, 1933.

Gunstone, F.D. "T.P. Hilditch, CBE, DSc, FRIC, FRS." *Journal of the American Oil Chemists' Society* 42, no. 9 (1965): a474–a530.

Gushue, R. *The Fisheries of Newfoundland, Retrospect and Prospect, an Address Delivered at a Meeting of the Rotary Club of St. John's, Nfld., September 12, 1946*. n.p., 1946.

———. "Newfoundland's Salt Codfish Industry Adopts the Pool Plan of Marketing." *Atlantic Guardian* 4, no. 1 (1947): 10–13.

Guy, R.A. "The History of Cod Liver Oil as a Remedy." *American Journal of Diseases of Children* 26, no. 2 (1923): 112–16.

Hampton, W.F. *Approved Methods of Handling Codfish for Salting and Drying.* Service Bulletin No. 9. St. John's: Department of Natural Resources, 1938.

Harding, S. "Stronger Objectivity for Sciences from Below." *Em Construção* 5 (2019): 173–92.

Harvey, D. "Resources, and the Ideology of Science." *Economic Geography* 50, no. 3 (1974): 256–77.

———. *The Limits to Capital.* London: Verso, 2006 [1982].

———. *The Enigma of Capital and the Crises of Capitalism.* Oxford and New York: Oxford University Press, 2010.

Harvey, M. "The Artificial Propagation of Marine Food Fishes and Edible Crustaceans." *Transactions of the Royal Society of Canada* 10, no. 4 (1892): 17–37.

———. *Newfoundland As It Was in 1894: A Hand-Book and Tourists' Guide.* St. John's: J.W. Withers, 1894.

———. "The Newfoundland Fisheries Commission." In D.W. Prowse, *A History of Newfoundland.* Portugal Cove–St. Philip's, NL: Boulder Publications, 2007 [1895].

Hatton, J., and M. Harvey. *Newfoundland: Its History, Its Present Condition, and Its Prospects in the Future.* Boston: Doyle & Whittle, 1883.

Henderson, G.L. "Nature and Fictitious Capital: The Historical Geography of an Agrarian Question." *Antipode* 30, no. 2 (1998): 73–118.

Hewitt, K. "Exploring Uncharted Waters: Government's Role in the Development of Newfoundland's Cod, Lobster and Herring Fisheries, 1888-1913." MA thesis, Department of History, Memorial University of Newfoundland, 1992.

———. "The Newfoundland Fishery and State Intervention in the Nineteenth Century: The Fisheries Commission, 1888–1893." *Newfoundland Studies* 9, no. 1 (1993): 58–80.

Hiller J.K. "A History of Newfoundland, 1874–1901." PhD dissertation, Department of History, University of Cambridge, 1971.

———. "The Origins of the Pulp and Paper Industry in Newfoundland." *Acadiensis* 11, no. 2 (1982): 42–68.

———. "The Newfoundland Credit System: An Interpretation." In *Merchant Credit and Labour Strategies in Historical Perspective*, edited by R. Ommer. Fredericton, NB: Acadiensis Press, 1990.

Hjort, J. "Fluctuations in the Great Fisheries of Northern Europe Viewed in the Light of Biological Research." *Rapports et Procès-Verbaux des Réunions du Conseil International pour l'Exploration de la Mer* 20 (1914): 1–228.

Hoffmann, R.C. "Frontier Foods for Late Medieval Consumers: Culture, Economy, Ecology." *Environment and History* 7, no. 2 (2001): 131–67.

Holm, P. "The Dynamics of Institutionalization: Transformation Processes in Norwegian Fisheries." *Administrative Science Quarterly* 40, no. 3 (1995): 398–422.

Hong, R.G. "'An Agency for the Common Weal': The Newfoundland Board of Trade, 1909–1915." MA thesis, Department of History, Memorial University of Newfoundland, 1998.

Hoogeveen, D. "Fish-hood: Environmental Assessment, Critical Indigenous Studies, and Posthumanism at Fish Lake (Teztan Biny), Tsilhqot'in Territory." *Environment and Planning D: Society and Space* 34, no. 2 (2016): 355–70.

Hopkins, F.G. "Feeding Experiments Illustrating the Importance of Accessory Factors in Normal Dietaries." *Journal of Physiology* 44, nos. 5–6 (1912): 425–60.

Hubbard, J.M. "Home Sweet Home? A.G. Huntsman and the Homing Behaviour of Canadian Atlantic Salmon." *Acadiensis* 19, no. 2 (1990): 49–71.

———. *A Science on the Scales: The Rise of Canadian Atlantic Fisheries Biology, 1898–1939*. Toronto: University of Toronto Press, 2006.

———. "Mediating the North Atlantic Environment: Fisheries Biologists, Technology, and Marine Spaces." *Environmental History* 18, no. 1 (2013): 88–100.

———. "Johan Hjort: The Canadian Fisheries Expedition, International Scientific Networks, and the Challenge of Modernization." *ICES Journal of Marine Science* 71, no. 8 (2014): 2000–07.

Huntsman, A.G. *The Ocean around Newfoundland*. n.p., 1925.

———. *Method of Handling Fish: I. The Processing of Dried Fish*. Bulletin No. 9. Ottawa: F.A. Acland, 1927.

Hutchings, J.A., B. Neis, and P. Ripley. "The 'Nature' of Cod, *Gadus morhua*." In *The Resilient Outport: Ecology, Economy, and Society in Rural Newfoundland*, edited by R. Ommer, 140–85. St. John's: ISER Books, 2002).

Huxley, T.H. *Inaugural Meeting of the Fishery Congress: Address Delivered June 18, 1883*. London: William Clowes and Sons, 1883.

Imperial Economic Committee (IEC). *Report of the Imperial Economic Committee on Marketing and Preparing for Market of Foodstuffs Produced within the Empire: Fifth Report — Fish*. Cmd. 2934. London: His Majesty's Stationery Office, 1927.

Ihde, A.J., and S.L. Becker. "Conflict of Concepts in Early Vitamin Studies." *Journal of the History of Biology* 4, no. 1 (1971): 1–33.

Innis, H. *The Cod Fishery: The History of an International Economy*. Toronto: University of Toronto Press, 1954.

Jeffers, G.W. *Bulletin No 18: Observations on the Cod-fishery in the Strait of Belle Isle*. Toronto: Biological Board of Canada, 1931.

Keough, W. "'Good Looks Don't Boil the Pot': Irish-Newfoundland Women as Fish(-Producing) Wives." *Signs: Journal of Women in Culture and Society* 37, no. 3 (2012): 536–44.

Kern, S. *The Culture of Time and Space 1880–1918*, 2nd ed. Cambridge, MA: Harvard University Press, 2003.

King, H. *The Marketing of Fishery Products in Newfoundland*. Economic Bulletin No. 2. St. John's: Department of Natural Resources, 1937.

Kimmerer, R.W. *Braiding Sweetgrass: Indigenous Wisdom, Scientific Knowledge and the Teachings of Plants*. Minneapolis: Milkweed Editions, 2013.

Kinsey, D. "'Seeding the Water as the Earth': The Epicenter and Peripheries of a Western Aquacultural Revolution." *Environmental History* 11, no. 3 (2006): 527–66.

Knowles, L.C.A., and C.M. Knowles. *The Economic Development of the British Overseas Empire, Vol II: Comparative View of Dominion Problems, Canada*. New York: Routledge, 2005 [1930].

Korneski, K. "Development and Degradation: The Emergence and Collapse of the Lobster Fishery on Newfoundland's West Coast, 1856–1924." *Acadiensis* 41, no. 1 (2012): 21–48.

Kosik, K. *Dialectics of the Concrete: A Study on Problems of Man and World*. Boston: D. Reidel Publishing Company, 1976.

Kothari, U. "Trade, Consumption and Development Alliances: The Historical Legacy of the Empire Marketing Board Poster Campaign." *Third World Quarterly* 35, no. 1 (2014): 43–64.

Kula, W. *Measures and Men.* Translated by R. Szreter. Princeton, NJ: Princeton University Press, 1986.

Kurlansky, M. *Cod: A Biography of the Fish That Changed the World.* London: Vintage, 1999.

Larkin, P.A. "Fisheries Management: An Essay for Ecologists." *Annual Review of Ecology and Systematics* 9 (1978): 57–73.

Laverty, P. *Silk Stocking Mats: Hooked Mats of the Grenfell Mission.* Montreal and Kingston: McGill-Queen's University Press, 2005.

Lever, M.A., O. Rouxel, J.C. Alt, N. Shimizu, S. Ono, R.M. Coggon, W.C. Shanks, L. Lapham, M. Elvert, X. Prieto-Mollar, and K.U. Hinrichs. "Evidence for Microbial Carbon and Sulfur Cycling in Deeply Buried Ridge Flank Basalt." *Science* 339, no. 6125 (2013): 1305–08.

Liedman, S.E. *A World to Win: The Life and Works of Karl Marx.* London: Verso Books, 2018.

Lodge, T. *Dictatorship in Newfoundland.* London: Cassell & Co., 1939.

Longo, S.B., R. Clausen, and B. Clark. *The Tragedy of the Commodity: Oceans, Fisheries, and Aquaculture.* New Brunswick, NJ: Rutgers University Press, 2015.

Lukács, G. "Reification and the Consciousness of the Proletariat." In Lukács, *History and Class Consciousness: Studies in Marxist Dialectics.* Translated by R. Livingstone. Cambridge, MA: MIT Press, 1971.

Macleod, M. "Prophet with Honour: Dr. William F. Hampton, 1908–1968, Newfoundland Scientist." *Newfoundland Quarterly* 81, no. 1 (1985): 29–36.

———. *A Bridge Built Halfway: A History of Memorial University College, 1925–1950.* Montreal and Kingston: McGill-Queen's University Press, 1990.

———. *Crossroads Country: Memories of Pre-Confederation Newfoundland, at the Intersection of American, British and Canadian Connections.* St. John's: Breakwater Books, 1999.

Macpherson, N.L. *Technical Investigations of the Dried Codfish Industry.* St. John's: Fishery Research Commission, 1932.

———. "Vitamin A Concentration of Cod Liver Oil Correlated with Age of Cod." *Nature* 132, no. 3322 (1933): 26–27.

———. *The Dried Codfish Industry.* Service Bulletin No. 1. St. John's: Fishery Research Commission, 1935.

———. *Newfoundland Cod Liver Oil.* Service Bulletin No. 3. St. John's: Department of Natural Resources, 1937.

Malpas, J., and A.F. King. "Pioneers of Geological Exploration, Mapping and Mining in Newfoundland." In *Early Science in Newfoundland and Labrador*, edited by D.H. Steele, 8–26. St. John's: Chapter of Sigma Xi, 1987.

Maltz, A. "Casimer Funk, Nonconformist Nomenclature, and Networks Surrounding the Discovery of Vitamins." *Journal of Nutrition* 143, no. 7 (2013): 1013–20.

Mandel, E. *Late Capitalism*. London: Verso, 1978 [1972].

———. *The Formation of the Economic Thought of Karl Marx: 1843 to Capital*. London: Verso, 2015 [1967].

March, W.S. *Some Piscatorial Notes and Suggestions*. St. John's: "News" Job Print, 1895.

Mariátegui, José Carlos. "The Problem of Land." In Mariátegui, *Seven Interpretive Essays on Peruvian Reality*. Translated by M. Urquidi, 31–76. Austin: University of Texas Press, 1988.

Marx, K. *A Contribution to the Critique of Political Economy*. Translated by N.I. Stone. Chicago: Charles H. Kerr & Company, 1904.

———. *The German Ideology*. New York: International Publishers, 1970.

———. *Grundrisse: Foundations of the Critique of Political Economy*. Translated by M. Nicolaus. Harmondsworth: Penguin, 1973.

———. *Capital: A Critique of Political Economy, Volume 1*. Translated by B. Fowkes. London: Penguin, 1976 [1867].

———. *Capital: A Critique of Political Economy, Volume 2*. Translated by B. Fowkes. London: Penguin, 1992 [1885].

———. *Economic and Philosophic Manuscripts of 1844*. New York: Dover, 2007 [1844].

——— and F. Engels. *Collected Works, Vol. 42, Letters, 1864–68*. New York: International Publishers, 1987.

Mayo, H.B. "Newfoundland's Entry into the Dominion." *Canadian Journal of Economics and Political Science* 15, no. 4 (1949): 505–22.

McChesney, R.W., and B. Scott. "Upton Sinclair and the Contradictions of Capitalist Journalism." *Monthly Review* 54, no. 1 (2002): n.p.

McCollum, E.V., and M. Davis. "The Necessity of Certain Lipids in the Diet during Growth." *Journal of Biological Chemistry* 15, no. 1 (1913): 167–75.

——— and ———. "The Essential Factors in the Diet during Growth." *Journal of Biological Chemistry* 23, no. 1 (1915): 231–46.

McDonald, I.D.H. *"To Each His Own": William Coaker and the Fisherman's Protective Union in Newfoundland Politics, 1908–1925*. St. John's: ISER Books, 2008 [1987].

———. "The Reformer Coaker: A Brief Biographical Introduction." In *The Book of Newfoundland, Vol. 6*, edited by J.R. Smallwood, G.J. Power, and J.R. Thoms, 71–96. St. John's: Newfoundland Book Publishers, 1974.

McEvoy, A.F. *The Fisherman's Problem: Ecology and Law in the California Fisheries, 1850–1980*. Cambridge: Cambridge University Press, 1986.

McGee, H. *On Food and Cooking: The Science and Lore of the Kitchen.* New York: Simon & Schuster, 2004.

McPhee, J. *Draft No. 4: On the Writing Process.* New York: Farrar, Strauss, and Giroux, 2017.

Medical Research Council (MRC). *Report of the Medical Research Council for the Year 1921–22*. London: His Majesty's Stationery Office, 1922.

Mellanby, E. "An Experimental Investigation on Rickets." *The Lancet* 193, no. 4985 (1919): 407–12.

Meredith, D. "Imperial Images: The Empire Marketing Board, 1926–1932." *History Today* 37, no. 1 (1987): 30–36.

Merrifield, A. *The Amateur: The Pleasures of Doing What You Love.* London: Verso Books, 2017.

Mirowski, P. *The Effortless Economy of Science?* Durham, NC: Duke University Press, 2004.

——— and E.M. Sent. "The Commercialization of Science and the Response of STS." In *Handbook of Science, Technology and Society Studies*, edited by E. Hackett, O. Amsterdamska, and M. Lynch, 635–89. Cambridge, MA: MIT Press, 2007.

Mitchell, T. *Rule of Experts: Egypt, Techno-politics, Modernity.* Berkeley: University of California Press, 2002.

Møller, F.P. *Cod Liver Oil and Chemistry.* London: Peter Møller, 1895.

Moore, J.W. "Transcending the Metabolic Rift: A Theory of Crises in the Capitalist World-Ecology." *Journal of Peasant Studies* 38, no. 1 (2011): 1–46.

Moreton, J. *Life and Work in Newfoundland: Reminiscences of Thirteen Years Spent There.* London: Rivingtons, 1863.

Morris, E.P. "Cold Storage in Its Application to the Newfoundland Fisheries." *Newfoundland Quarterly* 22, no. 2 (1922): 30–31.

Morris, L. *Pressure Vessels: The Epidemic of Poor Mental Health among Higher Education Staff.* London: Higher Education Policy Institute, 2019.

Mukundan, M.K., P.D. Antony, and M.R. Nair. "A Review on Autolysis in Fish." *Fisheries Research* 4, nos. 3–4 (1986): 259–69.

Mumford, L. *Technics and Civilization.* Chicago: University of Chicago Press, 2010 [1934].

Munn, W.A. *The Cod Liver Oil Industry in Newfoundland.* St. John's: W.A. Munn, Manufacturers and Exporters, 1925.

Murray, J. *The Commercial Crisis in Newfoundland: Cause, Consequence and Cure.* St. John's: J.W. Withers, 1895.

Muszynski, A. *Cheap Wage Labour: Race and Gender in the Fisheries of British Columbia.* Montreal and Kingston: McGill-Queen's University Press, 1996.

Nash, C.E. *The History of Aquaculture.* Danvers, MA: Blackwell, 2011.

Neary, P. *Newfoundland in the North Atlantic World, 1929–1949.* Montreal and Kingston: McGill-Queen's University Press, 1988.

———. "'Wry Comment': Rhoda Dawson's Cartoon of Newfoundland Society, 1936." *Newfoundland Studies* 8, no. 1 (1992): 1–14.

———. *White Tie and Decorations: Sir John and Lady Hope Simpson in Newfoundland, 1934–1936.* Toronto: University of Toronto Press, 1996.

Newfoundland. *Report of the Commission on Fishery Matters.* St. John's: The Evening Herald Print, 1915.

———. *Rules and Regulations for the Manufacturing and Refining of Cod Liver Oil.* St. John's: Department of Marine and Fisheries, 1919.

———. *Statement of Policy by the Commission of Government, Newfoundland: Press Communiqué of the Seventh Meeting of the Commission of Government Issued Saturday, January 26th, 1935.* St. John's: Harvey & Company, 1935.

———. *Report of the Commission of Enquiry Investigating the Seafisheries of Newfoundland and Labrador Other than the Sealfishery.* Economic Bulletin No. 3. St. John's: Department of Natural Resources, 1937.

———. *Report of Fisheries Research Committee.* Economic Bulletin No. 4. St. John's: Department of Natural Resources, 1937.

Newfoundland's Fisheries; "Richer by Far Than all the Gold Mines of Peru," As Lord Bacon Declared Three Centuries Ago. n.p., 1910. Available at CNS, MUN.

Nielsen, A. *Report on the Cure of Codfish and Herring.* St. John's: Evening Herald Office, 1890.

———. *Directions for the Manufacture of Cod-Liver Oil.* St. John's: Bowden & Co., 1896.

———. *Directions for the Manufacture of Cod-Liver Oil, Part II: The Freezing Process.* St. John's: Bowden & Co., 1896.

Noel, S.J.R. *Politics in Newfoundland.* Toronto: University of Toronto Press, 1971.

Norris, L.C. "The Significant Advances of the Past Fifty Years in Poultry Nutrition." *Poultry Science* 37, no. 2 (1958): 256–74.

North American Council on Fishery Investigations (NACFI). *North American Council on Fishery Investigations Proceedings, 1921–1930*. No. 1. Ottawa: F.A. Acland, 1932.

———. *North American Council on Fishery Investigations Proceedings, 1931–1933*. No. 2. Ottawa: J.O. Patenaude, 1935.

O'Flaherty, P. *Lost Country: The Rise and Fall of Newfoundland, 1843–1933*. St. John's: Long Beach Press, 2005.

Orwell, G. *Why I Write*. London: Penguin, 2014.

Osborne, T.B., and L.B. Mendel. "The Relation of Growth to the Chemical Constituents of the Diet." *Journal of Biological Chemistry* 15, no. 2 (1913): 311–26.

——— and ———. "The Influence of Butter-fat on Growth." *Journal of Biological Chemistry* 16, no. 4 (1914): 423–47.

——— and ———. "The Influence of Cod Liver Oil and Some Other Fats on Growth." *Journal of Biological Chemistry* 17, no. 3 (1914): 401–08.

Outerbridge, L.C. *The Bait Supply: Observations and Suggestions Submitted to the Fishery Exporter's Association*. n.p., 1933.

Overton, J. "Economic Crisis and the End of Democracy: Politics in Newfoundland during the Great Depression," *Labour/Le Travail* 26 (1990): 85–124.

Parsons, L.A. "Bait Fish." In *Encyclopedia of Newfoundland and Labrador, Volume 1*, edited by J.R. Smallwood and R.D.W. Pitt, 115–16. St. John's: Newfoundland Book Publishers, 1981.

Plumptre, A.F.W. "Newfoundland, Economic and Political I: The Amulree Report (1933): A Review," *Canadian Journal of Economics and Political Science* 3, no. 1 (1937): 58–71.

Poovey, M. *A History of the Modern Fact: Problems of Knowledge in the Sciences of Wealth and Society*. Chicago: University of Chicago Press, 1998.

Pope, P.E. *Fish into Wine: The Newfoundland Plantation in the Seventeenth Century*. Chapel Hill: University of North Carolina Press, 2004.

Porter, M. "'She Was Skipper of the Shore-Crew': Notes on the History of the Sexual Division of Labour in Newfoundland." *Labour/Le Travail* 15 (1985): 105–23.

Porter, T.M. "Quantification and the Accounting Ideal in Science." *Social Studies of Science* 22, no. 4 (1992): 633–51.

———. *Trust in Numbers: The Pursuit of Objectivity in Science and Public Life.* Princeton, NJ: Princeton University Press, 1995.

Postone, M. *Time, Labor, and Social Domination: A Reinterpretation of Marx's Critical Theory.* Cambridge: Cambridge University Press, 1993.

Proceedings of the Convention of Licensed Codfish Exporters (PCLCE). St. John's: Department of Marine and Fisheries, 1920. Available at CNS, MUN.

Radical Science Journal Collective. "Science, Technology, Medicine and the Socialist Movement." *Radical Science Journal* 11 (1981): 3–70.

Reeves, W.G. "'Our Yankee Cousins': Modernization and the Newfoundland–American Relationship, 1898–1910." PhD thesis, Department of History, University of Maine, Orono, 1987.

———. "Alexander's Conundrum Reconsidered: The American Dimension in Newfoundland Resource Development, 1898–1910." *Newfoundland Studies* 5, no. 1 (1989): 1–37.

Reid, A.J., L.E. Eckert, J.F. Lane, N. Young, S.G. Hinch, C.T. Darimont, S.J. Cooke, N.C. Ban, and A. Marshall. "'Two-Eyed Seeing': An Indigenous Framework to Transform Fisheries Research and Management." *Fish and Fisheries* OnlineFirst (2020): 1–19.

Riggs, B. "Currency." In *Encyclopedia of Newfoundland and Labrador, Volume 1*, edited by J.R. Smallwood and R.D.W. Pitt. St. John's: Newfoundland Book Publishers, 1981.

Roberts, C. *The Unnatural History of the Sea.* Washington: Island Press/Shearwater Books, 2007.

Rogers, R. *The Oceans Are Emptying: Fish Wars and Sustainability.* Montreal: Black Rose Books, 1995.

Rompkey, R. *Grenfell of Labrador: A Biography.* Toronto: University of Toronto Press, 1991.

Rose, G.A. *Cod: The Ecological History of the North Atlantic Fisheries.* St. John's: Breakwater Books, 2007.

Rosenfeld, L. "Vitamine-Vitamin: The Early Years of Discovery." *Clinical Chemistry* 43, no. 4 (1997): 680–85.

Rozwadowski, H.M. *The Sea Knows No Boundaries: A Century of Marine Science under ICES.* Seattle: University of Washington Press, 2002.

Rubin, I.I. *Essays on Marx's Theory of Value.* Translated by M. Samardźija and F. Perlman. Detroit: Black and Red, 1973.

Ryan, S. *Fish Out of Water: The Newfoundland Saltfish Trade 1814–1914.* St. John's: Breakwater Books, 1986.

———. "The Introduction of Steam Transport into the Newfoundland Saltfish Trade during the Latter Nineteenth Century." Paper presented to the International Commission for Maritime History Conference: "Food for the World: Maritime Trade and Shipping of Foodstuff." Madrid, 28–31 Aug. 1990.

———. *The Ice Hunters: A History of Newfoundland Sealing to 1914.* St. John's: Breakwater Books, 1994.

Rygg, A.N. *Norwegians in New York, 1825–1925.* Brooklyn, NY: Norwegian News Company, 1941.

Sars, G.O. "Report of Practical and Scientific Investigations of the Cod Fisheries near the Loffoden Islands, Made during the Years 1864–1869." In *Report of the Commissioner for 1877, Part V*, edited by S.F. Baird, 565–90. Washington: Government Printing Office, 1879.

Schuyler, M. "The Etymology of the Dutch Word Kabeljauw." *Journal of Germanic Philology* 4, no. 1 (1902): 55–57.

Schwach, V. "The Impact of Artificial Hatching of Cod on Marine Research." *Historisch-Meereskundliches Jahrbuch* 5 (1999): 27–47.

———. "The Sea around Norway: Science, Resource Management, and Environmental Concerns, 1860–1970." *Environmental History* 18, no. 1 (2012): 101–10.

———. "A Sea Change: Johan Hjort and the Natural Fluctuations in the Fish Stocks." *ICES Journal of Marine Science* 71, no. 8 (2014): 1993–99.

Scott, J.C. *Seeing Like a State: How Certain Schemes to Improve the Human Condition Have Failed.* New Haven: Yale University Press, 1998.

Selwyn-Brown, A. "The Atlantic Voyage of the 'Michael Sars.'" *Newfoundland Quarterly* 8, no. 1 (1913): 1–3.

Semba, R.D. "On the 'Discovery' of Vitamin A." *Annals of Nutrition & Metabolism* 61, no. 3 (2012): 192–98.

Shapin, S., and S. Schaffer. *Leviathan and the Air-Pump: Hobbes, Boyle, and the Experimental Life.* Princeton, NJ: Princeton University Press, 1985.

Shea, A. *Newfoundland: Its Fisheries and General Resources in 1883.* n.p., 1883.

Sherman, H.C., and H.E. Munsell. "The Quantitative Determination of Vitamin A." *Journal of the American Chemical Society* 47, no. 6 (1925): 1639–46.

——— and S.L Smith. *The Vitamins.* New York: Chemical Catalog Company, 1922.

Shortis, H.F. "Paper 144: History of the Cod Liver Oil Industry in Newfoundland." In *Shortis Papers*, Vol. 4, Part 1. n.p, 1906.

Sider, G. *Between History and Tomorrow: Making and Breaking Everyday Life in Rural Newfoundland.* Peterborough, ON: Broadview Press, 2003 [1986].

Sinclair, U. *The Brass Check: A Study of American Journalism.* Pasadena, CA: Published by the author, 1919.

Simmel, G. "The Metropolis and Mental Life." In *The Blackwell City Reader*, edited by G. Bridge and S. Watson. Oxford and Malden, MA: Wiley-Blackwell, 2002 [1903].

Simpson, L.B. *Dancing on Our Turtle's Back: Stories of Nishnaabeg Re-creation, Resurgence, and a New Emergence.* Winnipeg: Arbeiter Ring, 2011.

Smith, T.D. *Scaling Fisheries: The Science of Measuring the Effects of Fishing 1855–1955.* Cambridge: Cambridge University Press, 1994.

———, J. Gjøsæter, N.C. Stenseth, M.O. Kittilsen, D.S. Danielssen, and S. Tveite. "A Century of Manipulating Recruitment in Coastal Cod Populations: The Flødevigen Experience." *ICES Marine Science Symposia* 215 (2002): 402–15.

Small, L.G. "The Interrelationship of Work and Talk in a Newfoundland Fishing Community." PhD thesis, Department of Folklore and Anthropology, University of Pennsylvania, 1979.

Smallwood, J.R. *The New Newfoundland: An Account of the Revolutionary Developments Which Are Transforming Britain's Oldest Colony from "The Cinderella of the Empire" into One of the Great Small Nations of the World.* New York: Macmillan, 1931.

Smith, N. *Uneven Development: Nature, Capital and the Production of Space*, 3rd ed. Athens: University of Georgia Press, 2008 [1984].

Sohn-Rethel, A. *Intellectual and Manual Labour: A Critique of Epistemology.* London: Macmillan, 1978.

Solemdal, P., E. Dahl, D.S. Danielssen, and E. Moksness. "The Cod Hatchery in Flodevigen — Background and Realities." In *The Propagation of Cod Gadus Morhua L*, edited by E. Dahl, D.S. Danielssen, E. Moksness, and P. Solemdal. Arendal: Institute of Marine Research Flødevigen Biological Station, 1984.

Solnit, R. *Hope in the Dark: Untold Histories, Wild Possibilities.* Chicago: Haymarket Books, 2016.

Starosta, G. "The Commodity-form and the Dialectical Method: On the Structure of Marx's Exposition in Chapter 1 of *Capital.*" *Science & Society*, 72, no. 3 (2008): 295–318.

———. *Marx's Capital, Method and Revolutionary Subjectivity.* Leiden: Brill, 2015.

———. "The Role and Place of 'Commodity Fetishism' in Marx's Systematic-Dialectical Exposition in Capital." *Historical Materialism* 25, no. 3 (2017): 101–39.

Steinberg, P.E. "Of Other Seas: Metaphors and Materialities in Maritime Regions." *Atlantic Studies* 10, no. 2 (2013): 156–69.

——— and K. Peters. "Wet Ontologies, Fluid Spaces: Giving Depth to Volume through Oceanic Thinking." *Environment and Planning D: Society and Space* 33, no. 2 (2015): 247–64.

Stickney, R.R. *Aquaculture: An Introductory Text.* Wallingford, UK: CABI, 2009.

Stockwood, W.C. "Clouston, John William (1869-1956)." In *Encyclopedia of Newfoundland and Labrador, Volume 1*, edited by J.R. Smallwood and R.D.W. Pitt, 455. St. John's: Newfoundland Book Publishers, 1981.

Svåsand, T., T.S. Kristiansen, T. Pedersen, A. Salvanes, R. Engelsen, G. Nævdal, and M. Nødtvedt. "The Enhancement of Cod Stocks." *Fish and Fisheries* 1, no. 2 (2000): 173–205.

Sverrisson, A. "Small Boats and Large Ships: Social Continuity and Technical Change in the Icelandic Fisheries, 1800–1960." *Technology and Culture* 43, no. 2 (2002): 227–53.

Tait, J.B. "Harold Thompson, 1890-1957." *Journal du Conseil International pour l'Exploration de la Mer* 23, no. 2 (1958): 151–54.

Taylor, F.W. *The Principles of Scientific Management.* New York: Harper & Brothers, 1913.

Taylor, J.A. *A Report on the Development of the Fisheries of Newfoundland.* n.p., 1924.

Taylor, J.E. "Burning the Candle at Both Ends: Historicizing Overfishing in Oregon's Nineteenth-Century Salmon Fisheries." *Environmental History* 4, no. 1 (1999): 54–79.

Templeman, W. "Fisheries Research." In *Encyclopedia of Newfoundland and Labrador, Volume 2*, edited by J.R. Smallwood, C.F. Horan, R.D.W. Pitt, and B.G. Riggs, 167–74. St. John's: Newfoundland Book Publishers, 1984.

Terkel, S. *Working: People Talk about What They Do All Day and How They Feel about What They Do.* New York: New Press, 2004 [1972].

Thompson, E.P. "Time, Work-Discipline, and Industrial Capitalism." *Past & Present* 38 (1967): 56–97.

Thompson, H. *A Survey of the Fisheries of Newfoundland and Recommendations for a Scheme of Research.* St. John's: Newfoundland Fishery Research Commission, 1930.

———. "Fishery Research in Newfoundland." In *The Book of Newfoundland, Volume 2*, edited by J.R. Smallwood, 211–13. St. John's: Newfoundland Book Publishers, 1937.

Todd, Z. "Fish Pluralities: Human–Animal Relations and Sites of Engagement in Paulatuuq, Arctic Canada." *Études/Inuit/Studies* 38, nos. 1–2 (2014): 217–38.

———. "Refracting the State through Human–Fish Relations: Fishing, Indigenous Legal Orders and Colonialism in North/Western Canada." *Decolonization: Indigeneity, Education & Society* 7, no. 1 (2018): 60–75.

Waddell, J., and E.L. Rohdenburg. "The Provitamin D of Cholesterol. 1. The Antirachitic Efficacy of Irradiated Cholesterol." *Journal of Biological Chemistry* 105, no. 4 (1934): 711–39.

Waterman, J.J. *The Cod.* Torry Advisory Note No 33. Rome: Food and Agriculture Organization, 2001. Available at http://www.fao.org/wairdocs/tan/x5911e/x5911e00.htm; accessed 7 Aug. 2018.

Wendt, D. "The Man with a Fish on His Back: Science, Romance, and Repugnance in the Selling of Cod-Liver Oil." *Chemical Heritage Magazine* 28, no. 1 (2010): 32–36.

Werskey, G. *The Visible College: A Collective Biography of British Scientists and Socialists of the 1930s.* London: Allen Lane, 1978.

———. "The Marxist Critique of Capitalist Science: A History in Three Movements?" *Science as Culture* 16, no. 4 (2007): 397–461.

Whiteley, G. "Marine Research and the Scientific Method." *Newfoundland Quarterly* 31, no. 4 (1932): 28–31.

———. *Northern Seas, Hardy Sailors.* New York: W.W. Norton, 1982.

Whiteway, L. "Inception of the Newfoundland Department of Fisheries." *Newfoundland Quarterly* 45, no. 2 (1956): 29–43.

Wingate, T.R. *A Study of the Newfoundland Bait Service, Volume 1.* n.p, 1971. Available at CNS, MUN.

Wolf, G. "A Historical Note on the Mode of Administration of Vitamin A for the Cure of Night Blindness." *American Journal of Clinical Nutrition* 31, no. 2 (1978): 290–92.

Wright, M. *A Fishery for Modern Times: The State and the Industrialization of the Newfoundland Fishery, 1934–1968.* Toronto: Oxford University Press, 2001.

Young, R. "Science Is a Labour Process." *Science for People* 43/44 (1979): 31–37.

———. "Marxism and the History of Science." In *Companion to the History of Modern Science*, edited by R.C. Olby, 77–86. London: Routledge, 1990.

Zilva, S.S. "The Action of Ozone on the Fat-soluble Factor in Fats: Preliminary Note." *Biochemical Journal* 14, no. 6 (1920): 740–41.

——— and J.C. Drummond. "The Cod Liver Oil Industry in Newfoundland." *Journal of the Society of Chemical Industry Transactions* 42, no. 18 (1923): 185T–88T.

———, ———, and M. Graham. "The Relation of the Vitamin A Potency of the Liver Oil to the Sexual Condition and Age of the Cod." *Biochemical Journal* 18 (1924): 178–81.

——— and M. Miura. "The Quantitative Estimation of the Fat-soluble Factor." *Biochemical Journal* 15, no. 5 (1921): 654–59.

——— and ———. "A Note on the Relative Activity of the Fat-soluble Accessory Factor in Cod-Liver Oil and Butter." *The Lancet* 197, no. 5085 (1921): 323.

INDEX